WET EYES
& Caring Hands

The Intersection of Prayer & Compassion

P. Douglas Small, Editor

Produced by Alive Publications
USA
PO Box 1245—Kannapolis, NC 28082

ISBN 978-0-9820115-3-9

Cover design by Jackie Britton
Layout and interior design by Jackie Britton

Third printing — July, 2011

Printed in the United States of America

Table of Contents

Acknowledgments

This book would have been impossible without the cooperation of David Lorency. Yet throughout the process of writing and research, he chose to remain in the shadows, pointing to others as the examples of compassion and outreach. No one can deny the important place of Operation Compassion. It has become a formidable, charitable ministry, one of the largest in the nation out of thousands. It is teaching by example, leading our pastors and people to embrace care in a way not known before. It is, in fact, offering to us a pattern for a quiet reformation of our evangelism.

I am grateful to the pastors who contributed information. I offer an apology since there are so many more that could have been profiled. The pastors whose churches are the spotlight of this book would readily confess that their compassionate outreach is not necessarily the best or the greatest. It is the simple story of how God has led them, and what has developed out of humble obedience.

Compassion ministries change to meet changing needs. They are extremely dynamic. They require people willing to act now, by faith. Risk takers. The complex at Central Parkway, designed to house women, now cares for others—***change***. The facility that Bruce Deel miraculously acquired in Atlanta was not originally designed to serve as a shelter for the homeless—***adaptation.*** The outreach to the Navaho nation was not in the plans when the Appalachian Dream Center was raised to touch coal country—***expand.*** Jerry Lawson did not go to Glory Hill with the idea of benevolence on his mind—***revolution***.

One of the recurring themes in this little book is the story of how pastors themselves were changed. In almost every case, something happened to them and in them before it touched their people and went through their congregation or ministry to their community. Gary Sears was changed by the unconditional love of a little girl who innocently wanted to minister to him. Bruce Deel backed into his role as he simply attempted to be faithful—and in that process grew himself. Jerry Lawson had a moment when he saw himself in the Father's arms, a moment acted out by two members serving a poor and decidedly hopeless man. Their love, their embrace, their treatment of the malodorous man was to him stunning, and transforming.

Barry Clardy, over an open Bible in prayer, was moved from superficial and tactical "how to" approaches in ministry to a servant-based approach that had at its core his own personal transformation. He learned that loving Jesus was his highest call, and only then could he pastor the sheep belonging to Jesus. He discovered the greatest desire of the Father was not to make him a better and more effective pastor, but the pure pleasure of the relationship itself.

Again, I am grateful for the opportunity to have collected this collage of stories—to encourage the conversation of bringing more of our congregations to the "intersection of prayer and compassion." The impact of these churches, the reach of their programs, is stunning. It is an untold story —and a powerful story. As you read this book, my prayer is that you will conclude, if these churches can do this, your church can do this, or at least, some of this.

Prayer and compassion ministries are not optional. They are conjoined to the Great Commission, the final command of Christ. And yet, the completion of this task is impossible without prayer, and without an incarnational dimension to the gospel we preach.

— P. Douglas Small, Editor

How To Use This Book

1. Use the book as a 12-week study guide.
2. You may want to begin with a small group who have expressed an interest in compassion ministry or the leaders of your pantry ministry.
3. Each chapter has a small discussion guide that can be used to guide dialogue and reflection.
4. During the course of the study, explore other churches or ministries in your area that are doing compassion-based ministry. Take a field trip. Go visit them.
5. On one evening during the study take your group on a "plunge"right into the heart of some need, into a world they have not seen, one they might avoid, yet just on the other side of the city. Get a good look at the harvest. Pray. Ask God what your role might be.
6. Make arrangements to video conference, with one or more of the pastors in this book, their churches and leaders. Have them share their story. Ask questions. Develop a mentoring relationship with them.
7. Create a map of your city noting pockets of poverty, high crime, youth hang-outs, the needy spots. Pray over the map as you add data. Ask God for direction. Make prayer over the map, the gathering of data regarding your city, a critical part of your weekly gathering. Collect news clippings. Study your city. Find out about its history—its spiritual history.
8. Remember, it is never a cup of water or a piece of bread that changes a life. It is a cup of water *offered in the name* of the One, who is Himself, the Bread of Life. Your business is not commodities. It is compassion that leads to the salvation of souls.

The Great COMMITMENT

Therefore I exhort first of all that supplications, prayers, intercessions, and giving of thanks be made for all men, for kings and all who are in authority, that we may lead a quiet and peaceable life in all godliness and reverence. For this is good and acceptable in the sight of God our Savior, who desires all men to be saved and to come to the knowledge of the truth. I Timothy 2:1-4

The Great COMMANDMENT

He (Jesus) answered, "'Love the Lord your God with all your heart and with all your soul and with all your strength and with all your mind;' and, 'Love your neighbor as yourself.'" Luke 10:27

The Great COMMISSION

And Jesus came and spoke to them, saying, "All authority has been given to Me in heaven and on earth. Go therefore and make disciples of all the nations, baptizing them in the name of the Father and of the Son and of the Holy Spirit, teaching them to observe all things that I have commanded you; and lo, I am with you always, even to the end of the age." Amen. Matthew 28:18-20

The Great COMMITMENT

Paul exhorts that we pray for all men beginning with civil leaders and those who are in some position of authority. And somehow, the atmosphere of prayer impacts the culture itself, leading to a state of general tranquility and ultimately to the salvation of men and women, and to their knowledge of truth. The well-spring of cultural transformation, and of the change of hearts and minds necessary to see evil restrained, and truth enshrined, is prayer. First, prayer, in the form of supplication, an imploring yet pliable plea for God's intervention. Second, worshipful prayer. Third, intercession—the act of getting between God and some need, of pleading as if we were the hurting person, of declaring into and over some situation the will of God. All wrapped in a spirit of gratitude. Such prayer is seen by heaven as a good and acceptable thing; it is what God expects. Prayer—rising from every quarter and corner of the city. Prayer— that takes before the throne of God the name of city leaders and people of influence. The heart of the king is in the hand of God, and prayer is the evidence that we, His disciples, believe that. And it is also the means by which we, as kingly priests of heaven, invite the intervention of God into our time-space world. Without prayer, God could act. But with prayer, we know he does act! Cultural change begins at the intersection of prayer.

The Great COMMANDMENT

Christians are not marked merely by their own love–but by God's love. We never love God into loving us more. Nor do we elicit his affirmation by our love for others. Both postures – loving God and loving others – are the essence of religion. But not that of true faith. The difference is more than subtle. Christianity is not about our love, but about God's love. He loves first. He loves best. He loved us while we were yet sinners, and he loves those who wildly and carelessly sin around us, those who damage themselves and others by sin. What a mystery. Transformation happens when we ourselves are constrained by such love, and drawn into transforming truth. Love overwhelms us, but truth sets us free. The process begins, not with our love improved, but his love imputed, and then overflowing, shed abroad in our hearts, creating an inner flood. And a dialectic begins. He loves us, and with that love – agape– we love him back. Out of the overflow of that glorious cycle, we come to love others as we are being loved. Our deeds of kindness, our acts of benevolence, are evidences of God's wild and unrestrained love for us and those around us. Because it is Divine love given away, and not merely commodities, a blanket or a bowl of soup, the Great Commandment requires a connection to the Great Commitment.

The Great COMMISSION

The last command of Christ was for us, those He had saved, to embrace the discipline (to become disciples) necessary to fulfill our obligation to Christ. Others must be told, the nations – every ethnic stream of people – must yield a harvest of disciples. We are first to proclaim, to share the good news. The mere conversion of people is not our goal. After their confession of faith, we are called to join them in the public declaration of their new loyalty, to teach them all we know, to mentor them in the ways of the Lord until they are observing his commands in behavioral ways, and until they themselves are disciple makers. The truth we share is not a composite of ideas, but a person. Such truth sets men free. Love bonds us to Christ, but truth liberates us both from the world, to new living patterns. The Great Commission cannot be shared with mere words. It is not fulfilled only by the proclamation of principles, but also by their incarnation. The Great Commission may be the words we say, but the Great Commandment, love, is the music. Without love, the truth will not ring true. The transformational power of the Great Commission is evidenced by people living out the Great Commandment.

We PRAY ... We LOVE and CARE ... We SHARE!

"Now this was the sin of your sister Sodom: She and her daughters were arrogant, overfed and unconcerned; they did not help the poor and needy." —Ezekiel 16:49

"Command those who are rich in this present world not to be arrogant nor to put their hope in wealth, which is so uncertain, but to put their hope in God, who richly provides us with everything for our enjoyment. Command them to do good, to be rich in good deeds, and to be generous and willing to share. In this way they will lay up treasure for themselves as a firm foundation for the coming age, so that they may take hold of the life that is truly life —1 Timothy 6:17-19

"But You, O God, do see trouble and grief; You consider it to take it in hand. The victim commits himself to You; You are the helper of the fatherless." —Psalm 10:14

"You have been a refuge for the poor, a refuge for the needy in his distress, a shelter from the storm and a shade from the heat. For the breath of the ruthless is like a storm driving against a wall." —Isaiah 25:4

Operation Compassion

Operation Compassion is now one of America's Largest Charities, and in some rankings, regarding efficiency of investment dollars, is number one. In overall rankings, it stands in the company of ministries such as Food for the Poor, Feed the Children, and World Vision, non-profits with which the ministry now partners. The reach of the ministry is global. It is among the first responders to natural disasters and catastrophes. The extensive network of partner ministries within the denomination and without is staggering. The amount of goods managed annually is almost $250 million.

1

Building A Hope and A Future

Marissa was only four years old when she was invited to tag along with an older sister to the outdoor market. Standing in a sea of vegetables and meat, Marissa's sister told her to stay put while she picked up a few special items. Marissa waited—

and waited. To her dismay, her sister never came back. She had been abandoned. Local authorities classified Marissa a *"foundling"* and placed her in a temporary shelter facility in nearby Manila. Daily, she hoped that someone from her family would come for her. No one did. Unfortunately for Marissa, not one inquiry was made in the next three years. But there was hope for Marissa. God's promise found in Jeremiah 29:11 applies to orphans as well! *"For I know the plans I have for you, declares the LORD, plans to prosper you and not to harm you, plans to give you hope and a future."*

At the age of seven, Marissa was transferred to Samaritan's Place Homes for Children in the town of Silang, in the Cavite Province of the Philippines. There, Marissa found a family and staff eagerly waiting to embrace her and make a positive difference in her life. Day after day, she was lovingly nurtured and personal care was given. She learned about the Lord. At the age of 11, Marissa became legally available for permanent placement through adoption.

Father absence is a major cause of child poverty. 75% of poor children live with one parent, typically the mother. Annually, 1.5 million children are born out of wedlock. If fathers married the mothers of their children, three-quarters of poor households with children would immediately be lifted out of poverty.

Samaritan's Place Homes is a unique outreach for children founded by Marc and Marilen Morris to reach into the pool of 250,000 or more abandoned street children in the Philippines. They rescue children, minister to their needs, and when possible, place them with permanent caring families. Marc and Marilen also offer their children a unique international adoption awareness program. Marissa participated in such a summer hosting program. Traveling with other Samaritan's Place children, she stayed for one month with a loving Christian family in America's west. She fell in love with her host family. And, the family fell in love with her.

The experience was about to change her life forever. After Marissa

Street Kids

Street kids in Brazil had become epidemic in the 1980s and 1990s, and Brazilian 'death squads' made up of off-duty police officers routinely murdered them. One count placed the death toll of such children aged five through 17, at 5,644 in a two-year period. Organizations such as the International Center for Research and Policy on Childhood says the death squads are less common now. That is not a perception shared by the street kids. If they are discovered in a neighborhood to which they do not belong, they may still get a beating—or worse. Executions of kids under 18 in poor communities still occur. The street kids are one group, and the gangs are another. They are often pressured to join a gang, one that makes money by illegal activities. If the youth resists, he is at risk. Street kids run from gangs, and gangs prey on them. It is another kind of extermination.

With the war on drugs and gangs by the police, the more innocent street kids get caught in the escalating violence. Sadly, many of these same kids, especially in Rio de Janeiro, are fleeing the same drug wars that plague the slums where there are shootings every day. They soon learn that life on the streets is seldom an improvement. At best street kids are shunned or verbally abused by the public. At worst they are threatened, sexually abused, or beaten by police.

returned to the Philippines, the host family decided to pursue the legal adoption of Marissa. They completed rigorous legal and domestic requirements, filed the necessary documentation with both the US and Philippine authorities, and three months later, as the children of Samaritan's Place were preparing to experience a fun day at a local amusement park, a call was received from the host family. Marissa's was asked her to be their "forever" little girl. She would be abandoned no more!

"*It was like seeing rays of sunshine and joy,*" according to Samaritan's Place Founders Marc and Marilen Morris. The *foundling* had been found and the tapestry of Marissa's life to be filled with hope for the future had been completed. This would be one little abandoned child that would not have to go through life without a father and mother.

More Street Kids

Godoy's parents were always fighting. At the age of eight, his grandmother took him home with her. When she died, he chose to live on the streets, rather than go back to living in the war between his parents. He reflects on the day when, as an adult, he will have his own home, his own family, and sons. And he doesn't want them to grow up like him, in a house at war, or to have to live on the streets. He wants something better for them. May God help him survive to live out that dream.

"There are only two things that take away the fear [of violence]: drugs and the presence of God," explains baby-faced Godoy. The difference is stark, worlds apart in our minds. For them, it is living in a moment with a deep and full awareness of God or medicating themselves with drugs due to fear. They vacillate between the two. Godoy stashes a can of paint-stripper under his torn shirt. It's his medicine, a crutch, an addictive habit. But he knows there is something better, "With God by your side you don't even feel hungry."

But using drugs has become a survival strategy to forget stressful conditions and hardship of life on the street. If you go to Rio, it is impossible to ignore the clusters of scruffy street children who beg at traffic lights. You find the same scene in faraway places like Jakarta or Nairobi, all over India. In Rio de Janeiro, it is as much a part of the landscape as the statue of Jesus Christ that towers above the chaotic city.

In Brazil, the country's richest 10 per cent control nearly 50 per cent of its wealth, according to the World Bank. At the bottom of the poverty pile are the street kids, trapped in a cycle of drug abuse and physical violence from which there seems little possibility for escape.

Jefferson is a street kid. He often watches other children going home from school with their parents in the afternoon, playfully running along. He doesn't understand why he was not afforded such an opportunity. Fábio Campos de Oliveira survived the streets. He lived there for10 years, but not without consequences. At the age of 18, he was caught in the crossfire of a failed robbery. A bullet shattered his right leg. Now, at the age of 23, he bears his street wounds. He will never forget the moment. "There were five of us and we saw a man coming out of the Bingo Hall with a big bag. We started to follow him but a security guard came out and spotted us ... We didn't stop and another guard came out and began shooting," he recalls, pointing to a thick bullet scar still coursing across his thigh. They were mistaken as complicit with the robber.

A Century Earlier

Travel almost a century earlier and around the globe to the year 1922. The automobile was a brand new experience for most Americans and a ride in one was like Disneyland to a kid. With World War I over, the industrial revolution was driving a new world economy. These "Happy Days" were commonly referred to as the Roaring '20's. But not everyone was going to be privileged to take a ride into a dream life. For four year-old Margaret and her baby sister, a ride across town ended as a trip into a strange and different world, the beginning of a nightmare that many orphaned children faced in the early 1900's. On that day, Margaret was very excited to get a ride in the T-model and take a trip with her trusted uncle. *"I loved him like a father,"* she recalled later in life. *"Our own dad did not return from WWI ... and since mom died from TB, we had no one else but my uncle and aunt (mom's sister). We knew they loved us! But as little kids, we didn't understand the difficult realities they faced ... or we would face as orphans."*

Margaret's uncle drove his T-model to a house near the present North Cleveland Church of God. Margaret was completely unsuspecting. This was just another visit with family friends. The sound of children playing in the backyard attracted her. She didn't think twice about venturing there to join the playful activities. *"They were very, very nice and seemed to enjoy playing with me."* Margaret's innocent trust, her naïve confidence in family ties, was about to be shattered. Soon she heard the T-model engine crank up.

10.6 million children die each year before reaching the age of 5. Some 1.4 million die simply due to a lack of safe drinking water and adequate sanitation.

She ran to the front yard and watched in bewilderment as her uncle's vehicle quickly pulled away, down the street and over the hill, without her. *"I stood there and watched for the longest time as tears fell from my eyes. Why was he leaving me behind?"* She had just been abandoned. She would grow up in the small homes that eventually became the Church of God orphanage.

The average age of a homeless person in the United States is just nine years of age, and there are many kids below the age of nine living on the streets. Some live with a homeless parent or family, but most are trying to survive on their own. Currently there are 1.3 million homeless and runaway street kids in the United States, not counting children who were forced out of their homes, abandoned by the foster care system, or are part of a homeless family.

The story of both Margaret and Marissa are indeed sad, two different children so alike and yet separated by time and distance. But there is a connection between the stories, one with a decided silver lining. Such a painful trauma as abandonment cannot be erased. Margaret would remain in the Church of God orphanage for 14 years, never knowing a

Street Kids Cont'd

Fabio is now a disc jockey at a local radio station and the subject in the movie, *City of God*. He survived, but he cannot forget the 18,000 kids who will sleep somewhere on the streets in Brazil tonight. He graduated from the school of survival. There, on the streets, he learned humility the hard way. He learned to share, and to trust, and yet, to discern. He learned about true friendship.

Street kids unofficially marry as young as 12. They are looking for a sense of stability and companionship, the sensation of family. But the violence that separates and threatens is always looming. Street girls with scarred faces are far too common. They are marked by a boy or man who felt they betrayed him.

Recently, a number of street kids were again the target of murders by thugs, shocking the city. Fearful for their own lives, the kids have taken to banding together to provide a protective vigil throughout the night, chanting rap lyrics, and smoking. "If everybody went to sleep at the same time you never know what might happen." There is God, a Creator, a reliable Father, who watches over them, too. Where are His followers, His agents, the Church? (Source: http://greatreporter.com/mambo/content/view/387/; GreatReporter.com, *Rio's Desperate Street Kids Fear Annihilation*, Written by Tom Phillips and Thais Viallela (Tuesday, 17 May 2005; accessed February 28, 2011).

mom and a dad as God intended. And she would never forget her story. She told it to her children, and then to her grandchildren. One of her grandchildren was Marilen Morris, the wife of Marc, the founders of Samaritan's Place. Because of Margaret's life testimony, Marissa and other orphan children in the Philippines are now being rescued from abandonment, blessed with a home, and given a chance to be adopted by a loving, caring family.

Marilen says, "It was Margaret's dream that every orphan child have a father and mother. And now, it is possible through Samaritan's Place to open a door for that possibility." Jeremiah 29:11 is not wishful thinking; it is a reality, a promise for everyone, including orphans![1]

A Gospel with a Heart

Pentecost is known for its fervency—fiery preaching and ardent prayer, enthusiastic evangelism, and sober calls to holiness. But those things never existed alone. R. G. Spurling would acknowledge that the 10-year journey of prayer and study that became the wellspring for the birth of the Church of God was about finishing the Reformation. It was about moving beyond the creeds to the bedrock of Biblical authority itself, beyond liturgical forms to heart-felt connection with God. But he would also make a stunning declaration. Luther, he would declare built the reformation *on faith,* when he should have founded it *on love.* What a dramatic declaration. Such an insight did not come from Smokey Mountain vistas, but from a higher position—one of knees bent in humble prayer over an open Bible. Love and compassion were marks of the movement from the beginning. It was with love that the small group responded when persecutors came. It was because of love that they refused to prosecute hostile neighbors who barred them from one building and then, to technically avoid the violation of a law forbidding the burning of a church building, they dismantled the building and burned its component parts. File charges? Send them to prison? No! They were neighbors.

2.2 million children die each year because they are not immunized.

It was love that led to the early founding of a home for orphaned children. It was December 17, 1920, when four young children were placed in that small frame house in Cleveland, Tennessee, in the care of Lillian Kinsey. This home was eventually named Orphanage Number One and thus was born the Church of God's ministry to homeless children. The number of children in their care quickly increased. Two more homes were added and eventually a large facility capable of housing several hundred children was constructed on 119 acres of land south of town. It became known as the Church of God Orphanage with a mission to provide shelter for homeless children.

In 1949, the orphanage relocated to Sevierville, Tennessee, on property formerly occupied by the Church of God Bible Training School. Today, the **Smokey Mountain Children's Home** provides care for at risk children and teens through its Residential Care and Foster Care programs, providing family counseling, individual therapy, educational

opportunities, and structured group living. [2]

Now that one home is a flagship, complete with counseling ministries, a widow's home, and a variety of other services. In North and South Carolina are two additional homes. And around the world are similar ministries. Based in Bristol, Tennessee, Children of the World Ministries Inc. is a Christian charity that provides monitored safe havens—a network of orphanages and children's missions for youngsters who have no place to go due to devastating natural disasters, civil wars, or disintegrating societies and homes. It is a cooperative between the Lazarus Foundation, Operation Compassion, Church of God World Missions, and Care Ministries.

John Gregory, Founder of the Lazarus Foundation, declares, "We currently serve the needs of thousands of children in 15 facilities found in 12 different countries on five continents." The effort is momentous and yet so modest in the face of 143,000 million destitute, orphaned or abandoned children worldwide, a number equal to almost half the population of the US. Sadly, the number is growing. Children of the World declare that every minute, 23 more children become orphaned, 12 million annually.

Operation Compassion

Operation Compassion, a non-profit international disaster relief charity, has emerged as a powerful force demonstrating the connection between the *Great Commandment*—love and care, and the *Great*

Commission—the good news of Christ's love. *Forbes* magazine recently named Operation Compassion, for the second consecutive time, the most efficient benevolence agency in the nation out of 1.4 million other charities. In the case of Operation Compassion, 100% of expenses goes directly to global programs. For 13 years, this ministry has been quietly gaining a national and global reputation for its selfless and efficient network of care outreaches.

US households with children report food insecurity at almost double the rate for those without children, 21.3 percent compared to 11.4 percent.

In the Church of God, *Operation Compassion* is synonymous with Dave Lorency. As he nears the completion of four decades of ministry, he is in his element with a dynamic ministry to the underprivileged and poor around the world. He began on the streets of Virginia Beach, Virginia, where he started Youth Challenge Outreach and served as Chaplain to the Norfolk City Jail. That effort became an umbrella ministry for numerous coffee houses, servicemen's centers and beach ministry stations, all an attempt to reach youth as they descended on local beaches.

During the next five years, riding the wave of the Jesus Movement, the ministry reached thousands of youth, and grew to employ nine full-time and 70 part-time staff members. Soon, the Virginia Beach effort went international. The Osborn Foundation donated evangelism vans complete with sound equipment, and David and his family headed to Mexico, holding crusades and establishing churches.

The world's low income countries, almost half of all people, account for just 2.4% of world exports.

At first, with 1,500 donated Bibles, then three million Bibles, Bible portions or tracts, they were armed and dangerous. At one point, more than 11 million tracts were taken into Mexico. God guided his steps and ordered his paths. Dave Lorency would probably have never guessed that Virginia Beach was only the basic training of a global ministry he would lead that would touch the world. He and his family served in more traditional settings as well, pastoring three different congregations across America. In each pastorate, parishioners were encouraged to look beyond themselves and see the needs of their community.

A missional perspective is a part of his DNA. He served for a season at the state administrative level in evangelism and church planting, starting many ethnically diverse congregations. But in the end, it was compassion that drove him.

In 2000, David Lorency was selected to serve as Executive Director of *Operation Compassion,* David has guided and directed the growth and development of Operation Compassion from a small charity handling less than 100 semis per year to a charity that now handles thousands of semis loaded with commodities. In 2006, he was chosen to serve as President of the organization.

For every donated dollar, the ministry turns it into $88 of commodities for charitable use. Operation Compassion was at the forefront of response following the devastation caused by Katrina. When tornadoes ripped through Oklahoma, Operation Compassion trucks rolled in that direction. The Indonesian tsunami, the devastating 2011 flooding in the Philippines, Hurricane Mitch that ravaged Honduras, the 2010 earthquake in Haiti—all involved massive attention by Operation Compassion.

22,000 children die every day around the world. One child dies every 4 seconds, 15 every minute. It is like the 2010 Haiti earthquake or the 2004 Asian tsunami occurring every 10 days. The toll is 8 million a year.

Within 24 hours after the Haiti earthquake, Operation Compassion had mobilized relief, and within days, food, commodities were being distributed. A million shoes were given away, and 10,000 tents offered as temporary housing for families. From a bakery and two mobile kitchens, 10,000 meals were served during the height of the crisis. Hundreds of huge transfer-truck size containers flowed into the ravaged nation with medical supplies, sleeping bags and essentials. It was the compassion of Christ, in action as thousands of bottles of water given in his name. The "Giving Hope to Haiti" project was one of the largest projects of the ministry.

Operation Compassion is really a network of compassionate ministries operating throughout the nation and around the world. Churches are critical partners when an emergency occurs. The ministry has produced a handbook to assist churches in the partnership, the *Master's Mandate,* available online.

Around the World The Church Grows Where Care Ministries Grow

In the 1970's, the Mount Paran Church of God was the denomination's largest congregation. And it was listed at one time as the fifth largest congregation of any denomination in the nation. The worship was electrifying, the preaching relevant and Biblical, the singing inspiring, the programs of the church top quality. Its impact reached across Atlanta and around the world. Since that era, Church of God congregations across the nation have exploded in growth—and the same is true around the world. Now, Mount Paran is seventh on the list and the only US congregation found on the "top-ten list" of the largest of some 35,000 Church of God congregations around the world. The others are outside the US.

Surprisingly, the largest is in one of most hostile spots to Christianity on the face of the earth, Indonesia, the largest Muslim nation on the planet. There, a recent international Care Conference was conducted drawing thousands in attendance. Leaders from around the world with a burden for benevolence programs were in attendance to explore the three-fold vision—"Becoming, Reaching and Providing." The conference concerned itself with reaching society's most vulnerable victims who need compassionate care and providing methods of ministry to facilitate patterns of progress to escape the oppressions of poverty, sickness and social despair. The mission was "to challenge people who have the capacity to care to release their hearts and gifts to people around the world who have been impacted by centuries of diverse global peril." The conference was held at the Sentul International Convention Center (SICC) in Jakarta, the home of the 250,000 member congregation, the largest Church of God in the world.

Around the world, Church of God World Missions operates 174 orphanages, and 1,252 feeding ministries for the hungry. Proverbs 29:7 declares, *"The righteous care about justice for the poor ..."* Jesus charged that one of the measures of true kingdom people would be our record of care for the alien or foreigner among us, the homeless, the naked, the sick, and those in prison. Such people are to be looked after, cared for, and protected by kingdom people. We are to be advocates for the disadvantaged, intercessors, and beyond that, to provide tangible care. *"I was a stranger and you did not invite Me in, I needed clothes and you did not clothe Me, I was sick and in prison and you did not look after Me."* And then He will proclaim, *"Inasmuch as you cared for the least of these, you cared for Me."*

The dollars spent on cosmetics in the US annually, is enough to fix the sanitation and water needs of the world. Europe and America spends millions annually on perfumes, an amount equal to the additional funds needed to provide basic global health care and nutrition for all.

Isaiah 58:10 urges, *"Spend yourselves in behalf of the hungry..."* Quite a challenge. There is a personal price involved, and beyond that, a personal investment. Such action is not merely because of the need itself. Rather, it rises out of the nature of God. Psalm 68:5 declares of Yahweh, *"A Father of the fatherless, a Defender of widows is God in His holy habitation."*

We behave in caring ways because God, our Father, is a caring God. Our benevolent acts are evidences that we are His children. Psalm 146:9 notes, *"The LORD watches over the strangers (foreigners, noncitizens, aliens); He relieves the fatherless and widow."* His eyes are on such needy people. Our watch, our prayer moments before Him, should also embrace such needs. Like a man on a watchtower, we see battle action, the wounded as they fall, and we cry out to God in their behalf. Prayer is the means by which we see what God sees. We join Him on the watch. He watches, then He comforts. He observes, then He acts. We follow His lead.

Isaiah 1:17 counsels, *"Learn to do good; Seek justice, Rebuke the oppressor; Defend the fatherless, Plead for the widow."* This is the prophetic and cultural mandate of the people of God. The absence of such action by the righteous was proof of their apostasy. In a culture lacking justice, oppression multiplies. The poor are victims. The fatherless grow in numbers. The society descends into chaos and implodes. This is the condition about which Isaiah warns.

7.8% of US seniors living alone—884,000—(almost a million) are food insecure.

Malachi 3:5 anticipates what is coming, *"And I will come near you for judgment; I will be a swift witness against sorcerers, against adulterers, against perjurers, against those who exploit wage earners and widows and orphans, And against those who turn away an alien—because they do not fear Me,"* says the LORD of hosts. God will judge His own people. He will take the witness stand. The land is now filled with witchcraft. Families have disintegrated. Truth, even in court, is perverted by false testimonies and payoffs. The poor are exploited by cheap and withheld wages. Widows are multiplied and have no advocate in a culture that provides inadequate care.

The social framework is falling apart. Street kids multiply. Without caring parents, they fend for themselves, forming substitute families. Civilization is no longer civil. It is beyond ill-mannered and vulgar. It is indecent and destructive.

Sadly, it is not always an irreligious people who behave in such ways. In Mark 12:40, Jesus warns those "*who devour widows' houses, and for a pretense make long prayers. These will receive greater condemnation.*" How can it be that those who pray long prayers also exploit. Their faith does not affect the way they treat others. The sensitivity of God to us should manifest in us and through us as kindness to

Vincent de Paul, Helper of The Poor

Vincent de Paul was born in 1580, a peasant. An intelligent lad, his father sent him off to be educated. He was ordained at 20, and when he was 30, his post brought him into contact with peasants. He became concerned for their needs, physical and spiritual. In a confessional, a dying peasant pleaded for forgiveness for years of dishonesty. Vincent was disturbed.

He began to preach to peasants the importance of confession, repentance, forgiveness, and the love of God. He drew such crowds of penitents that other priests had to be called to assist. When a neighboring church offered a pulpit to a more fashionable and aristocratic crowd, he did not change his message.

Returning to Paris, he worked among prisoners. In 1625, he founded the Congregation of the Mission, a community of priests devoted to work in the small towns and villages. In an age not noted for "interdenominational courtesy" he instructed his missioners to treat Protestants as brothers, without condescension or contentiousness.

Wealthy men and women who came to him were organized into a Confraternity of Charity who cared for the poor and sick. The Archbishop offered him facilities to provide retreats six times a year for hundreds of ministry candidates annually.

Out of his Confraternity arose an order of nuns called the Daughters of Charity, devoted to nursing those who were sick and poor. Many babies were abandoned in Paris. Vincent established an orphanage for them, and often wandered through the slums, looking for abandoned babies.

He appealed to the King for more honesty in government, and the King created a Council of Conscience with Vincent at the head. A noblewoman became furious with Vincent because he refused to nominate her son as bishop. She threw a stool at him. He left the room with blood pouring from his forehead, and commented to a companion, "Is it not wonderful how strong a mother's love for her son can be?" He died September 27, 1660

others. But, it did not.

The first great crisis in the New Testament church had to do with the neglect of widows. The Acts church had a daily feeding program, and when it missed ethnic widows, an intense and potentially divisive complaint was registered. Care for the disadvantaged was an important component of the ministry of the early church, and yet never to the exclusion of prayer (Acts 6). James, the brother of Jesus, and the Bishop of the Jerusalem Church, urged, *"Pure and undefiled religion before God and the Father is this: to visit orphans and widows in their trouble, and to keep oneself unspotted from the world"* (James 1:26-27).

Around the world, the Church of God World Missions program operates 33 widows' homes, 26 medical clinics, and some full-service hospitals. More than half of the congregations outside the USA, some 15,000, have a benevolence ministry of some form. They are growing. They are serving. They are reaching out. They exist for the people in their community, and not merely for themselves.

Discussion Guide

Big Ideas

- Out of Margaret's pain came compassion, and out of her abandonment experience came Samaritan's Place home. She tasted pain, and through her granddaughter, who never forgot the family story, kids now in pain are being rescued.
- Father absence is a major cause of child poverty. If fathers married the mothers of their children, three-quarters of poor households with children would immediately be lifted out of poverty.
- For every donated dollar, Operation Compassion turns it into $88 of commodities for charitable use.
- After the Haiti earthquake, a million shoes were given away, and 10,000 tents offered as temporary housing for families. From a bakery and two mobile kitchens, 10,000 meals were served during the height of the crisis. Hundreds of huge transfer-truck size containers flowed into the ravaged nation with medical supplies, sleeping bags, and essentials.
- Sentul International Convention Center (SICC) in Jakarta, the home of a 250,000 member congregation, is the largest Church of

God in the world. It was built to serve not only the congregation, but the city—a city full of Muslims.

Notable Quotes

- She would be abandoned no more! *"It was like seeing rays of sunshine and joy."*
- The average age of a homeless person in the United States is just nine years of age, and there are many kids below the age of nine living on the streets. Currently there are 1.3 million homeless and runaway street kids in the United States.
- Spurling, the leader of the movement that became the Church of God, observed, "Luther, built the reformation *on faith*, when he should have founded it *on love."*
- 10.6 million children die each year before reaching the age of 5. Some 1.4 million die simply due to a lack of safe drinking water and adequate sanitation.
- Eight million dollars is spent on cosmetics in the US annually.

Questions for Consideration

1. Consider the plight of the street kids in Brazil and the "death squads." Could such a thing happen in the US? How can we prevent it?
2. Take a few moments to survey Isaiah 1 and the social conditions that exist. Then look at his charges against the people of God themselves. Do you think there is any parallel to what Israel was experiencing and America today?
3. If the brother of Jesus was right and "*Pure and undefiled religion before God and the Father is this: to visit orphans and widows in their trouble, and to keep oneself unspotted from the world*" (James 1:26-27), are we practicing pure religion in the churches of America?
4. Did you know that around the world, under the Church of God World Missions banner, we operate 33 widows' homes and 26 medical clinics, among them full-service hospitals?
5. What do you think about our churches around the world growing while we are stagnant here in the US? Further, more than half of those churches carry on some form of a compassion-based ministry effort.

Hurricane Katrina

Katrina was one of the most horrific natural disasters of our time. The hurricane brought straight-line winds in excess of 150 miles per hour. Thousands were displaced, and within hours New Orleans was underwater. It appeared that the whole city might be wiped out. In the aftermath, the nation watched the stranded and frightened multitudes—some on housetops, others reported to be in attics, some on the ramps leading to the New Orleans Superdome. The government failed miserably in its response. But from all over the nation, the church rushed to the troubled city of a dubious reputation. The testimony of the love and care of believers was powerful.

The Lord's Prayer calls for an alignment of heaven and earth, *"Thy kingdom come on earth as it is in heaven..."* God intends for His church to be living examples of Himself on the earth. The government had its teams of bureaucrats with trailer keys and red tape. The church transformed sanctuaries into makeshift homes and set up serving stations under tents offering free food and quick medical care. Blankets and baby bottles came with clean-up crews and

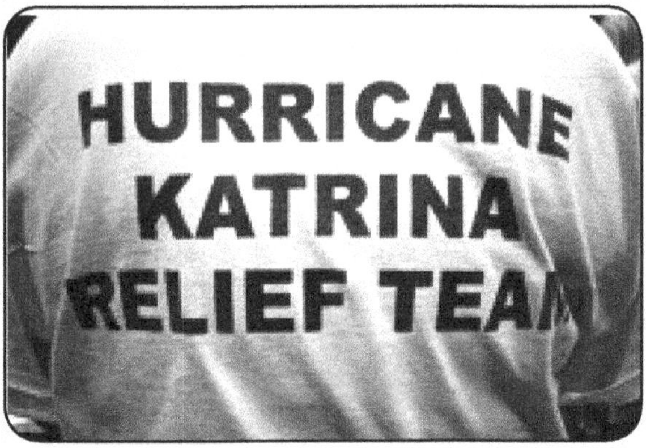

prayer teams. And Operation Compassion was in the midst of it all offering a serving, blessing, caring and loving approach to benevolence so needed to a region in shock. The tangible personal kits and food was an important component, but the power of prayerful touch, hands joined in prayer, and a reassuring hug, were symbols of the heart of God for the victims.

The Church of God, through Operation Compassion and the Chaplains' Commission, along with local agencies, were among the early responders. Relief sites spread throughout the region distributing food, water, ice and essentials. Willing volunteers worked and offered prayer. The stories of grateful survivors were powerful. For some, a life spared the storm led to a soul saved for eternity. Relief lines began to form at the multiple sites as early as 6:30 a.m. and were loaded with people of every conceivable description. The common denominator was need. The rich and poor were equally devastated. Expensive luxury cars ended up in the same line with dilapidated, aged, pickup trucks. Prostitutes and millionaires were in the same line, their hand out and their hearts open. Storms level the social ground. Needs draw diverse individuals toward the same door of hope.

Bill Isaacs was the Administrative Bishop for the Church of God in Louisiana, but during the crisis, he often worked the relief line, greeting, instructing and encouraging. "You never knew who would respond or what they would say. Most were polite and kind. A few were insensitive and a bit ungrateful. Others were desperate for hope, needing to understand things would soon be better. There were often tears and times of deep reflection," he recalls.

Whatever the disposition of a person, the teams prayed "hope and peace over the recipients and attempted to demonstrate God's presence." One day, Bishop Isaacs was driving through the region, praying and asking God for wisdom and the resources to respond. He felt God whisper that we "should be the 'living, visible presence of Christ'" in all we do. The "living, visible presence of Christ"—quite a mission. For two years, Operation Compassion carried on relief work in connection with the Church of God State office. Bill said, "We made sure our work was representative of Christ and pointing hungry souls to the Savior."

During that season, prayers of intercessors and warriors became a lifeline to all in the region, a support for the thousands of volunteers who came to serve from across the nation. Bishop Isaacs recalls, "I saw several key things that occurred as a result of our praying and working."

Compassion

We developed strong feelings of compassion for those who were the benefactors of our praying. The relief effort in the Gulf Coast was a prayer effort, and those who prayed aligned themselves with God's heart of compassion. Bill remembers, "I watched the fiasco at the Convention Center in New Orleans as the government tried to marshal resources to meet the needs of people. The violence and chaos were clearly the result of an institutional approach to benevolence. The people were treated as objects with little compassion. Food was distributed like farmers feeding cattle. There was not an attempt to provide dignity to the effort or compassion.

Across town at the New Orleans center, food was given with a smile and a big "God bless you!" People were made to feel they mattered. The difference was that our volunteers were praying before they served, and prayer allowed them to experience a compassion that transcended the needs, and opened windows of opportunity for communication and spiritual investment."

Discernment

In 2 Kings 6, Elisha prays that the eyes of Gahazi would be opened. In moments of warfare and confusion, more is going on than meets the eyes. And prayer is the means by which God provides the deeper and greater insight. Bill Isaacs remembers, "As I prayed, new insight came into the situation and we were able to more effectively minister to people. God allowed us in a small part to see what He saw."

Provision

The storm caught New Orleans unprepared, as it did the Federal Government, even with the science of meteorology. "But," Bishop Isaacs conjectures, "I believe it was God who moved on David Lorency and Operation Compassion, and other similar ministries, to position the resources needed for our early efforts. God knew what was needed before the essentials were evident to us. I was constantly amazed at provisions that were readily available. We would gather and pray for something very specific that was needed, and then learn that help was on the way, even before we had asked. If Katrina taught me anything, it was that God owns everything and everybody." Bishop Isaacs wrote a book, What Our Storms Teach Us. In it, he talks about Pat, a wanderer who volunteered at the facility in

New Orleans. His eclectic style was mind boggling. His uncanny sense about cutting through red tape and getting provisions was puzzling. When a civic service was delayed and created a special challenge, Pat would hustle off and the red tape would disappear. When a family came needing special supplies for an infant and we were out, Pat found supplies somewhere nearby. He became the "minister of procurement." He always knew where to find what was needed.

He showed up at the center when we needed him, and one day, as strangely as he came, he was gone. He was no angel. Pat was a bit eccentric, but we learned that God was providing everything we needed through the hands of a curious outsider.

"All of us were simply His instruments. As we prayed that God would use us, He did and allowed us front row seats to the manifestation of His grace, mercy, compassion and love to hurting people. This was God at work through us and despite us. We made many mistakes along the way but God insured that our mistakes were not fatal because we prayed and I believe He knew and heard our hearts. This was not about us. The story of God's compassion toward fallen man began long before you or I came to this earth and it will continue after we are gone. What we are blessed to experience is the call to the front lines of life—to engage in prayer and experience the opportunity to represent Him in everyday life to those who are most in need."

If my people, which are called by my name, shall humble themselves, and pray, and seek my face, and turn from their wicked ways; then will I hear from heaven, and will forgive their sin, and will heal their land. Now mine eyes shall be open, and mine ears attent unto the prayer that is made in this place. II Chronicles 7:14-15.

And great multitudes came unto him, having with them those that were lame, blind, dumb, maimed, and many others, and cast them down at Jesus' feet; and he healed them: Insomuch that the multitude wondered, when they saw the dumb to speak, the maimed to be whole, the lame to walk, and the blind to see: and they glorified the God of Israel. Then Jesus called his disciples unto him, and said, I have compassion on the multitude, because they continue with me now three days, and have nothing to eat: and I will not send them away fasting, lest they faint in the way. And his disciples say unto him, Where should we find so much bread in the wilderness, as to fill so great a multitude? And Jesus said to them, How many loaves have ye? And they said, Seven, and a few little fishes. And he commanded the multitude to sit down on the ground. And he took the seven loaves and the fishes, and gave thanks, and broke them, and gave to his disciples, and the disciples to the multitude. And they did all eat, and were filled: and they took up of the broken meat that was left seven baskets full. And they that did eat were four thousand men, beside women and children. And he sent away the multitude, and took ship, and came into the coasts of Magdala. Matthew 5:30-39.

Speak up for those who cannot speak for themselves; ensure justice for those being crushed. Proverbs 31:8 (NLT)

Those who mock the poor insult their Maker; those who rejoice at the misfortune of others will be punished. Proverbs 17:5 (NLT)

The rich and poor have this in common:
The Lord made them both. Proverbs 22:2 (NLT)

Jesus told him, "If you want to be perfect, go and sell all your possessions and give the money to the poor, and you will have treasure in heaven. Then come, follow me."
Matthew 19:21 (NLT)

Humphrey Humanitarian Ministries

Roy Humphrey is a veteran missionary, who at the age of retirement, launched Humphrey Humanitarian Ministries to focus on the Filipino people after a triple national disaster. The ministry was founded to reach lost and poverty stricken people and now extends throughout East Asia. The ministry provides medical care, water-wells, and operates a feeding ministry, children's home, a school, and more.

2

Making A Difference One at A Time

On June 15, 1991, Mount Pinatubo, on the island of Luzon in the Philippines 55 miles northwest of the capital city Manila, came alive, resulting in the second largest volcanic eruption of the twentieth century. Some 800 people were killed and 100,000 were immediately homeless. The ferociousness of volcanic activity was accompanied by a magnitude 7.8 earthquake centered 62 miles to the northeast of the Pinatubo region, no small matter itself. For three months, a series of smaller earthquakes had provided clues. But for 30,000 people who had built their modest homes on the flanks of the volcano, there was nowhere to go.

Six days before the eruption, scientist issued a stern warning and 25,000 people were evacuated. The next day, on June 10, Clark Air Base, a U.S. military installation near the volcano, was abruptly and permanently evacuated. The 18,000 personnel and their families were transported to the Subic Bay Naval Station. Most were returned to the United States. Clark Air Base became a ghost town. Natives watched the familiar trucks leave the area forever, and settled in to face a triple disaster virtually alone.

Americans spend about $50 billion on pets and their upkeep annually.

If a severe earthquake and nine hours of eruptive volcanic activity were not enough, nature had another player. Tropical Storm Yunya passed 47 miles to the northeast and generated huge amounts of rainfall. Suddenly the ash spewed upward, was coming down on the heads of the residents across the entire island. In places, the ash deposit was more than a foot. At least a quarter of those who died were victims of the weight of collapsing roofs.

Angeles City would have fallen on hard economic times due to the closure of the US Air Base, but now it faced greater calamity. As personnel of the abandoned military base and their families fled for their lives, the Amerasian children, fathered by military men stationed there only temporarily, helplessly watched their departure. A handful of civilian remnants chose to stay. All braced for the unpredictable eruption.

Roy and Ann Humphrey had in a previous season of their life served at the Ministry to the Military Center adjacent to the base in Angeles City. After the eruption, they returned to survey the damage. Tons of ash had altered the landscape. Some towns were buried. Angeles City had once been a bustling and thriving community, blessed by the proximity of Clark Air Base. Now the once sprawling and well-kept base was covered with *lahar*—gray ash particles. It was vacant with only a few vibrant residents. Thieves looted all that was left on the base. There was little restraint against the lawless looting. They carted away furniture and stripped once habitable homes of anything valuable. The abandoned base and adjacent housing area became a haven for criminals and drug addicts. The irresponsible found shelter in the very place that had existed to restrain evil. Worse yet, Plaridel II, a housing subdivision attached to Clark, and the Air Base itself, became a dumping ground for "victims of salvage"—a term for summary execution by vigilantes.

The silent killers, poverty and preventable diseases, are a daily catastrophe that never make the headlines.

Roy Humphrey's work with the Ministry to Military was already legendary—serving in Guam, Japan, Germany. He had already given a lifetime, beginning his work with men in uniform in 1957. But it was in November, 1995, that his scheduled visit to Angeles City transitioned into something very significant. What do you do with a Ministry to Military Center after all the military personnel have left the region? The volcano had inflicted severe damage to the center.

One morning, during that November visit, Roy was awakened at 3:00 AM. He heard a voice declaring, "Don't give my people away!" Suddenly awake, he was shaken. He attempted to return to sleep, to revisit the dream-state in which he had heard the voice. He discovered that it was no dream at all. Awakened, he had heard the voice of God more clearly than before. He sat stunned on the side of the bed, shaking from the experience.

Suddenly, he had a vision of what he was called to do in the Pampanga area of the Philippines. God gave him a mission and simultaneously the heart necessary to accomplish the assignment—a heart loaded with love and concern for the Filipino people. Roy recalls, "It was forceful and abounding." The depth of passion he had always felt in his ministry to men and women in uniform, a role he thought he would fulfill for the rest of his life, was suddenly reassigned by the Holy Spirit. God had other plans, and Roy backed into them. "Feed my people!" the Lord commanded. "Rebuild my house!" And finally, "Evangelize!"

He knew there had to be a place (II Chronicles 7:15), a base of operation, a place that honored God's name. A place where people would humbly pray and advocate for righteousness. And, somehow from that place, grace would flow and heal the wounded land. He could see the many hungry, seeking souls, and inadequate resources, but somehow God would multiply the loaves and fishes (Matthew 5:30-39), and perhaps he would bring miraculous changes to lives as well. "If you will follow me in this mission, I will provide for your needs and feed the people as I did in Matthew."

The effects of divorce on children are devastating – they are they poorer than before the divorce, a mother's income drops by a third, even with child support, they suffer higher rates of failure in school, school drop-outs and illiteracy, drug and alcohol abuse, delinquency, early sexual promiscuity and out-of-wedlock births, more illness and more psychological problems and treatment.

After this riveting night of revelation, at 6:00 AM, when it was barely light, three pastors knocked at his door, uninvited, though certainly welcome. Pastors Bong Tiru, Eileen Abasolo and Rex Lorico provided pastoral care at the center. Roy opened the door, and heard one of them exclaim, "Oh, Papa Roy, please don't give us away." These were the same words he had heard by the Spirit, three hours earlier. The Holy Spirit was directing in a rather dramatic manner. The pastors confessed that they had been praying through the night, deeply concerned, that with military personnel gone and the center damaged, that it would be closed. They knew it provided much hope and help in an area that had little optimism. From the center, a care and feeding program had begun for the virtually abandoned Amerasian children. And the center was serving as a house of worship and place to deploy workers to minister in the still deeply stressed region. The vision of the pastors, their very words were confirmation to Roy that God had plans for the Clarkview Center. The four sat down to plan a future that would look very different from the ministry profile of the center in the past.

John and Gilda Ordillo, a Filipino couple, had also been deeply concerned about Clarkview's future after the eruption and the closure of the base. They also had a vision for the area. Together, they decided to stay and offer hope, rather than abandon the remnant that remained and the depressed population victimized by Mount Pinatubo. As the Ordillos and the Humphreys worked side by side, the seeds of Humphrey Humanitarian Ministries were sown. Soon, the genuine love and dedication, the sheer and almost blind commitment of the Humphreys began to impact the people. Natives began to work with them to bring change to the area.

1.1 billion have inadequate access to water and 2.6 billion lack basic sanitation. Two-thirds survive on $2 a day, one-third on less than $1.

As the Humphrey's faithfully labored, God blessed. He validated their ministry with miracles of salvation, physical and emotional healings, and all the while, he expanded the vision of what could be done to impact the abandoned people and place. They could feel the breath of God bring new life and joy into the ministry. Those who at one time had been devastated and were hopeless, were now pressing through their sorrows and praying, reaching out in faith to God. It was like watching nature respond after devastation with fresh, tender growth.

A Center for Operation

With the base abandoned, the center needed to close or redefine its mission. Roy had heard from God—he could not close the facility. His ministry had always been the military; now it would be what the military left behind. Before them were the fatherless, thousands of victims who had not adequately recovered from nature's triple-disaster, and an entire city reeling from a flagging economy. About 42,000 people had lost their jobs, not counting an additional 79,000 jobs that had depended on the US facility. Business slowed down. Revenues dropped from US $13.8 million in 1991, the year of abandonment, to $5.8 million in 1992, reaching a low of $2.4 million in 1993. Cities came to a complete standstill. A large number of the population packed up and moved to other parts of the country, but the poor and the children of the streets, had nowhere to go. They needed hope.

At least 80% of humanity lives on less than $10 a day.

The focus of the center transitioned to serve those left behind, food services and basic care began a focus to US veterans who remained, the children, victims and more. No one in need was turned away, including native Filipino families.

In the early months, friends of the center worked untiringly to clear debris and prop up the roof under the weight of the ash. Many of the workers were not military related families. They had lost their own homes in the tragedy and found the center as a place of hope. They tried with all their might, to preserve it. Roy and Ann rolled up their sleeves and worked with this team. God gave them a love and vision for their needs.

In the faces of the Amerasian children were traces of their US fathers, now absent. A fatherly duty to protect and care for these children burned in his heart. His integrity became a declaration, evidence of care and concern. Ann prayed, and Roy worked next to the Filipino people, matching their work ethic, refusing to exempt himself as some kind of outside superior. His labor was intense and his spirit revealed untiring tenacity.

More than 1 billion people live on less than a dollar a day. The children and these families are imprisoned by poverty that has robbed them of hope.

Gilda Ordillo confessed, "Before Pop Humphrey came to work with us, we were used to missionaries waving money and commanding us to do this or that as they stood under their umbrellas and fans in comfort from the heat. We were so taken back by Papa Roy that we tested him. We wanted to see if he would work alongside the Filipinos in the hot sun. Not only did he withstand the heat. His stubbornness showed as he maintained his daily workout and wouldn't finish until someone else put their tools down first. He and Mom are not missionaries—they became one of us. They are family."

A daily stream of hungry, hurting people showed up at a facility still in partial ruins. Which was primary? The needs of the people or the place? It would take $200,000 to complete the repairs to the center. Somehow the money came in from appeals, from matching gifts, from churches and individual donors, from anonymous sources. Not unlike Nehemiah, they built with one hand and fed the hungry with the other. They completed the practical challenge of repairing the facility without abandoning the mission of caring for the people.

The poorest 40% of the world's population accounts for only 5% of global income. The richest 20% account for 75% of world income. That gap widens each year.

On May 25, 1999, the Humphrey Ministry center was dedicated in honor of Roy's father and mother, Joe and Annabelle Humphrey. In some ways, Roy was living his parent's dream. They had a heart for missions, though they had never been able to serve themselves. Sons and daughters, who believed in Roy's work, and saw the challenge of his present vision, pooled resources to purchase the land to begin the Humphrey Humanitarian Ministry Center. Four lots were purchased to raise a place of worship, and create a home for Amerasians and other street children. For Roy and Ann, with other members of the Humphrey family, the outreach center honors Joe and Annabelle and is testament to saints like them who love missions and quietly carry a burden for the world.

What was once a desolate and abandoned place, inhabited and illegitimately claimed by thugs and thieves with other unsavory characters is now the center of an educational, charitable, civic and spiritual institution, a place where residents can experience peace and feel secure

– thanks to Humphrey Humanitarian Ministries. There they come to know God's love and care, the hopeless get hope. Futures once bleak and barren are now infused with new enthusiasm and vigor. A once despondent people, now have been empowered to redefine their future.

Feeding the Hungry

Once the center was up and running, Roy could now more clearly assess how it might be most effectively used. All around were evidences of need, particularly the street kids. Angeles City is known around the world, and particularly in the Far East, as a haven for hedonism. The rough city, particularly the Bilabago region known for its abundant bars, is often said to be more awake at night than during the day. It is a collage of more than a hundred hot-spots for sin. The population is now approaching 300,000 and some call the city the entertainment capital of the Philippines, particularly with regard to club life.

According to UNICEF, 22,000 children die each day due to poverty—they die quietly in the poorest villages on earth, far from the cameras and conscience of the world. Their deaths are invisible to most of us.

Not all the residents find the glitz and clamor of the high-life clubs accessible or even desirable. They live a world away and struggle with daily felt needs. As Roy watched women walk long distances for fresh water only to return with contaminated water, lacking purity, he determined that one of the first projects would be a well for the poor on a piece of land he acquired only for that purpose. The enquiring people would ask, "Whose well is this?" And Roy would respond, "This is your well!" He could have built a small chapel on the land, but instead he created a neighborhood meeting place—a water well, and he gave it to the poor. A "well ministry" to other areas of the city would also take place. Everyone was not ready for the radical water of life, but everyone was thirsty on hot days, for water—and when they came to the well they knew it was there because someone representing Jesus had dug it to express his love and care for them.

Now eight wells offer water in the name of the Lord. The "Home and Abroad" ministry reach of Roy Humphrey is stunning (www.homeandabroadmininstries.org). The vision is simple—to extend the hands of God to those in need. The mission—to continue showing the love of God ... both home and abroad!

Eileen was one of the children the Humphreys impacted. They became her sponsor and provided financial assistance for her through high school. Eileen remembers Roy's dream question, "What is something you have always wanted that you thought you would never have?" When you are reared in poverty, your dreams can be terribly trivial —at least to others. For Eileen, standing across from the first McDonald's she had ever seen, her dream was to go inside and buy a hamburger. Unless you had the money to make a purchase, you were not allowed inside, the establishment's way of keeping street kids out. Eileen would stand at the door and breathe deeply each time it opened with someone entering or exiting. As she inhaled the savor of those hamburgers, she would say to herself, "Some day, some day, I'm going to get me a hamburger." She remembers when Roy loaded up a jeep full of kids and headed to McDonald's. Her longing was fulfilled. It was like going to Disneyland! Now Roy takes kids on regular visits—a rare treat for throw-away street kids.

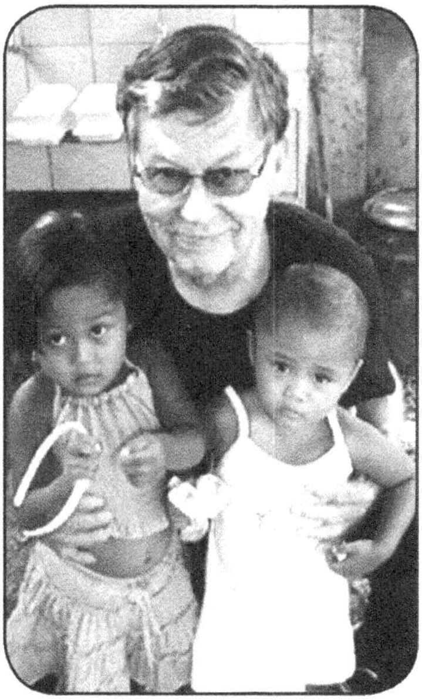

On a recent trip, Roy had 30 kids in the establishment. They were unbelievably well-mannered and quiet as they pressed into the restaurant. Everyone got a hamburger, fries, and a coke, and Roy made the rounds to make sure they were all served. He observed one little girl who had not opened her hamburger. He passed her again, and this time saw that her fries were gone but the hamburger was unopened on her lap, still in the wrapper. "Hon, don't you like your hamburger?" She smiled and responded, "Oh, yes, Papa Roy, I love my hamburger, but I have had one before. My little brother has never had one, and I am going to take this one to him." Roy commended her for her generosity. "Why don't you eat that one, and we'll get one for you to take to your little brother."

Once the feeding program was established, the Center quickly grew to provide daily meals for some 200 people, mostly children. Without the center, they would go hungry. In any given week, more than a thousand are served. All get healthy portions of natural and spiritual bread because the gospel is shared freely with all.

72 million primary school-age children in the developing world are not in school. Fifty-seven percent are girls.

Teaching Morality

The effect on the kids has been quite profound, and might be illustrated by one small experience. The occasional trip to McDonald's does not relieve the pain of chronic poverty and want from which the kids suffer. They still rummage through the dump looking for valuables, something they can recycle or sell, anything that translates to money to buy food or assist their families. Many of them attend school only if they can pay. One of those children came first to the feeding program, and then became a regular at Sunday School. Even on days, like that of his 10th birthday, when his grandfather offered to take him out for a treat, he wanted to be able to return in time for church. His heart was tender and even as a child, he was committed to practice what he was being taught.

Scavenging through the dump one particular day he uncovered a wad of money. He knew that it was a valuable find. With the money in his hand, the words from Pastor John Capati rumbled through his mind, principles from a Bible Study. The pastor had taught the children ownership, about respecting the rights of others, about not claiming what was not rightfully theirs. The call for respect and honesty created a crossroads. The simple "do unto others" ideas were suddenly no longer simple. His family could use the money. It was found in a dump. And yet, no one would purposely throw money away! Whoever had lost it must need it now more acutely than ever. Rather than run home with the money, he waited at the dump site. His stomach was churning from hunger, but he waited. Minutes turned to hours, somehow he knew he shouldn't leave.

The illegal narcotic trade is a $400 billion business globally.

Finally, coming toward him was a group of people, the Barangays, a mountain area people. A lady led them crying. She had obviously lost something, and the group had come with her to help her recover it. The money had been payment for a house, money that had not even belonged to the lady personally. Once the tender-hearted lad heard the story, saw the tears, witnessed the frantic search for the lost item, he smiled and surrendered it to the woman, with only the reward of knowing he had done the rightful thing.

Asked later, if he regretted the action, if he would do it again, he smiled and declared his firm conviction that he had done the right thing, and he felt in his heart that God rewarded him for obedience to the principles he had been taught from Scripture. Such transformations from self-centered living toward a loving concern for others, especially in a world where survival instincts tend to drive behavior, is nothing but miraculous. It should come as no surprise that now the child has led his entire family to faith in Christ. The entire family are faithful members of the local church.

Providing an Education

With education at a premium, one of the key strategies to provide for the kids was educational assistance. The feeding program kept them alive for another day, but it could not address their need for the future. And education was their ticket to a better life! Roy started a "Student Sponsorship Program." It wasn't long until they raised funds to assist 150 children. Without their assistance, these children would not be able to attend school, and would be trapped in poverty.

Some 28% of children in developing countries are undernourished, underweight and stunted in physical growth. The bulk of the deficit is in South Asia and sub-Saharan Africa.

Emily was one of the children, one among so many. A state-side couple signed on to sponsor the child. Emily sailed through school, and became a volunteer, she gave back. She is now a licensed teacher. A generational commitment, a little financial help, and a lot of love, and Emily was transformed from a victim to an agent of change. Sponsors come from all over the world, from Europe and the USA.

A donated van allowed the Humphrey's to provide transportation for 22 of the kids. In addition to educational assistance, the Center provides a range of social activities—a sports team along with other programs. All their funds are donated. Someone hears about need, and they provide the T-shirts or some other need. Chloe and Macey Jones became sponsors at the age of five and three, respectively. The two Filipino children they are sponsoring are their peers and are regularly in their prayers. At least once a year, letters are exchanged between the children and the sponsors, and pictures are provided. They save nickels and dimes to buy supplies, pay tuition, provide back-packs and all that is necessary for their distant friends. On birthdays and holidays they send presents. They have learned the joy of blessing and being a blessing.

Expanding Services

About 0.13% of the world's population controls 25% of the financial assets.

With abundant and needy children, poor and hungry, the daily feeding programs and educational assistance, didn't address all the needs. So God began to provide for other needs as well. In the '80's, the Humphrey's were serving at the servicemen's center in Seoul, Korea. It was there they met Dr. Ann Chang. She was touring Asia. Ann stayed for a season, teaching English, and then went to Lee University and on to Medical School.

But Ann never forgot the kindness of the Humphreys. With her new training and credentials, she became one of the first to journey to Angeles City with a team to provide medical services. On her first visit, more than 600 kids were given medical care, an experience most of them had never known.

If the whole world were a village of 100, 80 would live in substandard housing (67 would live on the streets of the village, half of them illiterate), 50 would suffer from malnutrition, 33 would not have access to clean, safe drinking water, 24 people would not have any electricity (Of those with electricity, the vast majority would use it only for light at night).

- **Medical Ministry**—Free medicine, medical check-ups, routine and minor treatment services are provided.
- **Eye Clinic**—In cooperation with the Philippine Cataract Foundation, free eye check-ups are provided to children who would otherwise never be served, and attention is given to the elderly with vision issues. These services have now been expanded to rural areas touched by the mission.
- **Dental Care**—Rich and Marcia Deem were a young military couple far from home when they first met Roy and Ann. Again in Frankfurt, Germany, their paths crossed. Marcia was trained in the dental field, and when she and Rich learned about the new Humphrey project, she arranged to get dental tools and supplies for the ministry, and now free dental care is provided monthly.
- **Humphrey Learning Center**—In 2002, it became apparent that there were too many kids to scholarship either to public or the more expensive private schools, so the Learning Center was created. Using a special international curriculum, one designed as a preparatory level program, and a host of volunteers, the center was opened to kids who could not pay for an education. A number of the volunteers and workers were children who had been previously sponsored. Each day, there is a sacred as well as a secular dimension to learning.
- **Humphrey Humanitarian Housing Project**—With the help of Men and Women of Action, a number of homes have been provided for victims of floods and storms. And the houses also provide a place for key workers in the various projects and outreach of the ministry.

- **Midnight Rescue**—Angeles City has a sad reputation as a "swinging city" with Fields Road, the street leading to Clark Air Base lined with bars and nightspots. Now, the base, after neglect for years, has been transformed into Clark Free Zone. Instead of attracting servicemen as clients, the area is drawing clients from around the world. Bars are abundant. Exploitation of the young extensive. The children are often vendors in the naughty atmosphere, peddling cigarettes, boiled peanuts, flowers or anything else to make a dollar. Children can be seen on the street as late as 2:00 AM and the small profits they make are either exploited by an adult or used to buy an extra handful of food or pay their school fees. Some are street-kids, totally homeless. Some support their mothers and younger siblings. The girls are the most vulnerable. Here they sometimes get their first taste of drugs or sniff of solvents – and the easy money only temporarily eases the pain in tough times. Some end up in abandoned buildings. Some become slaves to bad habits. Some are victims of their own hopelessness, and become suicidal. Midnight Rescue offers them an escape from the streets. Some are found on the streets. Others are found rummaging through dumpsters in the back allies, looking for discarded food. The hot meal, the smile, the kindness, and the prayer is the first light these night-life kids have seen in years.
- **Mountain Folks**—Near Angeles City are the Aeta people. They are an indigenous people group, primarily a hunting-gathering people, regarded as among the most skilled anywhere on earth in jungle survival. Many are small in stature, less than five feet tall! They have little understanding of things like money, personal property, or government law. Sadly, many, in part due to their proximity to Angeles City, have succumbed to lives of mendicancy or serfdom, panhandling or taking exploitative jobs for very little pay. These "Tribe People" are known in Angeles City for the sweet potatoes and bananas they bring to the streets for sale or trade for other commodities, supplies or additional food, such as rice. Some still live rather primitively, in huts comprised of little more than coconut leaves. They prize sheets and light blankets for cool evenings. Their lifestyle is essentially subsistence. Age and birthdays seem foreign to them. Their concern is daily needs. The outreach to these people is just one example of the missional ministries of the center.
- **Remote Ministry**—There are other groups in remote areas around Angeles City where the ministry is now providing some form of outreach—feeding of both children and their under-nourished parents. Many of these people live by collecting recyclable materials or scavenging through fields after a harvest. One meal a day is the goal, just daily bread, and they allow themselves to hope for

little more. The ministry reaches out to them with food, toiletries, clothes and other necessities, not to leave out, the gospel. Many of them are now Christians, regular members of the outreach church. Slowly, these people are affecting their culture as they walk in the light and alter their behavior in Christ-honoring ways. Roy calls it "doing the right thing" for their fellowman. Despite their daily challenges, their growing love for the Lord shines through. That love is demonstrated by those who serve with the Humphreys. The children and adults are hygienically challenged. The unconditional love, the absence of segregation between the workers and the needy, the city-folks and country-folks, those white and those dark, offer an embrace of people who others have valued very little, and that embrace is done in the name of the Lord. Roy says love, God's love offered by supernatural grace, overcomes the offensive sights and smells. He calls these souls "beautiful creations" to whom the deeds of kindness are a "bridge from God." This ministry now touches some 4,000 kids each month.

The goal of Humphrey Humanitarian Ministries is to reach every needy child through an expanding partnership with churches and other agencies that reach into Angeles City and radiate outwards into the remote rural areas. It may seem very small, but one hot, healthy meal per week can make the difference between life and death for some of these children. Even the schools will allow a gospel message when the ministry brings lunch for the children.

One at A Time

There is an oft told story of an old man walking on a starfish laden beach near the close of a day. As he carefully picks up one starfish after another, stranded on the beach at low tide, he tosses them back into the water. A young man jogging down the beach sees the noble effort of the graying senior, and draws near taunting him. "Old man, behold the multitude of starfish." As the old man picks up one more starfish and tosses him back into the water, the cynical youngster chides, "What difference will it make?" As the story goes, he probably didn't hear the wise old man's answer as he reached for

one more starfish, tossing him back to the sea, and muttered, "It made a difference for that one!"

Eileen is one that would have grown up in the poverty of Angeles City and might not have escaped, but she did. She went to middle and high school, with the tuition assistance. She sat at the table and fed from the hands of loving people like Roy and Ann. She tasted her first hamburger at McDonald's and thought she had achieved the zenith of her dreams. But, the Humphrey Humanitarian Center is a dream factory. There, she came to believe that with God's help "nothing was impossible."

The effects of divorce on children are devastating. Poorer than before the divorce, a mother's income drops by a third, even with child support. The children suffer higher rates of failure in school, drop-outs and illiteracy, drug and alcohol abuse, delinquency, early sexual promiscuity and out-of-wedlock births, more illness and more psychological problems and treatment.

Emily is a child who was also the recipient of a scholarship. Her sponsor, Linda Morrison, who now runs a prayer crisis outreach ministry in the USA, has become more than missions donor. She and her husband have taken an almost adoptive posture toward Emily. She finished high school, college, got her teaching certificate and has completed additional training, all with a goal of helping others as she was helped. Before her sponsor was found, Emily's single mom told her she could not return to school – there was no money. Roy learned about the situation and did an unusual thing. He challenged the children to give their "hamburger money" or whatever they had to sponsor Emily. They did, and she never forgot it. She and her husband teach, lead Bible studies and work with the ministry.

Leigh Savard became a volunteer and a team member. She inventoried supplies, stocked food, cooked and prepared meals, and served them. After serving meals at the center, Leigh would often load up her vehicle and head for remote areas, serving meals to needy children right on the street. Leigh declares that at times, more mouths abound than loaves and fishes, and somehow her supplies reach to the last child.

The feeding ministry now touches thousands of children and needy adults. In addition to hot meals served at the center and at remote places, there is a food distribution program, the educational scholarship and school ministry, the outreaches to the rural areas and mountain people, preaching and teaching ministries, the church and connections with partner congregations, the ministry to the military personnel who remain and the Amerasian children. There are the various medical outreaches, the water-wells— and more.

Each outreach picks up one more starfish—one more child, and

George Barna, Researcher

George Barna, the researcher, says 72% consider poverty to be one of the most serious social problems facing the United States today. And 67% claim some type of intentional and significant personal interaction with a poor person in the past year. This was particularly common among evangelicals (83%) and people who regularly attend a house church (84%).

A substantial number acted personally to provide assistance—clothing or furniture given directly to the poor (75%); a donation to an organization that addresses poverty (60%); food directly given (58%); prayer for the poor (55%); personal service to needy people (47%). Other responses included visiting institutionalized elderly or sick people who are not family members (40%); donating money to organizations that address poverty in foreign countries (31%); serving as a tutor or friend to an underprivileged child (30%); and helping to build or restore a house for a poor family (16%).

Atheists and agnostics emerged as the segment of people least likely to do anything in response to poverty. They were less likely to engage in eight of the nine specific responses measured, and were the faith segment least likely to participate in eight of the nine responses evaluated.

"makes a difference" for that one! The tireless spirit that characterized Roy when he stared down a depressed area reeling from the trifecta of a major earthquake, tropical storm and the second largest volcanic eruption of the last century, disasters all piled on top of one another, that same tireless spirit still grips him and Ann. Despite his recent bout with Large B-Cell Lymphoma and chemo, he isn't looking for a place to stop and sit down. There are too many starfish still on the beach. Maybe, he believes, he can help one more.

Discussion Guide

Big Ideas

- The direction that comes by the Spirit—in prayer, by dreams and visions, yet confirmed by Scripture! At times, it redirects a life and ministry.
- The plight of Amerasian children—do some research. Become more aware of this need.
- Joe and Annabelle Humphrey had a heart for mission. Roy, in some way, lived his parent's dream. As in chapter one, with Margaret, God seems to fulfill destiny and calling across generations. What he starts in the heart of one, he finishes in the lifetime of another.
- Standing in the ruins of the aftermath of the volcano and earthquake, Roy refused to be captive to a mere maintenance and rebuilding mentality – he balanced outreach and care, while at the same time they rebuilt.
- What do you think a child rescue effort, in the heart of the night, in a morally crude place like Balibago would be like?

Notable Quotes

- ❖ One morning, during the visit to the Philippines, Roy Humphrey was awakened at 3:00 AM. He heard a voice declaring, "Don't give my people away!"
- ❖ Americans spend almost $50 billion on pets and their upkeep annually.
- ❖ 72 million primary school-age children in the developing world are not in school. Fifty-seven percent are girls.
- ❖ Some 28% of children in developing countries are under nourished, underweight and stunted in physical growth due to a lack of nourishing food.
- ❖ Roy: "The feeding program kept them alive for another day, but it could not address their need for the future. And education was their ticket to a better life!"

Questions for Consideration

1. Talk about the direction of the Lord given to Roy Humphrey, how he reveals himself, how he speaks not only to us, but to others, in this case, at the same time. Does God want us to so clearly know his will that he could and would speak to us?
2. Talk about Roy's simply 'one child at a time' philosophy.
3. Is there something that Roy Humphrey is doing that your church could assist with? Have you visited his website, www.homeandabroadministries.org? Sponsor a new well? Build a new widow's home? Provide education for a child?
4. Is there something that Roy Humphrey is doing in the Philippines, that you could do in your back-yard?
5. Do you think ministry only emerges around exceptional people?

   Or do you think an exceptional God uses ordinary people—like you —but willing to sacrifice and risk, to follow a compassionate heart exposed to pain?

Then Jesus said to His disciples, "I tell you the truth, it is very hard for a rich person to enter the Kingdom of Heaven. Matthew 19:23 (NLT)

"He who gives to the poor will lack nothing, but he who closes his eyes to them receives many curses."
Proverbs 28:27

"A generous man will himself be blessed, for he shares his food with the poor."
Proverbs 22:9

"A faithful man will be richly blessed, but one eager to get rich will not go unpunished."
Proverbs 28:20

Jesus declared, 'This is how everyone will recognize that you are My disciples – when they see the love that you have for each other' (John 13:35 MSG)."

Daystar

Jerry Lawson has led the former "Glory Hill Church of God" for almost 10 years. The once single-cell congregation, now called "Daystar" has exploded to minister to thousands each week—in a decade. At the heart of their success is a culture of compassion. Jerry says the people taught him compassion. The church, the largest in its county, one of the largest in the state of Alabama, has a reputation as a caring congregation.

3

Reaching Out with Love, Acceptance and A Helping Hand

Over the past 10 years, Jerry Lawson has served as pastor of Daystar Church in Cullman, Alabama. It is now one of the larger churches in the state, and the largest Church of God congregation in less than a decade. Accompanying the phenomenal growth is its reputation, throughout northern Alabama, as a caring place, and nationally, as an example of a vibrant, growing, evangelistic church. The church has grown from under 100 to an on-campus attendance of over 2,000 in their worship attendance. Daystar has become a pace setting congregation, gaining notoriety on several fronts. One of the central keys to their success is a "culture of compassion" and a spirit of giving that has come to characterize the people. Lawson confesses, "I did not teach the people of Daystar to love and care for the hopeless in our community; they taught me." Here is the story.

On September 24, 2001, Jerry Lawson was welcomed as the new pastor of the Glory Hill Church of God, a 55-year-old congregation. The church was small, located on a dead-end street with less than a stellar history. Ahead were remarkable and unknown challenges. Yet, in that handful of faithful people, there existed a compassionate heart. Jerry described them as "a diminutive group of kind people with a huge empathetic core." They had vision but it had not been affirmed. The Administrative Bishop had told him, "Son, this is the only place I can send you. It isn't much, but if you will be faithful, I will try to find something better for you as soon as I can." Jerry would not need that kind of assistance.

Soon after Pastor Lawson's arrival in Cullman, he met Amy Speegle. Amy had been at Glory Hill all her life, a third generation member. She had a heart for the poor and less fortunate. Lacking financial resources for ministry, Amy found ways to compensate with a wealth of passion and purpose. She was not without the credentials of achievement and disciplines—her passion was not superficial and fanciful. She was an award-winning public school teacher, even though she had been out of college only a few years. She was gifted and caring, and her capacity for empathy and true passion seemed to reach the hurting on multiple fronts. Amy had achieved rapid academic and professional success without losing the sharp edge of spiritual sensitivity.

Before Pastor Lawson arrived as pastor, she had experienced a life changing vision. On her way to a college class, the presence of the Lord had suddenly flooded into her vehicle. God was so real that she was unable to continue driving. As she pulled off the road and began to weep, powerful images poured forth. She began to scribble down a record of the encounter and the impressions God was revealing to

Rich vs. Poor

According to DeNeen L. Brown, in a *Washington Post* article, "You have to be rich to be poor." The poorer you are the more things cost. Its takes more time. It costs more money. "The poor pay more for a gallon of milk; they pay more on a capital basis for inferior housing," says Rep. Earl Blumenauer (D-Ore.). They "... pay more for transportation, for housing, for health care, for mortgages." Without a car to get to a supermarket, they pay an extra dollar for it at the convenience market. They do the same for bread and bologna.

"Prices in poorer neighborhoods are higher. The cost of business there is higher—the volume is lower; the worker costs higher. When you are poor, you can't throw a load of laundry into the washing machine and do something else. You walk to the laundromat, hoping it is empty. You bundle laundry in sheets, your's and the kids,' and drag it to the corner. There is little to do while the multiple loads of laundry process. It will take a couple hours. When the poor ride a bus, it takes extra time to get on and off, to wait at the bus stop, to transfer to the next route bus."

Time and money. The poor pay more. Without money, you substitute time. Then you work extra hours, if you can, feeling like you are getting further and further behind. Both you and your money are squeezed. There is more hassle when you are poor—calls from the bill collectors, the landlord, the utility company. Wealthier people use direct deposit. The poor use a non-bank, check-cashing or payday loan institution—more time and money. The "payday advance" company charges an excessive fee and exorbitant interest.

Without a checking account, the poor pay for money orders to pay electric and phone bills, rent, and simple services. They pay a percentage charge to cash their payroll check. They are targets, easy prey, far too vulnerable and without justice. At the "payday" convenience office, the poor pay as much as a 10% surcharge per transaction. Then, to get it delivered in a timely way, more is required for electronic payment service. Why not open an account? Sometimes it is simply a matter of no government approved ID, no car, no driver's license. Sometimes it is matter of education.

The Poor Among Us

With the poor, there is often more month than money. And without collateral or credit, they can't get a loan—but they are desperate for a few dollars. So, there is the "payday" loan establishment. It's quick. It seems painless. Through the bulletproof glass, a cashier asks the applicant for a pay stub, an ID, perhaps another item, and the money is in their hand. The transaction fee alone is usually some 15%, but that is a worry for payday still seven days away. That is not the percentage charge for a year -- it's for seven days, although the terms can vary.

In simple terms, the effective annual percentage rate is over 750%. If you cannot pay the loan, you have the option of deferring payment for another fee, of course, another 750% interest charge. Only a few such experiences, and the rent or electric bill must go unpaid. The whole world is crashing in. If you paid a bill, but do not have proof—no cancelled check—you may not have the extra cash to pay it again until the matter can be cleared up. You have no wiggle room. One day you return to the payday institution to find it closed, but you don't have a means to get across town and clear up your debt with them. The poor pay more.

Pawn shops are only a degree better. Signature loans over car titles or valuables place the poor in a very vulnerable position. Douglas J. Besharov, resident scholar at the American Enterprise Institute, says, "There are social costs for being poor ... people who are poor are often more depressed ... people are so depressed they are not functional. 'I live in a crummy neighborhood. My kids go to a crummy school.' That is not the kind of scenario that would make them happy." Another effect of all this, he says, "Would you want to hire someone like that?"

The poor often stand at the supermarket counter hoping they have enough cash. They sometimes end up putting back the liter of soda, the paper towels, the deli food bought for that night. Is that enough? He hopes. He has no bonus discount card. At times, the poor sell their blood for a few dollars. No gas. No food. They go to a center that gives out boxes of food once a month. They look for vouchers from discarded newspapers. They'll gladly take dated commodities and day-old bread.

The rent they pay is higher than a mortgage would be, but they don't have the credit score to qualify for a loan, and if they did, they don't have the money for a down payment.

The Poor Cont'd

The poor would prefer a house, but a crowded apartment complex is all they find. The neighborhood itself will cost them more —a low-income neighborhood is a dangerous and expensive place to live. The cheaper housing is in more dangerous areas. Late at night, the streets are not safe, and sometimes that is true during day-light hours. They find it unsafe to take the dog out at night because of strangers up and down the street. At times, a stranger knocks on their apartment door. If they answer it, they get robbed, killed, or asked for money. If they're not at home, they may return to find an air conditioner or something else missing.

And just when they are getting ahead, they nudge above the poverty line, and all support is cut off. They no longer qualify for public assistance. Their gross income is suddenly a net loss. The system is insane.

The poor shop in thrift stores. They buy used appliances—no guarantee or warranty. It's cheap, but it may break down tomorrow. "People working who don't make a lot of money go to the system for help, and they deny them," one certified nursing assistant says. "They say I make too much. It almost helps if you don't work." She is paid $15 an hour as a nursing assistant—$600 a week. Her rent is $850. A two-bedroom unit in her area is $1,400. She sets aside $300 a month for special care for an 11-year-old son who is developmentally challenged. She rides a bus to work, adding an extra two hours to her daily schedule. Driving, it would only take less than 15 minutes. Rain or shine, she waits at the bus stop—the 15 minute interval stretches to 30. The poor wait in lines at bus stops. When you are poor, you wait, and you pay more. Adapted from an article by DeNeen L. Brown, "The High Cost of Poverty: Why the Poor Pay More!" (Washington Post: Monday, May 18, 2009).

her. In that moment, Amy had glimpsed at an array of unimaginable ministries reaching out of her small church. These mega ideas were incongruent with the reality of the small single-cell church on a dead-end street, and unbelievable considering the minute scope of the Glory Hill Church of God.

Undaunted by the "facts," Amy was certain that God had spoken to her. The small struggling congregation had a future, and so did she.

Amy started racing into the vision, feeling at times that she was riding a tricycle down the Autobahn. When she was on the edge of being overwhelmed or faced an insurmountable challenge, she kept her head down and peddled faster and faster toward the call, toward the fulfillment of the vision.

When Pastor Jerry Lawson came, one thing mattered to Amy, "Did the new pastor have a heart for those in need?" She wasted no time in putting forth the question. Pastor Lawson quickly answered, "Yes!" It was, of course, the right thing to say. With profound transparency, Jerry Lawson will confess, "Looking back today, I realize that I was unable to answer that question accurately that day because I did not really know what it meant to reach out to those in need." Like many pastors, he did not personally know any profoundly needy people. His work was with "church people." How could he be committed to the plight of the poor and disadvantaged? He, due the isolation and insulation of the institutional church, had never come to really know and understand such people. All of that was about to change.

Just 497 people control $3.5 trillion, over 7% of the world's Gross Domestic Product.

By the time Pastor Lawson arrived, Glory Hill was already ministering to several needy families. Amy had instituted a food distribution program called, "The Master's Hands." Jerry and his wife, Leslie, quickly rolled up their sleeves and became partners in the helping process. "We enjoyed helping people each month, and I really enjoyed the sense that my church was not like all of the other churches that just preach about caring; we were doing it." In truth, Jerry still lacked a personal connection with the hurting, the hopeless, those Jesus called "the least of these." The food distribution program was safe, risk-free, and without personal engagement. Before long that, too, would change.

It was a Saturday afternoon, food distribution day, and the small team had given away food, wrapped with prayer, to about 40 families, a significant group of people. The outreach mission was over for the day and the team was cleaning up. Pastor Lawson was anxious to get home to finalize plans for Sunday.

Just as the work was almost finished, another car arrived. Actually, it was more like moving scrap metal than a real car. It had obviously escaped notice by the Alabama Department of Transportation; it was hardly road-worthy. The two-toned exotic exterior was not a customized color job, just aged green and rust. Arriving in a cloud of smoke with trailing billows and more noises than a Southeastern Conference football game, the car came to a grinding halt just before everyone expected it to explode.

I wouldn't touch a leper for a thousand pounds; but I would willingly cure him for the love of God.
—Mother Teresa

Emerging from the car, Pastor Lawson recalls "... came the most physically filthy man I have ever laid eyes on. He was elderly, with a long and tangled white beard. His clothes were visibly in need of washing and his obscene odor was beyond description. The old man needed a bath so badly that his face was literally caked with dirt and grime."

A remarkable thing happened. Amy, and her husband, Roger, rather than explaining to the man that he had missed the distribution time window, they rushed out to meet him, and welcomed him as if he were a valued customer stepping into some fine boutique on Fifth Avenue. Pastor Lawson recalls, "Their demonstrated compassion was shocking. Their welcoming arms were astounding. I was stunned. Did they know this man?" If they did, if he were a friend or relative, that certainly raised questions about them!

But in the end, it was not questions about Amy and Roger than came to the fore, but the thoughts with which Pastor Lawson found himself grappling, "Who was this person? He looked ominous, if not dangerous. Were they not concerned for their own safety? Had they both lost their sense of smell?" They welcomed the man. No, they loved on him as if he was the one and only person to be served all day. Convenience was set aside, time demands were dismissed, service was offered as if to royalty. His trunk was filled with food, and then astonishingly, they actually strapped more food and commodities onto the top of his car. Now the vehicle was genuinely exotic.

Lawson was astounded and convicted. "I must admit that my heart was not in the right place that day," Pastor Lawson now confesses. "All I could think about was that soap and water are two of the most accessible and inexpensive resources in the world. Why wouldn't the old man at least clean himself up a bit?"

In truth, it was not the image of the old, unclean and unkempt man that was creating rumbles in the soul of Pastor Lawson—it was the seismic shifts, the convicting movements taking place deep inside his own soul. He had seen a stream of hurting people in the few months he had served at Glory Hill, but this encounter would change him forever. This was his first up close connection with a genuinely hopeless person. The inner pain of personal hurt does not begin with the body; it starts in the soul. Caring for such people, with a box of food is only the beginning. It may keep a body alive for a few more days, but it does not liberate them from the pit of despair. Not until the soul is touched is real outreach occurring. Amy and Roger were ahead of their pastor. They already knew that principle. And God had given them grace to begin to live it out.

Having loaded the car and secured the overflow items, Jerry was content that their duty to serve the needs of this elderly and untidy man was accomplished. They had exceeded expectations and were now serving in overtime. He was anxious to wrap up the day's work and retreat to his home office. He needed to get to the real business, sermon preparation.

Roger did not share that unction. In his mind, the ministry to this man was not complete. He insisted that prayer be offered for the scruffy senior soul before they released him, and that Jerry, as pastor, participate. What happened next rocked Pastor Lawson at his core. In a genuinely caring and personal way, one that he would soon learn to be characteristic, Roger insisted that all join hands creating a circle and pray for God to release miraculous power into the life of the aged man. Jerry remembers quickly repositioning himself. He took Amy in one hand and Roger in the other, isolating himself from direct contact with the soiled and smelly hands. Unashamed and without hesitation, as if it was their second nature, Amy and Roger gripped the grimy hands with love and evident compassion, completing the circle. Roger led the most beautiful prayer of hope. He prayed a blessing over the man and his family. It was sincere and touching, heartfelt and earnest.

But there was more. As he concluded the prayer, Pastor Lawson released the hands of Roger and Amy, but Roger refused to release the hand of the man. He would not let it go free. He held on, as if holding on to the hand of a dear friend. A moment later, he spontaneously pulled him close and gave him a bear-hug, as if he were a long-lost brother. It was an unbelievable moment.

Just 497 people control $3.5 trillion, over 7% of the world's Gross Domestic Product.

Pastor Lawson recalls, "I witnessed a change in the soul of a man like I had never seen before. With Roger's back toward me, I could see the man's dirty face, his chin over Roger's right shoulder. It happened all at once. Tears gushed from the senior's eyes in an unexpected explosion of emotion, so profound and sincere that I spontaneously joined in with tears of my own. I watched as those tears cut through the dirt and grime on his face like rivers creating new channels as they flow through a dry dessert. Suddenly, I knew I was in the middle of the story of the Prodigal Son. This, I thought, must be how the reunion between God, the Father, and a lost son really feels. Roger demonstrated the embrace of the Father—the reception of his lost, unkempt, unclean, pig-sty dwelling son. This is how the Father, God, feels about all of us."

Witnessing the embrace of this man and Roger, Pastor Jerry recalls, "I was seeing what it looked like in heaven when I myself came running to Christ, carrying the filth of my sin. And He received me, without regard to my condition, without being repelled or repulsed by sin's odor and corruption."

That day a pastor was changed, forever and completely. Love — God's *agape* love—was poured out in such a blind and disarming way. There was a harvest of humility, of brokenness that was unforgettable and life-changing. The entire experience became a metaphor of the call of Daystar. Lawson declared, "Everything God had planned for my future at Daystar was channeled through that one eye-opening moment. And from that day to this, Daystar's outreach efforts have mushroomed."

The vision of Amy Speegle, the mission of Glory Hill, given on that Spirit-filled day, on the side of the road, is coming closer to fulfillment. Today, about 400 families are cared for consistently by Daystar. The families are served by food distribution, clothing options, school supplies, and an array of medical assistance. At Christmas, there is an attempt to make sure children in needy families receive gifts in the name of Christ. Haircuts are offered, as is continuing education, job placement assistance, and much more.

The most valuable thing distributed, and the most powerfully impacting through all of Daystar's many outreach services is something very simple—*acceptance*. That is what happened, what had been demonstrated through Roger, spontaneously, near the beginning of Jerry's time at Daystar. But they would soon learn more about implementing a culture of acceptance.

In the early "Glory Hill" days, those who came for assistance waited in the parking lot. At times the line was long. Their food was passed through the door to them from the old fellowship hall. A culture of acceptance demanded that such a practice change. The poor and needy should not be kept outside. Within the first year, that was changed. Coming to a church for free food was humiliating enough. Requiring people to stand outside, waiting on their food added to their shame, and placed these fragile folks in an excluded position. That was clearly not the goal. No one intended to convey that signal–it was a blind spot.

The decision was made, all the "clients" would be brought inside. Moreover, they would be brought into the sanctuary, the most decorative room in the facility, and they would be welcomed with every amenity offered to members. One gesture of welcome was the offer of a cup of fresh coffee, but the tab to serve 1,000 plus needy people now streaming through their doors was pricey.

So they made another decision. If the people in need could not have coffee, neither would the workers. They would be no class division. The decision was simple—driven by reality of limited resources. At another level, the decision was quite profound. No volunteer would get what the church could not give the poor. Every decision was informed with the question, "How will this make our needy clients feel?"

Today, if you come to Daystar for food assistance, you are welcomed into the sanctuary, given a seat, and warmly greeted personally. In fact, there are multiple positive touches. An entire team of volunteers is assigned to greet each client and invest attention, care, and kindness into their lives. These volunteers are trained

to strike up conversations, to be sensitive to deeply personal matters, and offer prayer. Some of the most powerful moments in the outreach effort comes as a result of the context created, the quiet moments between a needy family and a volunteer who walks purposefully through the sanctuary looking for opportunities to share hope laced with grace.

In a further effort to make each needy client feel special, Daystar no longer hands food boxes to them. Each family is escorted to their vehicle and volunteers carry the groceries for them. After they are placed in the vehicle, a team member prays with them again. Prayer, Daystar believes, is the most powerful gift they give, the most potent thing they can do. The man or woman who came alone seeking assistance, humbled by their need, uncertain of what the experience might entail, leave in a sea of newfound friends, and with their need met.

A special team is trained to offer prayer to those in need. Members of a helping team carry food to the vehicle walking along with a prayer team member and the client. There will be one more prayer at the car, and perhaps the most personal moment yet. Carrying food boxes is a great entry-level ministry role, almost everyone can do that, and such volunteers get a front-row seat to watch the most important ministry—prayer. At Daystar, skeptical, shy, "food-runners" often turn into compassionate "prayer partners" after only a few short months. Witnessing the transactions between people in need, people with compassion, and the Holy Spirit is a contagious experience.

At Daystar, a box of groceries is not just a box of groceries. And a prayer is not just a prayer. The gift of a food box is a doorway that sometimes offers the privilege to walk into the heart of those in need, and in that sacred space, prayer is the greatest tool. It connects the hurting and desperate to God. Generic prayers are avoided. The goal is personal, informed, and purposeful prayers. So the prayer team is encouraged to ask questions without being invasive, to explore the needy state of the client, all within the bounds of their willingness to share. True intercession is empathetic, it steps into the pain of others, it feels their heartache.

The lowest income nations with 2.4 billion people account for only 3.3 percent of the Gross Domestic Product.

When prayer gives language to what others cannot say themselves, it becomes a powerful medium to connect them with God. Such empathy unites. It draws the wounded to the helper, and simultaneously to God. It bonds hearts. It reveals the heart of God to the person in need. It creates the sense of caring trust and hope. Members of the Daystar prayer team are encouraged to pray specific prayers so that people hear prayer that expresses their needy state and feel care. The goal is to find, by the Spirit, language that expresses the captured heart of God for the person, and express their heart as well.

Pastor Lawson often wanders the sanctuary on food distribution days, and wades into a sea of needy people. He says, "Prayer time is my favorite. I especially love those moments when a needy person is prayed over for the first time at Daystar. They have been shuffled through the system and handed off by every government and community program in our area. Though well-meaning, sometimes the workers in these agencies can lose the personal touch that hopeless people desperately need. When we tell them that they are loved, that they are important, and that we care enough to touch heaven with and for them, everything changes. In that moment, they finally believe that they are more than just a number. They matter. And this is when they realize, that we are the "real deal." We are not just posing as "do-gooders." Jesus declared, 'This is how everyone will recognize that you are my disciples– when they see the love that you have for each other' (John 13:35 MSG)."

There is nothing more central to our biblical mission than caring for the hopeless. Throughout the Scriptures, God encourages us to give to the poor, the widow, the orphan, the injured and the prisoner. Daystar confirmed God's direction for their church by their early experiences, but that was not the only source of direction. They searched the Scripture and the entire experience transformed the congregation into a caring church.

Roughly one in 10 of the persons counted among the poor by the US Census Bureau is either an illegal immigrant or the minor child of an illegal.

Pastor Lawson concluded, "In all the times Jesus and other biblical writers call us to give to those in need, there is never a specific pre-qualification imposed." Churches add their own qualifications and conditions, "Give to the poor ... if they really need it." Or, "Reach out to those in need ... as long as they did not do something to deserve their troubles." Yet, God, the perfect all-knowing Judge never asks for our opinions about who deserves our help and who does not. He simply says—help the poor, no matter what; it is an unconditional command. Knowing and allowing Him to be the judge of hearts lightens our load, it makes our responsibility simpler and easier.

Pastor Lawson notes, "We made a commitment to minister to whoever showed up at our door. And God gave us ample work to do." At times, the sanctuary would be full of needy families and the food warehouse not so full. Such times were always a test of faith. Had the team succumbed to fear and temptation, they might have counted the loaves and dismissed the less needy in the crowd. With less supplies than people, Amy would breeze through and say, "Guys, don't count how much food we have or how many are still waiting. Just keep boxing groceries."

As the doors were closed and the lights were turned out, everyone was doing the math in their head and knew what they had just witnessed was not humanly possible. There was another guest in the house that day – not a member of a needy family, nor yet a volunteer. God had come. And God had multiplied the loaves and fishes. No one had to be turned away. No one had to be discriminated against. No one had to be judged as less deserving.

> **Having been poor is no shame, but being ashamed of it is.**
> *Benjamin Franklin*

The outreach ministry volunteers at Daystar work with their heads down and their hands moving. It is how they have always served. Long before the phrase was famous, Daystar was chanting the mantra, "Yes, We Can!" From the earliest days, the commitment has always been, "Find a way to say, 'Yes.'"

- "Can we feed anyone who shows up for assistance?"—"Yes, we can."
- "Can we provide Christmas gifts for every needy family in the community?"—"Yes, we can."
- "Can we purchase school supplies for every child?" —"Yes, we can."

On one occasion, supplies were low, and distribution day was approaching. There did not seem to be a solution, but the team had learned to simply trust the Lord, not knowing how God would supply. Before distribution day, Amy was offered a semi-trailer load of collard greens. "Wow. Sure we'll take them," Amy mused. But collards came on a refrigerated truck. How would they preserve a semi-load of greens? "Yes, we can. We can handle your collard greens."

More than 33.3% of poor families had a financial difficulty last year, a late payment of rent or utility bills. Some 16% had phone or utility service discontinued or were evicted.

With distribution a week away, a solution had to be found or the gift would be wasted. Church growth had demanded the use of a portable classroom unit as a choir room. Someone observed, "That semi-trailer of collard greens is about the same size as the portable unit in which our choir rehearses—and it's refrigerated, too." The minister of music never knew what hit him. Drums, keyboards, and music stands were expelled and replaced with collard greens. The floor, walls and ceiling were lined to lower the temperature and crates of collard greens were stacked from floor to ceiling. A few days later, over 1,000 people were treated to fresh produce from the 'Master's Hands' at Daystar.

Daystar has multiple "collard stories," all bearing the fingerprints of God. A semi-load of frozen goods was dropped off unexpectedly and they stored food in homes and restaurants all around the county. Occasionally a trucker with a surplus load hears about the ministry at a local truck stop, and the "Master's Hands" are filled with food stacked on pallets for clients. Each time, someone stepped out in faith and said, "Yes, we will do whatever it takes to make that happen."

Some 1.8 percent of all US households "sometimes" did not have enough food to eat during the previous four months, while 0.4 percent "often" did not have enough food.

The "Snapple Story" is one of the most memorable. The church had been given a small box truck to transport food. Soon, there was a flood of free goods if *the truck* would come and pick them up. "It was as if a memo sent from heaven was circulating around the Southeast. Offers came from everywhere." Even when offers came at inopportune times, in the true spirit of caring, the team always answered, "Yes, we can."

Operation Compassion called with the offer of Snapple fruit drinks, if they could be picked up. The truck arrived, but the supply was more abundant than the little truck had been designed to handle. Six pallets of cotton balls wasn't the equivalent of six pallets of liquid Snapple. But in the true, "Yes, we can!" spirit, the six pallets were hand-stacked into the little box-truck. Under such a heavy load, the small truck handled like an army tank. Headed back from Tennessee, it struggled up little hills, and at times it appeared that it might not make it to the top. Pushing appeared to be a clear possibility. Twenty miles from the church, the little truck, just like "the little Choo-Choo,"was completely out of "Yes, I can!" Under the heavy load, the Snapple snapped all four tires. They simply blew out. Miraculously, God spared any injury or serious damage to either the little truck or the Snapple.

Of all the needed components to effective caring, Daystar believes the hand of God is the most important. The second essential is the faith to believe, that if they step out, and work hard, God will take care of the rest. Lawson declares, "Daystar is a truly inspirational place to serve. There are now more people serving in outreach ministries than were members of the church only a few short years ago. The operation almost runs on autopilot. Two thrift stores now completely fund the ministry. Effectively trained teams serve effectively and efficiently."

The focus remains on being a compassionate congregation,

Hunger in America

Canning Hunger was founded in 1992 with the goal of restoring people to nutritional fitness and healthy well-being while ending the demoralizing conditions caused by hunger. Canning Hunger is a privately funded non-profit organization. The organization has been celebrated nation-wide, written up in news articles and books, and the recipient of many awards. In 2002, Canning Hunger was selected by Disneyland Community Resorts Hotels as the top social service agency in Orange County, California

According to 2006 Hunger Study by America's 2nd Harvest, one in four people in a soup kitchen line is a child. More than 35 million Americans are food insecure, hungry, or at risk of hunger. And yet, 96 billion pounds of food are wasted each year in the United States, with 12.4 million children in food insecure households. While 64% of low-income children participate in a school lunch program, only 13% participate in a summer feeding program. Over half of the families that access food pantries have children under 18 in the home. 37 million people in America live below the poverty line, a rate of 12.6% of all Americans.

Thirty-five million Americans are food insecure, meaning their access to enough food is limited by a lack of money and other resources. An estimated 40% of poor families must choose between buying food and paying for utilities or heat. An estimated 35% of poor families must choose between paying for food and paying their rent or mortgage. An estimated 31% of poor families must choose between paying for food and paying for medication or medical care. Nearly half of all families that use a food pantry consist of working families with children.

Hunger is real in America, but not necessary … 107 babies die every day in the US due to hunger related causes. Kids with empty stomachs find it more difficult to learn. Sadly, seniors must choose between medication and meals. Most of the poor have jobs, but their income is not adequate. They run out of money before they run out of month.

"Those who help the poor honor God," Proverbs 14:31.

attempting to faithfully live out their mission. "We've found that the best place to put our focus is on the hopeless. Those are the folks we believe the eyes of Christ are on. When we see them we discover again how much farther we have to go to fulfill our role of being compassionate, of reaching God's plans for our congregation. We understand that each time we give a cup of cold water in Jesus' name we are giving it to Him. Each time we feed a hungry person, we are feeding Him. And each time we provide for a single mom, we are doing it for Him."

Lawson has become a sought after speaker, ministering to tens of thousands, mentoring hundreds of pastors. But he will tell you that the greatest honor he has been given is leading a caring congregation where people can find love, acceptance, and a helping hand from Spirit-filled prayer warriors who believe in the impossible in their own lives and can believe the same for others as well. He pastors at the intersection of prayer and care. And his church is exploding.

Discussion Guide

Big Ideas

- Daystar is an example of at least one 55-year-old congregation that met on a dead-end street and found the grace of God necessary to come alive!
- The 'Masters Hand" is the food distribution ministry of Daystar. They also run a Thrift store.
- Daystar insists that their primary ministry is not commodities that feed the body for a day, but prayer that can feed the soul for eternity. Care without prayer is crippled. It is not whole. The goal is not to connect people to compassionate Christians and churches, but to God Himself. That can only happen with prayer.
- The poor pay more, wait more, are inconvenienced more—and their victimization multiple.

Notable Quotes

- Jerry Lawson says, "I did not teach the people of Daystar to love and care for the hopeless in our community; they taught me."
- Jerry describes the people of Glory Hill as "a diminutive group of kind people with a huge empathetic core." His perspective of them, coupled with humility, may have allowed them to teach him.
- US households with children report food insecurity at almost double the rate for those without children—21.3 percent compared to 11.4 percent.
- Lawson speaking of the Speegles: "Their demonstrated compassion was shocking. Their welcoming arms were astounding. I was stunned ... They welcomed the man. No, they 'loved on him' as if he was the one and only person to be served all day."
- 7.8 percent of US seniors living alone, 884,000, almost a million are food insecure

Questions for Consideration

1. The Daystar story is one of the people teaching a pastor, not with words, but with lifestyle actions. Talk about what a true pastor-people partnership looks like.
2. How important is respect for a pastor, for the church and the people he leads in the formula of church growth and community impact? And conversely, how important is the respect of the people for their leadership?
3. Do you develop and operate care ministries to become known as a compassionate church who reaches the lost? Or, do you become known as a caring church and reach the lost because you have committed yourself to operate care ministries? What is the difference?
4. Discuss Jerry's personal moment when he saw himself dirty and offensive, and yet in the Father's arms, while Roger held an elderly and quite dirty man. Can we really give meaningful love and care until we are humbled by the depth of God's love for us? Is that what levels the ground between the caregiver and the needy?
5. Talk about Daystar's "Yes, we can!" attitude. Is it blind? Unrealistic? Does your church have a "Yes, we can!" attitude?

What's A Holiness Pastor Like You Doing in New Orleans During Mari Gras?

Dr. Dean Hackett is a pastor! A respected pastor. But in the season of Mardi Gras, you may find him in the middle of six million partiers who flood the streets of the French Quarter in "The Big Easy." He is neither the only preacher nor Christian that attends the veritable pagan pageant. Due to the confrontational evangelism that is carried on by a handful of dedicated, but misguided zealots, authorities are considering creating a "Christian-preaching free zone."' Such a move would be an unfortunate precedent. But Dean is not found among those with the bullhorns.

He is with a gentler group comprised of some 240 college students from around the nation. They gather in New Orleans for one purpose, to take the good news to the streets. The special approach to outreach is part of the School of Urban Missions, whose main campus is in Oakland, California, with 25 cohorts in cities across America. The school requires unique evangelism practicums. But what they experience in New Orleans is a class all to itself. Millions, not thousands, but millions are shoulder to shoulder, crowded into a concentrated section of the city, all of them in various stages of inebriation and with wild outfits ranging from ballroom gowns, celebrity replicas, and nothing but body paint.

The students pile into the streets, take precise positions on Bourbon Street near Canal Street. Their stationary positions on the street create a human maze through which the revelers then have to walk. Captains are mobile, serving as "watchmen" and engaging in surveillance of the whole, by prayer walking the area, crying out to God for salvation, and staying alert to spiritual attacks that can arise on the street.

The objective of the team is to bring revelers face to face with the mercy, grace, and love of God. There are resistant hecklers, but the disciplined students are patient and steadfast. Full of tender boldness, they come face to face with one person and then another in rapid succession. As a person pauses in front of them, they look for the open door to share hope. The atmosphere hardly seems conducive to soul searching. And yet, last year, 550 first time commitments were made to Jesus Christ.

Dean reported, "One of the student teams saw a blind man using a cane with the assistance of an aid coming toward them. They asked if they could pray for him. He agreed. After a few minutes of prayer, the students asked him to raise his dark glasses and test his eyes to see if there was any change. He raised his glasses and said, 'Oh my. It is clear.' Then he exclaimed, 'I can see. I can see clearly.' Two other students prayed for a man with a serious back injury. Suddenly that man began bending over again and again declaring, "I am healed. I am healed." There were several significant healings on Bourbon Street, during Mardi Gras.

For five days, Jesus walked the streets of New Orleans. He stood among the rough and raucous crowds through His body, the Church. Multitudes turned Him away. Thousands did not see Him, blinded by sin. But hundreds welcomed Him and opened their hearts for the first time. Almost 500 additional people renewed a commitment they had made previously.

Each night, the team gathered to review what had taken place during the day. They rehearsed the encounters of light and grace that had taken place that day, right in the middle of one of the nation's wildest parties. There were celebration shouts and tears of joy flowing liberally among the students each evening after "Taking it to the streets." Testimonies abounded. They had seen the greatness of God's love and mercy. *"Lord, You are good and Your mercies endureth forever. People from every nation and tongue, from generation to generation, we worship You, hallelujah, hallelujah. We worship You."*

The light belongs in the darkness! The salt has to connect with the corruption. Where does the darkness flourish near you? Where is the light most desperately needed in your city?

Dr. Dean Hackett serves as the lead pastor at Living Faith Church in Hermiston, Oregon, and is a member of the State Council of the Pacific Northwest.

"Who shut their ears to the cries of the poor
will be ignored in their own time of need.
Proverbs 21:13 (NLT)

Command those who are rich in this present world not to be arrogant nor to put their hope in wealth, which is so uncertain, but to put their hope in God, who richly provides us with everything for our enjoyment. Command them to do good, to be rich in good deeds, and to be generous and willing to share. In this way they will lay up treasure for themselves as a firm foundation for the coming age, so that they may take hold of the life that is truly life. I Tim. 6:17-19.

Do not overwork to be rich;
Because of your own understanding, cease!
Will you set your eyes on that which is not?
For riches certainly make themselves wings;
They fly away like an eagle toward heaven.
Proverbs 23:4-5

"'When you reap the harvest of your land, do not reap to the very edges of your field or gather the gleanings of your harvest. Do not go over your vineyard a second time or pick up the grapes that have fallen. Leave them for the poor and the alien. I am the LORD your God."
Leviticus 19:9-10

Mount Olive Church of God

When Gary Sears went to the Mount Olive Church of God it was a relatively small church on a rural road outside the little town of Cleveland, Tennessee. In the congregation, he discovered a passion for care—and he cultivated it. The church exploded. Multiple building programs followed, taxing the limits of their property. So a multi-campus model is now being pursued. Aggressive outreach events are an extension of his heart. He is a compassionate pastor with a compassionate church.

4

Kindness Is A BLAST!

Gary Sears is a pastor, not merely to a congregation, but to a city. Twice a year, he serves as a volunteer Chaplain at the local hospital. It is part of his commitment, to pastor the city, and not merely an individual congregation. Sears declares, "We are called to a city, not just to a church or organization. Paul answered the call of Christ, and with his apostolic team engaged entire cities. He did not simply mingle at the local synagogue." The vision given to Paul by the Holy Spirit, called him to a region, "Come over to Macedonia and help us" (Acts 16:9). The early church understood the importance of the city. Jesus ministered in the villages and to their surrounding areas. He walked *among* the people sharing the love to a lost and hurting world. The Great Commission strategy *began with a city,* Jerusalem. Ministry is to be in the public arena in order to connect with those who truly need an encounter with Christ.

The title of this book, *Wet Eyes and Caring Hands,* speaks of the Mount Olive journey to move toward pastoring a city and not confine ministry within the four walls of a church building. Graduating from Lee College, Gary began a personal journey of transformation from serving in the role of a *pastor doing care* and outreach, to becoming a *pastor with compassion.* At Central Parkway in Cincinnati, he was experientially marked in an irrevocable way. His outreach role forced him into the streets of Cincinnati, and the experiences would mold his perspective of compassionate ministry.

Life for city children is getting worse—25 percent of New Yorkers are children, 762,000 live in poverty, 181 new babies are born into poverty daily. 10,000 children are on New York streets, a number that has doubled in 20 years.

With a tender heart, he remembers tasting his own tears frequently in those early years. His exposure to first-hand sorrow and pain jolted his sensibilities. The substandard living conditions, the poverty and want, the pulsating need of people into whose eyes he looked arrested him. He could never escape it. He felt the pain of those who lived on the streets or in housing that was definitively deficient. He remembers soberly thinking,"I would never want my family to live in this." But for those who lived there, no other alternative was available. No one who works with the poor and disadvantaged intentionally wants to differentiate themselves or offer assistance in a condescending manner. Humility is the wellspring of healthy empathy, and healthy empathy is the touchstone of sincere compassion.

But there was that one Christmas, one moment of turning that Gary would never forget. A moment that revealed him, that forever changed him. He had taken a group of teens to visit families along the church's bus routes. The teens were distributing food baskets and Christmas gifts to one particular family. That experience would become a life changing event for Gary Sears. He and the teens carried the food basket into the depressing apartment. Inside it was cold and decidedly dirty. For one of the bus families, however, this was home. Suddenly, with a room full of guests, another resident of the apartment decided to go public. A large rat ran across the floor. Neither the family nor the kids even seemed to notice. Gary jumped. The experience was so common, so ordinary, the appearance of the rats so routine, they had come to accept their presence.

Some 13% of the poor had a family member who needed medical care, but did not get it due to a lack of funds. About 7% ran out of food in a four month period.

The next Sunday, Christmas Sunday, Gary was working the same bus route. He was helping one of the little girls from that family onto the church bus. As she approached, she held a napkin with something protectively wrapped inside. Everyone found a seat except her. As Gary encouraged her to be seated, she insisted, "I have a gift for you." For her, this was a huge moment— an expression of gratitude, a "thanks" offering. Overwhelmed with anticipation, she demanded her moment. Gary had a sense of what was about to unfold, and attempted to evade the public moment, to acknowledge the gift, but postpone the inevitable opening. "Thanks. I will open it later." But she insisted that it be opened then and there. Inside the crude wrapping paper were homemade cookies baked from items in the food box that had been delivered just the day before, delivered to the dirty, rat infested apartment. "Thank you!" Then Gary again told his little friend, with as much gentleness as he could muster, "Better get into your seat now." But the benevolent little girl insisted on a shared moment, on the somewhat public celebration of her gift. Filled with inner joy, she couldn't wait to see his reaction. She challenged Gary beyond words with her incorrect English. "Ain't you gonna eat it now?" she pleaded. Gary was holding food he feared might be contaminated, and simultaneously looking into the eyes of a small child who simply wanted to give back, since he had given to her family. She was mirroring ministry. She had caught the gift of giving; she had been infected by it. She was demonstrating what had made her heart and that of her family so glad the day before. Suddenly, Gary saw his own reflection in her actions. Her simple act was an expression of his love and kindness, and that of the church. Battling the reality of a weak stomach and holding the cookies, all he could remember was the condition of that dirty apartment and the sight of the rat running across the floor. He had no appetite for cookies, at least not those cookies.

Feeding America reported an increase in demand over the previous year in 74 percent of pantries, 65 percent of kitchens, and 54 percent of shelters.

But that day he had a breakthrough. He experienced a moment of God's grace shown to him in a new and empathetic way. His eyes filled with tears, and he took a bite of the cookie, and thanked his little friend. She would never know the transformation she had innocently but catalytically put into motion. *To give* is to remain in *an empowered position*. It is one thing to be an empowered helper, but it is quite another to watch the unempowered become themselves agents of grace and give gifts.

To receive, especially from those to whom you have given, *requires greater grace*. It demands the ability to create room for their gifts and to humbly receive them, and that may be the greatest component of compassionate ministry. It is not a mere subsidy that is exchanged; it is *the exchange of people* that transforms. The ground is leveled. The poor and needy are granted peer status. That social transformation is at the heart of the gospel.

Among the children of illegal immigrants, the poverty rate is 37 percent.

On that day, Gary could see more clearly the difference between the people and their need state. He recalls, "That day, I moved *beyond pity*, and I *experienced the compassion of God* for others, the kind of compassion Christ had for those in need of a shepherd. A pastor's heart for the distressed in the city was born in me." That day, he was humbled, not by giving, but by receiving; not by being the one empowering the lesser, but by making room for another to empower. True compassion demands the powerful become peers with the poor. This is a reenactment of the incarnation—God among us, God as carpenter, God living in Nazareth, God wrapped in flesh, touched with our infirmities.

In Acts 10, Peter was preaching to the Gentile gathering at the house of Cornelius. This was not Peter's typical audience. He was bagels and lox, and this group was ham hocks and yeast bread. But a vision, paired with an extraordinary series of events, had compelled him to this setting, and all that overnight. Suddenly, Gentiles would know the same riveting sense of God's presence that Peter and those in the Upper Room had known. Peter learned by the experience, that God would show no favoritism, that he was God of Jew and Gentile, willing to touch any city or people group, any geographic area or nation that would accept the gift of His Son. Jew or Gentile, God loves them all. There is no wrong side of town to Jesus. There is no 'excluded other'.

Peter declared, "God anointed Jesus of Nazareth with the Holy Spirit and with power, who went about doing good and healing all those who were oppressed by the devil, for God was with Him" (Acts 10:38). Pentecostals see only the miraculous dimension of this passage or assume that "doing good" and "healing" are synonymous. We are too often narrowly inspired by a some great 'miracle working ministry' that oozes with the supernatural. Young Pentecostal preachers often focus exclusively, myopically, on the miraculous – with a sincere desire to see

God open blinded eyes, heal the lame and raise the dead. Longing for a supernatural dimension in his ministry, Gary recalls, "I realized *only God could do miracles.* I had been waiting to do ministry in a way that was impossible without supernatural intervention, without a supernatural dimension I had not known. I was allowing my ministry to be held hostage until I stepped into some supernatural zone for which I had longed, but not experienced. And yet, in the same passage that contained the note about 'healing'—a supernatural intervention of God was also a note about 'doing good.' The first was outside of my power. The other was within it. I couldn't heal, but I did have the power to do good." This simple but profound insight became a defining inspiration for the kindness outreach of the Mount Olive Church of God.

A recent study found that poor folks—households earning under $13,000 per year—spend about 9% of all their income on lottery tickets.

Jesus went about "doing good!" That was the foundation of his earthly ministry. In the last verse of John's gospel we read, "And there are also *many other things* that Jesus did which if they were written one by one, I suppose that even the world itself could not contain the books that would be written" (John 21:25). Gary Sears came to believe that these "other things" were the benevolent "good deeds" of Jesus, not as sensational as the miraculous, but far more numerous.

Kindness and love are gifts that don't demand a cash investment. Mark Twain said, "Kindness is the language which the deaf can hear and the blind can see." We can all show a little kindness and a lot of love. A Russian proverb declares, "A kind word is like a spring day." Demonstrating the kindness of God involves no hard cash cost. A smile may light up the life of someone who hasn't received one in a long time. Opening a door is a gesture of kindness, inclusion, and graciousness. They are snapshots of God. They are moments from the life of Christ that ooze through our lives, reflecting the kindness of Jesus interacting with the woman at the well; the pause under the sycamore tree and the affirmation of Zacchaeus. He refusal to judge the woman caught in adultery. He gave dignity to the lad with an inadequate lunch and the immortalizing of his simple gift. Here is Jesus—sensitive, caring, forgiving, inviting and more. And that is how He wants us to be.

The journey from mere tears of sadness over the hurt of others to tears of prayerful concern, which moves us to action and engages our hands, is worlds apart. But the beginning point for a laborer in the harvest field is first to see it. The church needs to find ways by which more people will see needs with such impact,that the experience brings tender tears.

In the early days, Gary often gave a significant portion of his ministerial paycheck away, almost recklessly. He was living by Spurgeon's mantra, "Carve your name on hearts!" He would take people home with him, and their hard luck story would move him to tears. His tender heart made him vulnerable. He recalls, "If it were not for God, his mercy and gracious protection, Charlotte and I would have been in worse shape than many of the people we helped." How you remain tender without becoming cold and callous, tough and resistant to needs, is a critical balancing act.

Gary soon found out that "wet eyes" alone would not help him fulfill the biblical mandate to care for the hurting and helpless. Only when "caring hands" were added did it become possible for a church to fulfill God's command to go into all the world and touch the hurting. The commitment to care for the hurting and reach out beyond the four walls of the Mount Olive sanctuary was in response to a praying congregation. Little happened until the church began to deliberately and specifically pray about community needs. Those needs were not obvious at first. But persistent community-focused prayer allowed God to inform hearts. Only then did the church translate prayer into purposeful action.

In the early days, there was one woman, one catalyst. She was a wonderful woman affectionately referred to as "Big Mama". That woman birthed in the entire congregation a burden for the poor. Single-handedly, she inspired individuals to collectively begin to act in behalf of the less fortunate. She moved people beyond a genuine, heartfelt sorrow for those in need to concrete action. Tears were not enough, neither were prayers. The church needed to start doing something about the needs around it.

"Big Mama" started a little "closet of care" under the steps of the old Mount Olive church balcony. From that place, she fed hundreds. All that Mount Olive does in terms of food care and distribution grew from that humble root. Today, there is a weekly endeavor whereby the church feeds and provides help for families from a facility called "Compassion Corner." As congregational concern and compassion grew, others became involved. Long after this wonderful lady's passing, her legacy lives though many others who care for those in need. A Chinese Proverb observes, "A bit of fragrance always clings to the hand that gives roses." Like Mary, the gift of the contents of our alabaster box can't be contained—it transforms the atmosphere of the whole house. Everyone ends up smelling sweet.

A survey by the US Conference of Mayors involving 92% of cities cited unemployment as one of three major causes of hunger.

"Big Mama" had a ministry of baking pies for anyone she heard was sick. It was her medicine. Even folks who had received bad news got a "Big Mama" pie—a sedative. And her pies were tantalizing. The irony of her ministry is that she offered to others what she herself could not enjoy since she was diabetic. She never used a recipe, at least not a written one. It was a pinch of this and a handful of that. She just knew how to mix the ingredients. So when the Lord called her home, everyone was sure only heaven had her pies, and those here would have to wait to taste them again. Her recipe died with her.

No one knew that a granddaughter, who loved helping her, had caught her gift. One Pastor Appreciation Day, Gary received a great gift from the granddaughter, a pie that looked and tasted like "Big Mama's." As if made in heaven by the sweet saint herself, the secret ingredient was there as well, that measure of love baked into each pie. Someone once said, "The true meaning of life is to plant trees, under whose shade you do not expect to sit." Interestingly enough, the granddaughter who now carries on "Big Mama's" ministry is also a diabetic. She offers to others, what she herself cannot enjoy. And that spirit is at the core of Mount Olive's compassion. It is genuine *agape*.

In 2006, Pastor Sears wrote *Operation Kindness—Kindness is a BLAST!* using the word "BLAST" as an acrostic

- **B**-e Available
- **L**-ove People;
- **A**-cts of Kindness;
- **S**-eed Planting; and
- **T**-ime Well Spent.

In this book he shared the journey that led the Mount Olive congregation to focus not only on *in*-reach (**edification**—*caring for one another*) but to also turn to *out*-reach (**evangelism**—*going into the highways and byways, inviting souls to come in*), an expression of the heart of God for the lost and hurting. Gary believes, "If you will make yourself available to God through tears of prayer, He will turn you into a loving person who, through showing acts of kindness and sowing seed, will in time produce souls for the kingdom of God." That is the strategy for the Mount Olive outreach ministry.

According to Pastor Sears, each church should have a plan to reach out to and into the city touching the needy. Every church has been called by God to reach their city, county, country and then around the world. In the opening words of the Book of Acts, the short history of the church's beginnings, Jesus charges His followers: *"But you shall receive power when the Holy Spirit has come upon you; and you shall be witnesses to Me in Jerusalem* (the immediately local city), *and in all Judea and Samaria* (the surrounding country/county; the ethnic pockets nearby; the displaced and disadvantaged), *and then to the ends of the earth* (around the world)" (Acts 1:8). The mandate is not optional. It is the responsibility of every church to protect the reputation of a good name that commends the church to its community, opening doors for ministry in the streets and across town where church members live and do their business.

The teen suicide rate and the divorce rate have tracked each other, going up 300% in the last 30 years.

Even if the reputation of a church has been spoiled, the importance of a good name, of integrity with the city, is so important that it should be redeemed by the church and pastor willing to work at it. In one city, a congregation faced a difficult time financially. Eventually, the church along with the founding pastor, declared bankruptcy. Sadly, the media grasped the story and the heart-rending narrative was in the headlines for days. The church was helpless. There seemed to be no solution.

Soon the scintillating tale ran out of wind. But that was not the last word in the narrative. That pastor made a trip to every creditor and pledged that he and the church would repay every penny—with interest. His intent was noble, but few believed that he could fulfill his pledge. They were wrong. Today, the pastor and the church continue, now as a mega-church ministry with greater impact than before. They have a television ministry, a university, and a soul winning congregation with honor and reputation for integrity. They kept their word. They paid their debt in full and reclaimed the virtue of a good name in their city. Because of their diligence, God has now given them a ministry that reaches around the world.

The Mount Olive vision is an outreach program to the city of Cleveland, Tennessee, driven by kindness. The menagerie of sharing events has grown to be quite diverse. The church has offered free car washes and handed out bottles of cold water. It encourages its people to witness on Sunday by giving generous tips to a waiter or waitress along with an occasional extra blessing. No tipping of less than 20 percent. They encourage paying for the order behind them when ordering at a fast food drive-though. After paying, they leave a card to be handed to the vehicle behind them that declares that the act of kindness was done to show the love of Jesus.

All of these tactical endeavors are to position their people to gain the right to share the love of Jesus. Someone once said, "No one cares how much you know until they know how much you care." John R. W. Stott, the great missionary leader said, "Social responsibility becomes an aspect not of Christian mission only, but also of Christian conversion. It is impossible to be truly converted to God without being thereby converted to our neighbor."

The prayer and outreach pastor has developed a plan to reach from the church to surrounding neighbors by sending prayer teams to determine the needs of those living closest to the church facility. Martin Luther, the Great Reformer charged, "It is the duty of every Christian to be Christ to his neighbor." In many neighborhoods, the church is the absentee, non-contributing neighbor.

- **Prayer**—The first team sent is always a prayer team. That team first prayer-drives the neighborhood and covers it with prayer, opening their heart to impressions that might come by the Spirit as they pray together. They submit a report of the prayer mission, including spiritual hunches, impressions from the Holy Spirit.
- **Research Team**—The second team is a fact-finding team. They collect empirical data, the obvious, visible needs. Does there appear to be elderly residents or young families? Are there homes in need of repair? Houses that just need the grass cut? Are there families who have some specific and particular need for assistance or care?
- **Personal Contact**—The third team sent is an information team. This team goes out on Sunday mornings during typical church attendance hours, so they can visit every home surrounding the area around the church facility, obviously with a focus on the functionally unchurched or shut-in. This team carries the gift of a local newspaper, a church bulletin, and a liter of Coke. They chat. They offer assistance, featuring the "good neighbor" and servant-heart of the church. If appropriate, they might pray, but the gospel is never forced. The goal is to establish a

relationship.

- **Action Team**—The final team is the Men and Women of Action. This team takes on projects that enable the congregation to demonstrate the love of Christ and win the lost to Him. These projects include everything from lawn ministry to roof replacement. All of these outreach efforts have one goal—to demonstrate the love of Christ and win the lost to Him, to share with a family in need and offer them membership in God's family.

In 2000, the number of US children, born without a father of record, reached 33% of all births, an all-time high. The greatest increase was among whites.

The Mount Olive strategy for moving from a church that simply "feels pity" for those less fortunate to becoming "compassionate change agents for Christ," and doing the good that He would do if He were here today, are included here:

Start With a Church Motto—"*A Church to Come Home To!*"

Find a statement that declares your church is interested in people outside of your four walls. Our church motto is *"A Church To Come Home To."* In Cleveland, a lot of people have church wounds. They are victims of friendly fire. The Mount Olive church serves as surrogate, expressing regret in behalf of brothers and sisters who have wounded others, unwittingly or even knowingly. Gary declares, "We try to let hurt people know that we, as representatives of the Church, and as a church, are sorry they have been hurt. We want to be the safe place that encourages them to come to a church that will genuinely care about them." We tell them, "Don't let past hurts keep you from coming home!"

Pastor Sears believes, "People need to clearly understand that the church cares because God cares—and we have to say that often. He tells the story about a church with a beautiful stained glass window displaying a shepherd reaching out to a lost lamb. The design was stunning, but it was only visible on the inside of the church, not outside where lost sheep are usually found."

Surround the Harvest

The obstacles a church faces in reaching a city can be overcome. In the process of moving forward to construct a 2,000 seat sanctuary, at the point of Mount Olive's greatest growth, they discovered that the public works infrastructure, specifically, the water lines, were inadequate to provide the necessary sprinkler and fire protection required for the building. They hit a seemingly insurmountable wall. Their building permit was denied, and it was a major blow to the congregation. They went to prayer and heard God say, "Surround the harvest." Mount Olive adapted, it changed its goal in order to "surround the city" with a multiple congregation and outreach model, to get closer to the lost in adjacent communities. Limitations can be overcome. Sears believes, "Whatever the need is—your church can fill it. The plan begins with prayer. Ask God for direction, for a strategy. Then watch God do something bigger than what seems possible, and certainly much bigger than we could begin to do on our own."

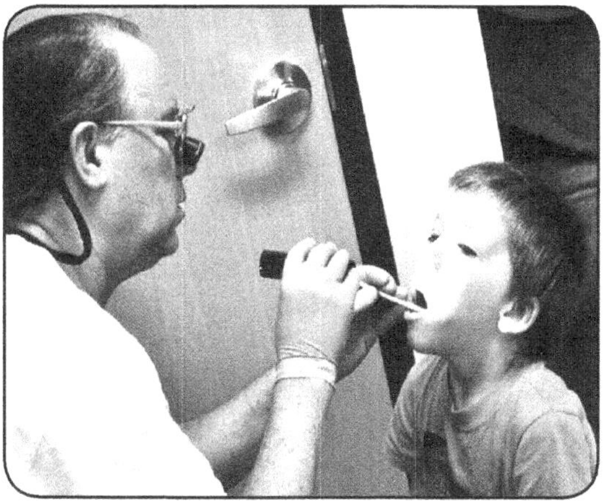

Care For What God Has Given and Reach Out For More

Pastor Sears reflects, "Our vision of reaching the city started with pastoral prayer rides across the city. My prayer partners have ridden thousands of miles crisscrossing Bradley County, and praying for God to cover the city with love, and to destroy the bondage of religiosity that has held us bound for far too long." Those relentless prayer drives were focused on schools and businesses alike, on various sectors of the city. Gary recalls, "We parked in neighborhoods that had high crime rates and prayed for God to intervene and bring deliverance. As we prayed *over* our city, God birthed in us a desire to go *into* the city and make a difference." Now, Mount Olive members are engaged in the community. They volunteer as workers in hospitals. They prepare food for families who have someone in an Intensive Care Unit (ICU). They supply food for the local homeless shelter. Volunteer teams repair homes and care for shut-ins. They volunteer for chaplain duty in hospitals, correctional facilities, as well as roles in the police and fire departments. All of this is to show the love of Jesus and earn them the right to share the salvation message.

Have a Party and Invite the City

Every July 4, Mount Olive has a large family-style barbecue and party for the entire city and county. Last year, over eight thousand people joined the fun. There were free games and rides for the kids as well as free entertainment for the adults, all culminating with a giant fireworks show to end the evening. Everything was free! This is a high-profile event, a huge doorway toward faith that the church creates for the community, done to earn the right to share Jesus, to make the declaration that the church cares about faith and family, about the nation and the city. Pastor Sears says, "We pray over all of the activities and our congregation is there to share the salvation message in an effort to win souls to Christ." John Wooden, the great UCLA basketball coach, and foremost Christian observed, "You can't live a perfect day without doing something for someone who will never be able to repay you." Sadly, the church is far too self-interested.

Children of the never-married do not have a high suicide rate, rather, they have a high homicide rate! Children who knew their father but lost him through divorce, grow up sad. Children who never knew their father, grow up angry.

Remember the Poor! The Clay Pot!

If you visit Mount Olive on Sunday morning, you may notice sitting on the platform steps below the pulpit is a small unadorned clay pot. During the offering, without fail, people will slip to the front of the building, and drop money into the pot. Children will come forward with nickels and dimes. Catherine Marshall, the beloved author and wife of the Great Pastor and Senate Chaplain, Peter Marshall would say, "No matter how little you have, you can always give some of it away."

Here is the story of the "clay pot" ministry at Mount Olive. During the recent economic turn-down, Pastor Sears was reviewing notes for the morning message from Luke 6:38, which says, *"Give and it shall be given you."* As he moved through the offices toward the sanctuary, he happened to see a clay pot sitting on the book shelf of his administrative assistant. He picked it up, thinking it might be an appropriate prop.

That Sunday morning he shared how, in the time of Christ, prepackaged things weren't sold in the marketplace. Shoppers carried their own containers to the market and then bargained with the merchants about price, quality and quantity. Once a price was established, the owner instructed a servant to pour the grain. The servant would pour the grain into the container, then press it down, and shake it until it settled into every corner of the vessel and the grain overflowed. Any grain that overflowed and fell into the servant's apron was his to keep. He, the servant, the disadvantaged, was blessed by the overflow. The question lingered, as if suspended in the air? Who do we allow to be blessed by our overflow? What disadvantaged person would find a few grains a blessing to help them get through their week? When our cup is full, do we consider others less fortunate?

Gary continued his message and placed the clay pot to the side of the pulpit. He was finished with it for the morning, but God wasn't. He had been calling for an extra measure of sensitivity for weeks. A few Sundays earlier, he called for a "Lean Year Offering," asking the people to give something extra to help families who had lost a job or were having a hard time. "One of my goals," he says, "is to infuse compassion in the whole of my congregation. People who allow themselves to be moved with compassion can be deeply used by God."

When he placed the clay pot on the floor, immediately, and in the middle of his message, a man came forward and placed a hundred dollar bill in the clay pot. As he kept preaching, others began to come forward, until virtually the entire church had responded, filling the clay pot! The congregation got it. It wasn't a *sermon*; it was a *message* for their church—and they responded. The 'clay pot' was left at the altar as a permanent feature. The first year it sat there, more than $100,000 was given through that simple portal alone to help hurting brothers and sisters in the Mount Olive congregation. Gary says, "We have answered these difficult economic times through the use of a clay pot. That's right ... a clay pot!"

During the last July Fourth gathering, a decision was made to introduce the clay pot to the community, the people who gathered for the summer holiday celebration. Gary told them the plan, "We will use these funds to assist anyone with a dire need. When funds are adequate, we will try to help." In a few moments, the pot was the recipient of sufficient funds to repair a car that had become the only home one family had. They were living in the vehicle. Not only was the car repaired, but adequate funds got them a place to stay. Another family needed work clothes, and that need was met. A brother and sister, both in wheelchairs, had recently lost another brother to death. With their own limited funds and needy state, they were not able to provide for his funeral and interment expenses. So the church assisted in caring for the brother in a proper way. They were both surprised and grateful.

Now the little pot had grown from meeting congregational needs to meeting community needs. The not so small effort at the July 4th gathering has spawned a new Mount Olive outreach to the county called "Community of Care." The church has discovered community and civic partners who are willing to collaborate in ways that reach those in need and without help. The result has been the gift of a new roof to a man whose house had otherwise been condemned. A financially distressed single mom received assistance with repairs to her home after she had

Global Hunger

The world is facing a hunger crisis unlike anything it has seen in more than 50 years. Almost a billion people are hungry—925 million. Every day, almost 16,000 children die from hunger-related causes. That's one child every five seconds. In 2005, there were 1.4 billion people in extreme poverty, but the World Bank estimates that the spike in global food prices in 2008, followed by the global economic recession in 2009 and 2010, has pushed that number to somewhere between 100-150 million people into poverty (United Nations Food and Agricultural Organization). While poverty has declined dramatically in East Asia and in India since 1981, Sub-Saharan Africa has seen little change with 51 percent of the population still living on less than $1.25 per day. The absolute number of people in extreme poverty has almost doubled since 1981, escalating now to 400 million (*World Development Indicators 2009*, World Bank Group, p. 69; http://data.worldbank.org/topic/poverty).

About 75 percent of the world's poor people live in rural areas and depend on agriculture for their livelihood. In 2008, nearly 9 million children died before they reached their fifth birthday. One third of these deaths were due directly or indirectly to hunger and malnutrition—inadequate nourishing food, or a lack of sufficient protein, vitamins, minerals and calories to support physical and mental growth and development. Childhood malnutrition brings irreversible harm— poor physical development, compromised immune function, and impaired cognitive ability. Around the world, 178 million children under 5 are stunted, low height for age. Of all stunted children, 90 percent live in just 36 countries, most of them in sub-Saharan Africa and South and Central Asia. In countries with these high levels of childhood malnutrition, the economic loss can be as high as 2-3 percent of Gross Domestic Product. The whole nation suffers.

The U. S. development assistance program to global hunger accounts for about 0.2 percent of our gross national income. Since 2000, U. S. poverty-focused development assistance has tripled, and currently totals about $28 billion (Bread for the World estimate), an amount that is less than 1% of the federal budget. In a recent twenty year period, the U. S. development assistance to support agriculture and rural development declined from 12 percent to 3.1 percent, a 75 percent reduction.

"They will hunger no more, and thirst no more." (Revelation 7:16)

been abandoned by her husband and left with children. The list of help projects continues to grow. Praise God! Mother Teresa once said, “We have forgotten that we belong to each other.”

What Can Be Done In Your City?

Pastor Sears says, “What can be done by your family of believers is only limited by your prayer life. When you begin to pray and look at your city through wet eyes, when you weep out of Spirit-led compassion for the hurting, then the creative Holy Spirit will birth ideas and action plans, and the simple ways your hands can express the compassion God feels for your community. I don’t know your community needs, but I do know, when you pray, your heart will explode with compassion and concern. I encourage you to consider initiating your own “Operation Explosion” in your community. Let *kindness* become a BLAST in your church!

“Look at your city through eyes of prayer and capture the vision of what God wants show you. When you see the harvest, with spirit-enlightened eyes, you will never drive through your city and see it the same again. Congregational members will bring spirit-infected ideas on how you can touch and then reach a city, county, country, until you reach literally around the world.”

The **Three W’s** of Mount Olive Ministries are **Weeping, Watching** and **Working.** Those are more difficult to actualize than to articulate as vision. But they could become your words, guiding your church to touch your city. Gary challenges other pastors, “If that happens, and it may not happen easily, there will be an explosion of compassion and practical care-based outreach.

Your congregation will move from a self-absorbed focus to one of sharing, and that is a major feat.” Zig Ziglar once said, “There are no traffic jams when you go the extra mile.” But sacrificial action always draws the fire of God. Pastor Sears is convinced that Mount Olive is not unique. “What follows compassionate and sacrificial care will be an explosion of growth that will fill your church with hungry hearts! That is what happened at Mount Olive.” Kindness, it turns out, is like a boomerang. It always returns home.

Discussion Guide

Big Ideas

- Acts 10:38. Gary suggest that we Pentecostals sometimes wait on the miraculous—which only God can do, rather than "doing the good" that is within our power. Agree or disagree?
- ***"BLAST"*** as an acrostic—***B-e*** *available;* ***L-ove*** *people;* ***A-cts*** *of kindness;* ***S-eed*** *planting;* ***T-ime*** *well spent.*
- The ***Three W's*** of Mount Olive Ministries are—***Weeping, Watching*** and ***Working.***
- Almost a billion people are hungry—925 million. Every day, almost 16,000 children die from hunger-related causes.

Notable Quotes

- We are called to a city, not just a church!
- She was mirroring ministry. She had caught the gift of giving; she had been infected by it. She was demonstrating what had made her hear and that of her family so glad the day before.
- To *give* is to remain in an empowered position ... to receive, especially from those to whom you have given, requires greater grace.
- That day I moved beyond pity and experienced the compassion of God. How do you "Carve your name on hearts!" (Spurgeon)

Questions for Consideration

1. In what way does your church engage the city? How could it begin to do so?
2. What do you think about Mount Olive's annual 4th of July party for the community?
3. Discuss how God used the exposure of Pastor Sears to the poor as a catalyst for the compassionate soul of his ministry? Would he have been the same without such a moment, such a transformation? Do you think we isolate ourselves too much?
4. "Big Mama" embodied compassion and modeled it. How can lay-led ministries embedded in the heart of the church become the seed-bed to "take-over" the church, changing its culture in a positive way? Do you have a "Big Mama" in your church?
5. Discuss how God used the giving spirit of the little girl to change Gary Sears. Can we really minister to the poor unless we are able to receive ministry from them?

Matthew 28:18-20, Isaiah 58, Matthew 25:31-46 and James 1:27

"Then He will say to those on His left, 'Depart from Me, you who are cursed, into the eternal fire prepared for the devil and his angels. For I was hungry and you gave Me nothing to eat, I was thirsty and you gave Me nothing to drink, I was a stranger and you did not invite Me in, I needed clothes and you did not clothe Me, I was sick and in prison and you did not look after Me.' They also will answer, 'Lord, when did we see You hungry or thirsty or a stranger or needing clothes or sick or in prison, and did not help You?' He will reply, 'I tell you the truth, whatever you did not do for one of the least among you, you did not do for Me.'"—Matthew 25:41-45

"No, this is the kind of fasting I want: Free those who are wrongly imprisoned; lighten the burden of those who work for you. Let the oppressed go free, and remove the chains that bind people. Share your food with the hungry, and give shelter to the homeless.

"Give clothes to those who need them, and do not hide from relatives who need your help. "Then your salvation will come like the dawn, and your wounds will quickly heal. Your godliness will lead you forward, and the glory of the LORD will protect you from behind. Then when you call, the LORD will answer. 'Yes, I am here,' He will quickly reply. —Isaiah 58:6-9. (NLT)

"Better a poor man whose walk is blameless than a rich man whose ways are perverse."
Proverbs 28:6

RIO (Restoration Int'l Outreach)

Ronnie Hepperly has been at his present assignment for a dozen years, and in that time the 100 year-old congregation, which numbered some 50 folks, has grown to multiple congregations and an outreach that touches South America and Africa. The church is now a network of congregations—with mission at the heart of their purpose. The exposure to a world in need was a catalyst for the culture change in the local congregation, creating a hunger to reach East Tennessee. They have effectively partnered compassion with outreach resulting in some 20,000 conversions each year.

5

The River—Healing Wherever the Water Flows

On Palm Sunday, 1998, Ronnie Hepperly went to a small church in Maryville, Tennessee called Foothills Church of God. That day, the members were given the opportunity to vote as to whether or not he would be their new pastor. Forty-two people attended that service—and the implications of their decision that day were obvious to no one. Foothills had been a small church existing for almost a hundred years. It had undergone numerous name changes and several moves—and other than those superficial changes, nothing had changed. It was the first pastorate for Ronnie and though other pastors had come and gone from Foothills, feeling less than successful, Ronnie was young and had not yet learned that he could fail. He didn't know the history of the congregation, their many struggles even to exist, much less grow and become influential and impacting. But, he wasn't looking back! Those who know Pastor Hepperly would probably agree that he is characterized by the power of audacious sincerity.

That day the Foothills Church made a decision that would change them forever. They selected Ronnie, and equally important, Ronnie accepted them. He threw his heart into the venture. And he immediately broadened their horizon, taking some with him to Mexico on a mission trip, an unfinished commitment from his work as an evangelist. That work would never be finished. Ronnie is really a pastor, with the heart of an evangelist. In Mexico, he baptized converts from an earlier trip. And he conducted another crusade, engaged in evangelistic work with his people in tow. The small core had now tasted something they had never known before—evangelism on the streets, up front and personal, lives changed, people following Christ in baptism.

> *"Even a tree has more hope! If it is cut down, it will sprout again and grow new branches. Though its roots have grown old in the earth and its stump decays, yet at the scent of water it will bud and put forth shoots like a plant.* Job 14:7-9.

What a promise from Job—at the scent of water the downed tree will bud and put forth shoots. It is a picture of a resurrection. Zechariah pictured Israel as a stump, a tree cut down, dead and lifeless. But, then in his vision, he saw a branch that came forth. There was new life. Israel would live again. Churches, written off, having existed like stumps in the forest, can live again. They can rise from what appears to be certain and decided death. They need "the scent of water" – the fresh move and stirring of the Holy Spirit.

Ronnie encouraged his congregation to find patterns and practices for ministry from Scripture. They adopted Matthew 28:18-20, Isaiah 58, Matthew 25:31-46 and James 1:27 as defining Scriptures. Therein was the job description for the church. Suddenly, a congregation that had seemed latent for years began to grow exponentially. In only three years, the small block building was no longer adequate to hold the crowds. They had already expanded to two services on Sunday morning, but still the small facility was unbelievably crowded. So they did the unorthodox. They simply moved outside—well, to a canvas tent that they acquired with the help of Dr. T. L. Lowery. On Easter Sunday, in 2001, they had their first 'tent service'. On a day that demanded sunshine, Maryville had a terrible rain storm. But despite the downpour, only a buoyant resurrection spirit was to be found under the tent, along with 500 people.

Almost half of all people in developing countries are suffering at any given time from problems related to water and sanitation.

For two years, the tent was their church. Other pastors might have become maintenance minded in such a season, concerned about getting through the transitional "tent" era and into a permanent facility, but Pastor Hepperly did the audacious opposite. He kept the congregation engaged in mission work. The people and the pastor conducted mission excursions. After Hurricane Mitch ravaged Honduras, they focused on the needs of that area, despite their own lack of a building. In Panama, they made a divine connection with Pastor Roberto Taton which launched a fruitful relationship, not only in Panama, but opened opportunities in many other nations of the world, where a partnership has been forged.

Some 20,000 souls have been saved each year during the past 8 years—160,000 people won to Christ. And 250 churches have been planted around the world. In addition, the little Foothills Church of God now offers ministry through 11 satellite locations in East Tennessee and some 130 outside the United States—"little" no more. That is really audacious. At the scent of water a forest is now growing.

Pastor Hepperly says, "It almost seems like an incredible dream." The church is now known as Restoration International Outreach (RIO), which in Spanish means *river*. So the church makes use of the river metaphor to describe how they operate.

A new sanctuary in Maryville is designed to seat 600 people. In addition, there is now a family life center. A fire destroyed their youth facility, but God always proved faithful and the distractions did not stop ministry. They continued to outgrow their facility. So, they purchased two additional church facilities for use, and the Church of God partnered with them and gave them the use of three facilities where congregations had failed. All the facilities are now being used.

At one time, to handle the crowds, they secured a larger tent, one that would accommodate 1,000 and for a season they moved into it. They have planted churches in the facilities of school buildings, clubs, community structures and God has continued to place his favor upon them. Why the success? "I have no question that it has been because of our focus on the Great Commission and alleviating suffering at home and abroad," notes Pastor Hepperly.

- **Katrina Outreach**—During the Hurricane Katrina tragedy, the church took 20 teams to help rebuild four buildings for area Church of God congregations, and they assisted other needy churches, and rebuilt several homes of widows. The more they adhered to the Scriptural mandate, the more God blessed them at home. Pastor Hepperly recalls, "It never made financial sense. It wasn't the reasonable thing to do—all the focus on missions and care for others. At times, it got a bit scary, but as we prayed for God to open doors, doors opened, and we stepped through them."

- **Public School Ministry**—At one time, they had 20 area public schools where organized devotionals were conducted each week.

- **Jail Ministry**—At 6:00 A.M. every Sunday morning for almost 10 years, they have held services at the Sheriff's office, regular services in the local jails, and a service in the 911 center. Their chaplain program works with the road officers, the SWAT team, and jailors.

Even the librarian at the jail is a volunteer from their church. Oh, the open doors. Ministry at jails and prisons is not merely a preaching action.

- **Celebrate Recovery**—The church has a *Celebrate Recovery* program for people with habits and hang-ups. Every Tuesday night trained volunteers meet with folks who, as a part of their sentencing, are required to participate in some kind of rehabilitation program. The Celebrate Recovery program is educational, teaching them about their addiction problem. But it also offers liberation through the delivering power of Jesus Christ. The program is similar to Alcoholics Anonymous, but unapologetic about Christ—the Higher Power. It is now among the most effective 12-step programs in the Maryville-Knoxville area.
- **The Isaiah 58 Project**—Another huge win is the Isaiah 58 Project. In 2010, Ronnie called an Isaiah 58 fast network wide, in all the RIO congregations, ministries and mission connections. For 21 days, revival services were conducted in different locations, including partner churches in Kentucky. The revival culminated with a tractor trailer load giveaway of food to the community. The effort was such a huge success that now at least one tractor trailer load of food is given away monthly at one of the network locations. The local newspaper has agreed to give free advertising for the effort. So, in the midst of economic downturn, help to hurting people has escalated, and the more that is given away, the more resources come in. Pastor Hepperly says, "Favor with the community, and the benevolence program, which has always been very strong, has grown by leaps and bounds. In the course of 12 months, after launching the Isaiah 58 Project, over 200,000 pounds of food was distributed to over 5,000 families. The gift of care, made tangible by the food boxes, gives us the opportunity to pray, minister and give Bibles to thousands of needy people. At times, people come to the Lord. At other times, significant personal ministry takes place. What is really special is to see the recipients of care turn into volunteers with the ministry."
- **Food Pantry**—The church also has a food-pantry where families receive emergency food throughout the week. The pantry ministry has been a blessing to hundreds of needy families. As volunteers box up the food, they chat, minister and pray with people, often

at a very intimate level. It is a common occurrence to see family members leave puddles of tears on the floor as they hear and feel the love of God and receive personal prayer. "Those moments of compassion and prayer are life changing for those serving and those receiving," notes Pastor Hepperly.

- **Christmas Outreach**—Between Thanksgiving and Christmas, the Isaiah 58 team sells Christmas trees to raise extra funds for a turkey and ham give-away to pantry families. Last year a single mom stopped by the church and asked if she could "have a tree." Her kids were begging for a real tree for Christmas, and she had no money for such a luxury. She had been all over town searching to see if someone would donate a tree to her family. The team gave her a tree and she broke down and wept. The kindness meant so much to her and her children. What a way to win the hearts of children. And the team was so blessed and touched to be the givers and find themselves inside a moment of profound gratitude and humility.

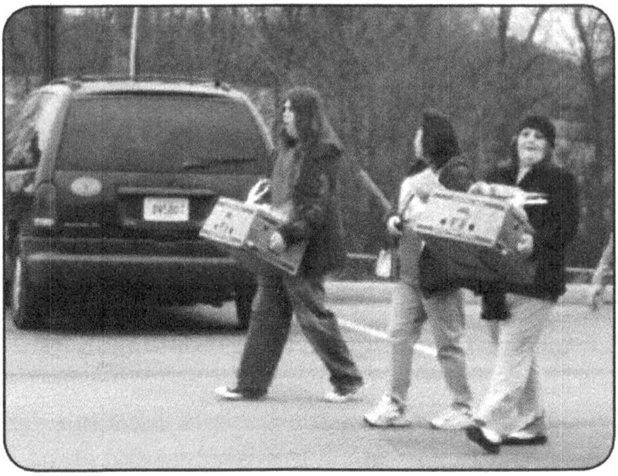

- **Widows Ministry**—The Isaiah 58 Project for this year includes new goals. The ministry will continue to deliver food to shut-ins and the disadvantaged, with a special new outreach to the widows in the community. They also hope to double the number of families served and give away two trailer loads of food each month.

Pastor Hepperly has been privileged to speak to groups of pastors and church leaders, teaching on evangelism and outreach. Dr. Raymond Culpepper recently showcased the ministry at an International Evangelism Conference. "These honors and open doors," Pastor Ronnie believes, "have come about by our obedience to the Great Commission and doing so in the spirit of Matthew 25. God's pattern works, and He always causes us to be productive and fruitful." The RIO ministry is largely made up of honest, hard-working, blue-collar people with little or no formal training in ministry, but with hot hearts and a lot of caring love to give away. Their obedience is a testimony that God honors His Word. For 12 years against insurmountable odds, God has kept His hand on this faithful band, multiplied their number, given them unbelievable success, and continued to bless them as they have allowed themselves to be a blessing. Pastor Hepperly noted, "I am very appreciative to the Church of God for allowing me the opportunity to do and be all that God has intended. My prayer is that I will reach my full potential as I lead the ministry entrusted to me." Audacious humility.

Female-headed households are twice as likely to be among the working poor than male-headed households.

The Prisons of Haiti—Two Months before the Earthquake

In October 2010, Josh Broyles, a young member of the RIO congregation, was sitting at his computer reading an article about the cholera outbreak in Haiti, a story that was going to change his life. The report described how cholera had spread into the Haiti prisons. A number of prisoners had already died. Josh recalls, "My head began to spin and tears filled my eyes." He had been trying to discern direction for a mission trip about which the Lord had prompted him. He had felt called to Haiti, then to Kenya, then to Haiti. He was undecided. How could he do three weeks of mission work in the two weeks of vacation time he was provided? Kenya was inviting. He had friends there. But God had other plans. Two weeks before Pastor Ronnie was scheduled to leave for Haiti, the missions director asked Josh if he could go and help the pastor with ministry activity there. Josh recalls, "I felt the Holy Spirit affirm this as the direction I needed to take." He immediately agreed.

The purpose of the trip was four days of intense prison ministry and then the construction of a new orphanage. Josh had never been on a mission trip with the pastor, but he had "heard the stories." The audacious pastor was dangerously adventurous. He lived on the edge. Josh was a bit anxious. He had never been in a prison nor even visited one, not even in the USA. His only preaching experience had been to a church crowd.

The advance team arrived in Haiti on Saturday. The pastor would join them Monday. On Tuesday, with the entire team on the ground, they loaded into a suburban and headed to their first assignment. When they arrived at the prison, they entered through a metal door cut through thick, high concrete walls. Entering the courtyard, he could see razor-wire weaving its way through the grass, roosters roaming freely, and a row of cell doors facing the courtyard. Someone yelled, "Grab an interpreter and go!"

Of the 1.9 billion children in developing nations, 640 million are without adequate shelter, 400 million do not have access to safe water, 270 million have no access to health care.

Josh paired up with Pastor Jacques of Haiti. He suddenly felt a sense of courage he had never experienced. He had no idea what to say to Haitian prisoners. He had never even been in trouble with the law. How could he relate? Deep inside, he sensed God would give him the words. As he approached the first cell, he was amazed to see 57 men crammed into a space roughly 15 feet by 25 feet. There were no beds, no toilets, no shower, no air conditioner, and no space to move. The smell was similar to a backed-up sewer. The "business bucket" sat just outside the cell door. It was the worst place Josh had ever seen in his life for human habitation. It was a place of despair. Hopelessness was in the air. The physical conditions were unthinkable and unimaginable.

With his mind reeling, Josh introduced himself and began to ask questions. "How many of you are in this cell? How long have you been here? Who has been here the longest?" Some had been there for five years. It was a hellhole. How could you survive in a place like that for five years? It would be an eternity. For 15 minutes, he shared the simple Gospel and gave an appeal. "Would anyone like to surrender their lives to Christ?" About half of the men raised their hands. He prayed with them and moved on to the next cell.

Here he was astounded to find 81 men in a cell only slightly larger than the first. Again, he shared the simple Gospel. All 81 men raised their hands to receive Christ! "What an amazing feeling," he recalls. "I left there with immense joy, strength, and courage but also compassion and pity for those men who were living in those horrid conditions." Two other prisons were more of the same—filthy and extremely crowded. And all with extraordinary results. Incredible ratios of conversion.

The trip was just prior to the Haiti earthquake that damaged or

destroyed eight of the nation's 17 prisons. They were ambassadors of grace days before calamity. When the earthquake came, 60% of the nation's 9,000 prisoners disappeared. One prison built for 800 held 4,300 at the time of the earthquake. Prisoners suffered from a lack of basic hygiene, malnutrition, and poor quality health care. Incidents of preventable diseases such as AIDS, malaria, and tuberculosis had become a serious problem.

Some 88 percent of the hundreds of incarcerated juveniles had been held for three years without clear charges being filed or a trial.

These people needed "good news" and the opening of the prison. An earthquake did it—but not before the gospel was preached to them. Of course, some died and they died "in Christ" because someone visited them in prison, as Christ commanded us to do. What if the team had not gone just a few weeks before the earthquake? Ronnie and his team demonstrated compassion. They shared the love of Christ. They passed out Bibles, gave away toilet paper, soap and other personal items to make living conditions a bit more bearable. Josh believes lives were changed that day, their eternal destinies amended, and his life was forever changed.

In Buenos Aires, 550 believers met in a train depot at rush hour. They began softly singing "Hallelujah!" The atmosphere of the station was dramatically changed. They boarded trains and fanned out into the city. They touched 7,000 people in one evening. 6,736 wanted prayer. 1,704 became Christians. Give the gift of prayer.

Destination—Panama

Sometimes the best laid plans are disrupted by the will of God. And somehow, prayer ends up in the mix of such confusion before God's will becomes as clear as glass. Sambu is a Central American community with a river that runs through it, bearing the same name, the Sambu River of Panama. A cultural collage finds some people there who are quite modern and others who appear to be stuck on a cultural continuum at least five centuries in the past. If you look around, you will find thatch roof houses on stilts. A semi-clad culture is still acceptable. A native pastor has tried to evangelize, to be obedient to God's call. But the rejection to his message has been severe. His resources have been limited. He has been taunted and ridiculed by neighbors and villagers. His small church met underneath his stilt house by the side of the river. It had no walls, and the space of less than 150 square feet was confining, even to a native population. The pastor was desperate, yet faithful and persevering.

He had heard that a group of Church of God people had teamed up to build several church buildings in Panama. Hearing such news, it was nothing less than miraculous. He had hope. He was inspired to make the long trip to the capitol to request help. As he prayed and prepared to go, to petition men for assistance, God was already at work.

A team from RIO had finalized plans to go to Panama. They had secured the funds to purchase materials to build a church. But at the last minute, security issues became paramount. It would not be safe for them to complete the planned mission. As the pastor in Panama paced the ground underneath his house passionately petitioning heaven for help with a church building, the team in the US processed their confusing and frustrating news. They too sought God about what they had perceived to be His will and the wall they had encountered.

Overall, illegal immigrants families constitute 5% of the U.S. population, but they are 10% of all poor persons in government poverty reports.

When the Panamanian pastor reached the capitol, he connected with Pastor Roberto Taton who had arranged for the RIO group to come to Panama. The unanticipated tense cultural problem had placed Pastor Taton in a difficult position. What would he do with the failed plan, with the large group of men who had invested a significant amount of money and arranged time off work to come to Panama and build a church facility? It was clear. God had other plans all along.

Quickly, the focus of the team was shifted to Sambu. And when the team of Panamanians and North Americans converged on the small community of less than a thousand people, they had the attention of the whole village. Half the team went to a mountainous area and built a new church facility in a very remote area called Cerro Knaife. They had only a small, and rather run-down, make-shift shelter they called a church. The area was so remote, most of the natives had never seen a white man. The team of RIO shaved heads was quite a spectacle. Lee Staley, a RIO jail minister was quite a sight all by himself. With a body covered in tattoos, a shaved head and huge ear-lobe holes, he was an attention getter! After he was saved, he had "Not Guilty" tattooed on his back in big letters along with the word "Forgiven." The writing on his shoulders and his belt line framed a picture of Jesus that covered the full length of his back, a picture of Jesus holding Lee, limp and helpless in his arms. He was a walking billboard. The villagers had never seen anything quite like Lee Staley.

Lee's team was in the remote mountain region, building a wooden structure for worship. The other team was in the river valley in Sambu, building a block building with a concrete floor and a metal roof. The poor, formally untrained pastor, as a result of his fervent prayers and desire to impact his village, was host to a large team of builders and preachers sent by God. The Lord had heard his plea.

Every night, until the new facility was built, the team met under the pastor's house for open air church services. With one light bulb and generator power, the mosquitoes and bugs were more plentiful than villagers. Still, church members and curious onlookers gathered. They heard the gospel. They saw the miracle of answered prayer. They watched a facility rise from the ground, a little church for which the whole village could to be proud.

The dedication service brought out almost everyone in the area. The pastor would be ridiculed no more. He had walked the ground and claimed it. He had called that which was not, as if it were, and now it was. He had responded in kindness when the villagers had mocked him. His prayers had brought people he himself did not even know from another continent to bless church and the village. It was clear. No one in the village had that kind of power and influence. As a result of his persistence in prayer, he had moved God to redirect the plans of the entire team.

RIO is a work in progress, a network of churches and ministries, birthed out of the passion and prayer of a pastor, and what began as a handful of people. It is a river, a movement, and they are riding the rapids, not sure of their destination, other than heaven. The boat always has room for more. And they are currently picking up people

If A Poor Man Comes ...

Tommy Jackson is the pastor of the New Heights Church of God in Longview, Texas. One particular Sunday morning when hundreds began to gather for worship, he was conspicuously absent. They had another guest, though, but certainly no peer to the pastor. It seems on that morning, a rather inebriated soul was trying to navigate his way across the busy highway that runs in front of the impressive Rose Heights facility. A number of parishioners were concerned that the obviously drunk dude might be injured.

"There was concern for the individual. We could tell that something was not quite right," said church member, Gary Treat. He finally made it to the parking lot—unshaven, wearing soiled clothes, and a ball cap with sun glasses. Walking toward the church, a stranger smelling of alcohol, he was welcomed into the facility and seated near the rear of the auditorium.

As it turned out, the "stranger" was Pastor Tommy Jackson in disguise. He wanted to find out whether people at his church practiced what they believed, so he came up with the unique exercise. How would his church react to a person in need in their own church? "This month, we have a series called 'Kingdom People.' The one distinguishing factor of a Christian should be our love," Jackson told his congregation.

Jackson had the police called to "haul him away" to see if church people might intervene. He played the part to the fullest. And, admittedly, some church members were wary, but others reached out to him, offering food and shelter, not knowing they were offering kindness to their own pastor, sprinkled heavily, not with holy water, but with Jack Daniels.

At the time in the service when the pastor was to come forward, Tommy revealed himself. "What are we doing to help those less fortunate, what are we doing to share God with others," that is the question church members were asking that day. Tommy says he was proud of Rose Heights. They passed the test. How would your church react?

on three continents. There may be rapids ahead, but God knows that. And when the rapids appear, the Lord will have a solution. Today, they are still riding the river, pulling drowning and dying people onboard. Their story is quite amazing—once a rather typical, small, single-cell congregation on a treadmill for decades, but now affecting thousands, small and single-cell no more. They are audacious.

> *Wherever the river flows, there will be many fish and ... the river will make the water in the Dead Sea fresh. Wherever the river flows, it will bring life. (Ezekiel 47:9 – GWT)*

Discussion Guide

Big Ideas

- A pastor with the heart of an evangelist!
- A Celebrate Recovery Program.
- The Isaiah 58 Project.
- Involvement in the Local Chaplaincy Program—jail ministry and ministry in and to the Sheriff's Department.
- The connection made by prayer—a poor pastor in Panama needing a place for his congregation to meet; and a planned church-building mission excursion, gone astray. How they found one another is a miracle, stumbling into the will of God. God does direct our paths.

Notable Quotes

- *"Even a tree has more hope! If it is cut down, it will sprout again ... though its roots have grown old ... and its stump decays, yet at the scent of water it will bud ..."*
- "It never made financial sense. It wasn't the reasonable thing to do —all the focus on missions and care for others" with all our needs abounding.

- Other pastors might have become maintenance minded in such a season, concerned about getting through the transitional 'tent' era and into permanent facility, but Pastor Hepperly did the opposite. He kept the congregation engaged in mission work.
- More than 35 million Americans are food insecure, hungry, or at risk of hunger. And yet, 96 billion pounds of food are wasted each year in the United States, with 12.4 million children in food insecure households.
- Kids with empty stomachs find it more difficult to learn. Sadly, seniors must choose between medication and meals.

Questions for Consideration

1. What role do you think the early mission trip taken by the members of the church had in redirecting their missional and congregational vision? What would happen if a significant number of your fellow church members went on a mission trip together?
2. Do you agree with Pastor Hepperly's assessment of their growth? "I have no question that it has been because of our focus on the great commission and alleviating suffering at home and abroad"? Does your church need an external focus?
3. It almost seems that many of the people involved in missions from RIO are learning on the run—thrown into the maze of ministry and suddenly, with an innocent and tender heart, they become immediately and deeply dependent on the Holy Spirit! And with astounding results. Is this the way your church does it?
4. Could the catalyst for change and growth in your church be found in reaching to those outside even with a small number inside – regardless of whether they respond, become members or even return thanks?
5. Discuss the difference between a 'maintenance' and 'mission' mentality?

Peniel Ministries

William (Bill) Henry, during the Nixon years, was a secret service agent assigned to the Diplomatic Team, working with Embassies and Foreign Dignitaries. He is a decorated Marine whose record in Vietnam left him with a Purple Heart, two wounds and a partial disability. He was raised on the tough side of Baltimore, the middle child among seven kids. His father, a gambler and less than adequate provider, left the family, and the step-father who followed him was abusive. It only hardened the core of young Bill. His mother took the children to church, but he strained the grace and the tolerance of volunteer Sunday School teachers and workers. "They didn't think they were getting through to me, I'm sure," he reflects now. His rebellious behavior was a veiled plea for love, but even he didn't recognize that then. "Momma made me go to church and to summer camps." Still, he admits, "A lot of that teaching, those values stuck, they got in there," referring to his heart and soul.

At 18, Bill joined the Marines and headed to Vietnam. His unit was the recipient of a performance citation. When he came home, he was disillusioned like a lot of young men from that era. Having avoided drugs all his growing up years, and even in Vietnam, returning he succumbed. "Partly to deal with real pain—the wounds—and partly to deal with emotional pain." At first it was marijuana and then cocaine. He was married and had children. With a disability from his battle injuries secured, he moved to work with the Government Security Agency, but his life spiraled out of control.

Coming to his senses, he and his wife found their way back to God, to church, and a stable family life, but was soon shaken as well. To compensate for all of his wayward years, he overinvested in the church-life and ignored his wife and family. That cost him his 20-year marriage and this time, he fell further than before. Homeless and disconnected from all family, he bounced around from one friend's house to another, from one homeless shelter to another soup kitchen. Sometimes he was with an equally destitute companion. Sometimes alone. He was back to alcohol and drugs. He was in and out of jobs. For seven years, life was a roller coaster. He had hit the bottom.

"I came back to church in that five-year season, but when I look back, I realize the church did not prepare me for life. It did not address the deeper issues of childhood, drug use, war, and the wounds he still carried. It did not disciple him." He isn't blaming the church. His work now is precisely in that arena, working with men and women who, too, hit bottom and need more than a sermon and a song book. He remembers during that season God started wooing him, calling him back. "Bill, what are you doing? Look where you are? Is this what you want? When you were serving Me, wasn't life better?" The inner voice was one of comfort, not condemnation.

His most recent arrest resulted in mandated treatment for 28 days. He came out of the program the same as he went in. "It didn't work!" he lamented. His parole officer invested in him emotionally, urging him to get help, to get well, to shake the addiction. Bill resisted. "I told him that if I wanted treatment again, I would only go to a Christ-based program."

The parole officer found Peniel Ministries. Bill still resisted, but six months later, he agreed, and on July 2, 1991, he arrived in Pennsylvania in the middle of the Church of God camp meeting. All the Peniel patients were in attendance. That night, Bill made a dash for the altar and God met him and changed his life. The addictions fell away, the chains were gone, and for the next 13 months, Bill received the counseling, the self-understanding, the deeper healing, and discipleship he had not received earlier.

When he graduated from the program at the age of 42, God spoke to him and told him, "Stay here! This is your home." It felt like home. The Spellman's wanted to be sure it was no emotional decision. They sent him home, but Bill now knew the voice of God. He came back. In the early years, he simply served. "I was the gopher!" he says. A member of the secret service detail, a decorated Marine—now a servant of the Lord. It was quite a promotion, really. The program had grown and developed him and he was still growing. He went back to school, graduated from college, got his credentials as a Certified Addiction Counselor, and went to work helping others the way he had been helped, one of seven counselors at the ministry.

He married Susan, now the Administrative Assistant. He is an elder at the host church and the two of them part of a staff of some 35 at Peniel Ministries. The 13-month residential program accommodates as many as 50 men or women. In addition, there is a family and out-patient component. Clients come from across the US and, at times, from the international community. Some are lawyers, teachers, and other professionals, a surprising lot ranging from age 18 to 60, but their lives became unmanageable. Some are blue collar singles, the ages of the clients have grown younger in recent years. Some have never known Christ, but at Peniel, they find Him the center of their healing regiment.

They leave and return to their families, their jobs, and over 70 percent of them to clean, liberated lifestyles, one of the highest success rates in the nation. The learning program is dynamic, bent to the client's needs. It covers everything from self-care to the basics, culinary arts to the art of drug-free living. College credit is now available for some of the learning. Top notch instructors now serve the program. A computer lab and library is a part of the amazing facility on the multi-acre campus. Their graduates are good fathers and mothers, some are pastors. They all participate in an after-care program. Each graduate develops social reentry goals and the counselors track the alumni, assist with after-program care, and connect them to a faith community. Bill has now reconnected with his children, and grandchildren.

Adopt A Foreign City

Pastor Richard Dial has taken almost 2,000 people to Ecuador, almost 200 annually for 16 years. They made a decision that they would adopt a foreign city. No missionary tourism. Each year, they serve sister churches in that city and the region. They have built 20 churches, two schools, opened the Hands of Compassion medical clinic free to the public, and constructed a children's development center.

Ministry at the **Cary Church of God in Cary, North Carolina**, reaches beyond Cary to another continent. Not only has it impacted Guayaquil, it has impacted every person who has made the trip. It has changed the character of the church's ministry in their own home town. The first year, Carl Dragstedt made the trip. He was an IBM executive, new to the church. Once there, he was assigned to a construction project in a remote village high up the mountain. The area was primitive—no facilities, no accommodations or modern conveniences. When Carl returned after days in the fine, black, volcanic dirt, the growth of his beard and condition of his clothing reflected difficult days without the means for adequate self-care. Richard was concerned, "Are you okay?" he quietly asked. He wondered, "Was the assignment too much, too fast?" Pastor Dial waited for a response.

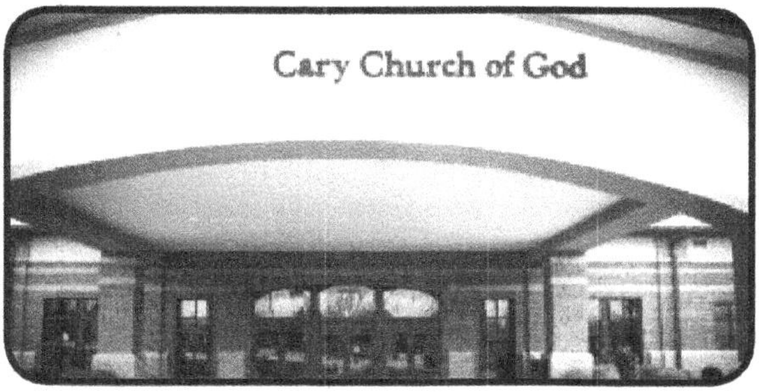

"The greatest experience of my life!" Carl said, choking back the tears. "Of one thing I am sure. Next year, wherever I live, I will be back in Ecuador!" Each year, until his death, he returned. The cry of the church has now become, "One thing I know. Next year, I will be back in Ecuador."

What one thing is God calling you and your church to do? As a person? As a congregation? What mission field, near or far, can you impact?

"If there is a poor man your brothers in any of the towns of the land that the LORD your God is giving you, do not be hardhearted or tightfisted toward your poor brother." Deuteronomy 15:7

"Speak up for those who cannot speak for themselves, for the rights of all who are destitute." Proverbs 31:8

The apostles returned to Jesus from their ministry tour and told him all they had done and what they had taught. Then Jesus said, "Let's get away from the crowds for a while and rest." There were so many people coming and going that Jesus and his apostles didn't even have time to eat. They left by boat for a quieter spot. But many people saw them leaving, and people from many towns ran ahead along the shore and met them as they landed. A vast crowd was there as he stepped from the boat, and he had compassion on them because they were like sheep without a shepherd. So he taught them many things. Late in the afternoon his disciples came to him and said, "This is a desolate place, and it is getting late. Send the crowds away so they can go to the nearby farms and villages and buy themselves some food." But Jesus said, "You feed them.""With what?" they asked. "It would take a small fortune to buy food for all this crowd!" "How much food do you have?" he asked. "Go and find out."They came back and reported, "We have five loaves of bread and two fish." Then Jesus told the crowd to sit down in groups on the green grass. So they sat in groups of fifty or a hundred. Jesus took the five loaves and two fish, looked up toward heaven, and asked God's blessing on the food. Breaking the loaves into pieces, he kept giving the bread and fish to the disciples to give to the people. They all ate as much as they wanted, and they picked up twelve baskets of leftover bread and fish. Five thousand men had eaten from those five loaves! (NLT: Mark 6:30-44)

The Appalachian DreamCenter

Michael Hartwell knows the hunger of poverty. He had his turn in the coal mines of West Virginia. He now works the food lines when needy people show up for help, but he always remembers what it was like to be in that line. His Appalachian DreamCenter is just that for thousands of people who find relief in a variety of ways throughout West Virginia. He is a pastor, with a church that cares about its neighbors—Christians and non-Christians. They were committed to make a difference for others, and now that difference is felt across the nation and into other countries as well.

6

Praying from the Valley of Despair

Michael Hartwell was raised as a coal miner's son in the hills of West Virginia. He knows the sustaining power of compassion from youth. When his father was injured in a mining accident, the local grocery store owner accommodated the family's need for food for several months during the season of recuperation. And then there were times when the paycheck just didn't last long enough and the government food subsidy program was their safety net. In his early pastoral ministry, he was the recipient of a much needed food basket by a local charity. He recalls standing in unemployment and food assistance lines as a young father. His frugal and godly grandmother canned food every summer to care for the sparse winter needs of her family. Their life was not one of reckless neglect, but one in which the best efforts sometimes fell short. Michael knows about life in a valley of despair.

The Appalachian Regional Commission was established to foster development in 397 counties in 13 states covering 165,000 square miles. The 2,000-mile-long Appalachian National Scenic Trail runs from Mt. Katahdin, Maine, to Springer Mountain, Georgia.

Coal mining is a dangerous occupation. Some 100,000 miners lost their lives in the last century due to accidents—an average of 1,000 per year.[3] His father lived with potential tragedy and often tasted injury—injuries that left the family without a stream of needed income. Michael recalls one Saturday evening when his Mom cooked a scrumptious dinner that he heartily enjoyed. Later, he overheard his mother telling his father the meal constituted the last of the food. There was nothing to feed the family the next day. His father's calm reply was, "The Lord will provide." Winston Churchill once said, "Success is not final, failure is not fatal: it is the courage to continue that counts."

Michael carried the secret to bed. Through the night, he worried about the needs of the family, "What would they eat?" This was one of the first experiences he had in prayer. He recalls, "My theory of God was that He was a Man who sat in the sky at a control board. The board had buttons for rain, thunder, sunshine and so on." He wondered, "Did the board have a button for food?"

To his amazement, the next morning there was a knock at the door.

A local grocery store owner brought enough food to last for a week. He heard the grocer tell his mother, "If there is anything else you need, get on the 'party Line' and let me know." The party line was common in those days. It was an arrangement that placed multiple homes on the same phone line. All had to share the phone and risked having other neighbors and folks in the community listening in. Everybody knew everyone else's business. "We enjoyed hearing the conversations of others. Life was good again—we had food."

Someone Came for Him

The Montcalm Church of God had a bus ministry. The bus lumbered by Michael's house Sunday after Sunday. One Sunday morning, he boarded the bus and was introduced to the Church of God. Once again, he was about to learn about the power of prayer.

As a typical teen, Michael had prayed for tests he had not adequately studied for, and for good grades. But, he was yet to learn of prayer's real importance and power. Like many West Virginia kids, he graduated from high school, and went to work in the coal mines, following in the footsteps of his father and grandfather. It was life in the valley of despair. Steady coal mine work was unpredictable. It would start and then suddenly stop. There was work, and then no work. There were high demands for coal and then no demands. Michael found himself, now a young husband and father, standing in food bank and work assistance program lines when the work stopped. He was in "the valley of despair with little hope." It was the local churches filled with generous and compassionate Christians who showed the more excellent way.

After his conversion as a young layman, he was taught the principles of Matthew 25 by Pastor Rex Ball. It opened a new world to him, a ministry with which he could readily identify. The church opened a clothing and food center. He and his wife were appointed to oversee the project. Enthusiasm for the ministry center was high, at least at the beginning. But as time went on, fewer parishioners felt the call to the ministry of care. Michael and his wife were soon carrying an inordinate burden.

Going For Others

He was still laboring in the coal mines when he met a fellow worker, a member of the Church of God. The concern for souls resonated with Michael. Soon he was beginning preparation to enter the ministry. Pastor T. L. Sizemore appointed him to assist with the food pantry of the Maybeury Church of God. There he received valuable training and a place to fulfill the burden to care for others, who like himself were at times in need. After several years of training at the Maybeury Church, he was appointed pastor of the Bluewell Church of God. With two children and more enthusiasm than was legal, he accepted the challenge. Counting the four members of his own family, the first Sunday saw seven in attendance. At Bluewell, he would encounter Johnny Gray, a coalminer-pastor who would add to what he had already learned about Matthew 25 principles. Johnny would teach him the importance of praying daily for the Lord's provision.

It was a faith walk. The small family lived in the basement of the church facility for several years, and from "poundings" (food gifts) from those that attended the church. The first Christmas was like those of his childhood— a hungry family with little food or means for provision. No one knew—but God. And when a holiday food basket came by means of a friend, it was an answer to prayer. And it was also a part of God's bigger plan. The ministry that put food on his table was based in Bastian-Bland, Virginia, and he would later learn, was an outreach of Dr. John Gregory. After seven years of a faith-walk in Bluewell, it was time to move to the infamous Logan County, West Virginia.

From the beginning, Michael led the church in offering assistance to the local community. The need was so great. With a disproportionate number of needy elderly folks, the church started a Meals-on-Wheels program. That core ministry is what developed into the "Appalachian Dream Center." The rural church was limited both in terms of space and finances. The small fellowship hall was commandeered as a food pantry. The congregation made the missional decision. The very real hunger needs of the elderly in the community were greater than the convenience of a fellowship hall. The sacrifice of fellowship space for community food and hunger needs continued for a number of years. Then Michael Hartwell met David Lorency who would provide assistance to build a network of care and compassion.

The Power of Partnership—Christmas to Appalachia

The needs were beyond food. Along with the multiple needs of the elderly, there were single parent homes who also needed more than a warm meal or a box of food. Some were living in homes badly in need of repair. With the assistance of Operation Compassion, practical care was now soaring to another level. "David Lorency," Michael noted, "gave us valuable teaching and assistance in helping to expand and fulfill our vision. We had now outgrown the food pantry operating from the small fellowship hall.

After much prayer, we decided to relocate into a larger facility. But where? We began our search, but every door was closed. No facilities were available anywhere that would meet our needs. And even if we had found some, we were searching by faith with no funds." Michael recalls, "We continued to pray, fast and work with what we had, being grateful. Then one morning, I heard of a vacant building in an adjacent town."

Michael would make multiple attempts to connect with the owner only to be informed the building was not for sale. Michael persisted. He explained his burden and that of the congregation to make a difference in the community. He told the unsaved owner of the facility he had no choice in the matter. He was "commanded" by the Lord to assist the poor. The owner relented and gave permission to use his building to coordinate their first Christmas giveaway in cooperation with Operation Compassion.

On that first "Christmas to Appalachia," not everything went without challenges. The first tractor-trailer arrived at the steep entrance to the building on a cold day with snow and ice blanketing the driveway. Undaunted, the driver carefully placed chains on his tractor-trailer tires, backed the rig up to the building. "Excitement filled the air and spread quickly through the entire area—the elderly, the single parents were going to have Christmas. It was a wonderful feeling. We were part of something bigger than ourselves."

When the morning of the first giveaway came, it was cold and the line was long. The staff was ready. The food, toys, and clothes to be given away were abundant. The day went well—a historic first—and the team was feeling great! Leaving the building that day, an elderly lady approached Michael, one of the last to receive ministry. "Do you have any candy, Pastor?"

Five states had significantly higher household food insecurity rates last year – Arkansas: 17.7%; Mississippi: 17.1%; Georgia: 15.6%; Texas: 17.4%; and North Carolina: 14.8%.

Michael recalls, "I will forever remember her words." The supply of food and candy had been depleted before she had been served. But on the greasy floor of the old building in which mining equipment had been repaired, was one more candy bar. It had been dropped and trampled. "May I have that candy bar?" she politely requested.

The day had been great—but after it was all over, the humble request for a damaged piece of candy was enough to break Michael's heart and renew his burden for the people of Appalachia. With gratitude for the use of the building, they expressed appreciation to the owner, secretly longing for permanent use, but it was not meant to be. God would provide another facility. This time, the building would not be a former mine equipment repair center, but one used to store hay and farm equipment. The ragged facility was a reminder they, too, were both in the repair and harvest business.

Though the days were exciting during the formative years of the Appalachian Dream Center, there was major warfare. Michael's wife had been diagnosed with cancer and was undergoing treatment. Still, she encouraged him to continue and not quit.

One morning, over the Book of Job, the Holy Spirit spoke to Michael that "the later years of the ministry would be greater than the beginning." That morning the house was quiet. The hungry needed to be fed. And he had a congregation to care for besides the needy in the community. The needs of his wife were increasing—and without a miracle she would soon be with the Lord, and he would be alone with a ministry to Appalachia. This was a tough season. Things would get worse before they got better. The owner announced that he needed his property. Once again, Michael and the Dream Center had to relocate.

They built a small two story building adjacent to the Church and there continued to serve the people of Appalachia. This building was called "Martha's House." But it was no match for the need. They knew it was only a temporary measure. They needed a Dream Center, a much larger facility. Michael learned that a local facility which had been the center to feed, clothe and provide furniture for needy coal miners was vacant. He prayed and then contacted David Lorency.

As Operation Compassion began the process of dialogue with the A. T. Massey Coal Company, Michael was led to go to the physical location of the property. He stood on the porch of the facility and poured out his heart in prayer. There, the Holy Spirit whispered that this would be the home of the Dream Center for Appalachia. As one dream came to pass, another died. Michael lost his wife to cancer. He poured himself into his work. He found comfort in comforting others. He knew pain. He was living with loss.

The Appalachian Dream Center

After months of prayer and negotiation, permission was given to use the facility now owned by the Appalachian Dream Center. It took a great deal of work to prepare the 40,000 square foot facility for ministry use—and then the real work began. One of the first projects was reroofing the house of the former pastor's wife, now a widow, and then an elderly couple's home.

Sometimes the assistance given to those outside is bittersweet. As Michael eagerly informed the congregation of those first projects one Sunday morning, an elderly woman, herself a member and regular in attendance, exclaimed, "Pastor, what about my house?" Her need was legitimate. Her house desperately needed a roof, so soon, after materials could be secured, volunteers reroofed her needy house. Later, they would build her a brand new home with the assistance of Operation Compassion.

During the 2010 Christmas Celebration at the Appalachian Dream Center, over 40 adults accepted Jesus Christ as their Lord and Savior. Over 400 food baskets with hams, along with clothing and toys were distributed. Though the early morning air was crisp and the temperature in the lower teens as Pastor Hartwell arrived at the Center, a long line had already formed hours before the doors were to open. The needs remain. For some, their greatest hope and only place of assistance, is found with the people of God.

The Appalachia Dream Center, a completely volunteer operation, has offered hope in the face of despair, bread to the hungry, a toy for a discouraged child, a coat for elderly widow, kindness to the poor, prayer for the sick, the presence of a caring God to the lonely for more than 10 years now. Through the efforts of Operation Compassion, thousands of Bibles have been distributed. Many of those were large print Bibles for people with impaired vision. *That bread* did not merely keep hunger at bay for a day; it satisfied for eternity. For some, it was their first and only Bible and a pathway to a deeper and more fulfilling relationship with Jesus Christ.

Standing in line, in December, 2010, were cold but excited Appalachian people. There was hope. Christmas would be kind, even in the valley of despair. God had heard their prayer for food and clothing, and toys for their children. An army of volunteers were getting ready to open the doors to the families of aging couples, to single parents, and to grandparents now caring for their grandchildren. Some come to the Dream Center having known only a life of hardship. Others come, having tasted success, only to have some life event steal it away. For both, the pain is intense, and the care received is an evident witness of God's love.

A senior woman approached Michael and confessed, "I thought I would never have to stand in a line for a handout, or for help from others." But there she was—life is fragile and unpredictable. Michael confesses that such statements of despair still affect him. But for the grace of God, anyone can end up in such a line. He recalls, "I stood in that same line 30 years ago. From the same valley of despair, I was crying out to God. Even as a young pastor, living in the basement of a Church Of God, with only 10 people attending and most of those my own family, I would haul heating oil in five-gallon buckets in order to warm the church on Sunday morning, and I would pray that the oil would last through the Sunday services."

Moving up and down the line of needy people, having had the personal experience of being in such a line made compassion both gentle and fresh. Michael prayed with one person and then another, reminding them that God is the One who gives the ultimate provision. Standing in front of the Dream Center, the entire crowd began to pray in unison "the Lord's Prayer." There were tears. There were hugs and voices saying 'Thank You!" Many of these people did not know the Lord, in a personal way. Before their experience at the Dream Center was over that day, some 40 would express faith in Christ.

"As I share these personal stories from my life as a son, a father and pastor," Michael reflects, "I would encourage anyone—pastor, layman whoever, to be a vessel of encouragement to others. No matter how deep your valley or how you are financially challenged, the God of Hope will provide. Many times I have been worn out, without resources and all around are needy hungry people as in Mark 6. They can't be sent away! We can't create space to be alone with Jesus and shut out the needy around us."

Some come to the Appalachian Dream Center with empty cupboards. They need only enough food until some promised but delayed subsistence arrives. The Dream Center is the difference between the hunger in those days for both seniors and children. Floods are a seasonal reality in the hills of West Virginia, and almost every spring when the snow melts, small creeks become raging rivers and people lose their homes, some for days, and some forever. Again, the Dream Center is a place to which they can turn!

During the summer of 2010, major floods brought havoc to the state. The needs were so overwhelming that the Dream Center's stockpiles were woefully inadequate. Within 12 hours, Operation Compassion had completed the first delivery of emergency supplies. And those who were emotionally devastated, many having lost their homes and a lifetime of possessions, could dream again.

Prayer turned five loaves and two fishes into truck-loads of supplies, as in Mark's gospel. Jesus was in Appalachia, and He was again caring for the needy through His body, the Church. Thousands were assisted in a two-week period following the disasters. Michael has learned from his early walks by faith, that "the meal barrel may be bare, but faith in God makes all the difference. God is our source," he urges, "not man. And with such a caring God and ready helpers, there will be an abundance to feed, clothe and house the multitudes."

What he learned in walking by faith with his family and small congregation, he now uses to dream, by faith, for a needy state called West Virginia in Appalachia. What he learned, walking alone, after the death of his first wife, was that God was a friend indeed, a comforter, a very present help. And he also learned that God still knew his needs. Last year, he gained a helper, a new wife to share the adventure to Appalachia.

The Appalachian Dream Center is a distribution complex and sometimes a temporary home to flood victims or those who, in the winter, lose their homes due to a house fire. In the Christmas season of 2010, a mother and child were forced to the center due to fire. They lost everything. It was the fourth family at the center in a three-week period, all victims of house fires, all having experienced the loss of furniture, food and clothing.

Go West, Young Man! Appalachia and the Navaho Indians

As if Appalachia and a new wife was too small a challenge, after much prayer Michael felt their mission needed a mission of its own. With limited resources, a small team went to the land of the Navajo, the First Americans—in Gallup, New Mexico. There, with the small mission team, Michael and his new bride celebrated their first wedding anniversary and dedicated the "First American Dream Center." He had little idea God was about to stretch his Appalachian roots. Under the direction of David Lorency of Operation Compassion, he would soon serve as the director of the facility. Now a two-story facility is in place with a ministry kitchen and two apartments for staff.

Operation Compassion recently opened a warehouse to distribute food to the "forgotten people."

The first Christmas banquet, in partnership with the Director of Southwest Indian Ministries and Operation Compassion, was a great success. And the first Christmas food basket and toy giveaway took place. Ministry partnerships and networking is multiplying the effort to assure that no one goes to bed hungry, cold or lonely on the reservation. On some days, as many 130 hot meals are served to the First Nation people. In addition, there is a clothing and Bible Ministry, all possible because of the mentoring and equipping of local church members who are willing to serve as missionaries to the needy. Now the Appalachian Dream Center is able to send trained leaders and helpers to the First American Dream Center to facilitate and equip the Navajo leaders there. Another couple, who for five years had gone to serve the Navajos as short-term missionaries, have now taken on a full-time pastorate on the reservation. Michael, by use of technology and internet communications, directs both centers.

Michael's West Virginia church stands as an exit point from Appalachia's Valley of Despair. They are still praying and ministry to the needy is owned as a continuing call on their local church. It is not a fad in which they experimented—it is part of their call to fields both familiar and to those unknown, near and far. They love Michael, but they have learned not to hold him too tightly in order to give him away to the needy.

A handful of key leaders serve the ministry in sacrificial and bold ways. The pastor of benevolence, Malcolm Floyd, his wife, Robin, and a teenage son have relocated to serve the ministry in New Mexico. Robin Floyd serves as executive secretary for the ministry and Malcolm III, doubles as a communication technician. Carolyn Floyd is the kitchen manager. Broderick Baldwin is the warehouse manager and his wife, Stephanie, are overseers of the clothing distribution and media ministry.

> *Jesus came and told His disciples, "I have been given complete authority in heaven and on earth. Therefore, go and make disciples of all the nations, baptizing them in the name of the Father and the Son and the Holy Spirit. Teach these new disciples to obey all the commands I have given you. And be sure of this: I am with you always, even to the end of the age."*
> *—Matthew 28:18*

Don't Wait for Them to Come—Go Get 'Em!

"At an earlier time in my life, I wanted to curl up and quit, but God was calling me and this church out of its self-preoccupation, to engage

> The **Verdunville Church of God** is the staging post for all the benevolent ministries of the Appalachian Dream Center. "The church, Michael Hartwell declares, "is not a place 'to go to' but rather 'to go from!' From the church, came the outreach center, the systems used by the center, and the volunteer force. These men and women have learned that 'this kind comes only by much prayer and fasting.' Dependence on the Holy Spirit, by prayer, is the most important lesson-skill taught. So much energy and effort is required in this front-line type ministry that it is crucial for the participants to 'recharge their batteries' regularly."

a hurting and needy world," Michael recalls. And God's pursuit of the lost through us is relentless. Through the ministry of the Appalachian Dream Center, not only are hot meals served, but clothing and shelter is also being provided. And other ministries have been birthed as well.

In Harrisonburg, Virginia, drugs and prostitution were practiced openly 24 hours a day. Dan and Renee Garber, leaders of the Potter's House Worship Center, began a ministry to impact victims of sexual and substance addiction. The partnership between the center and the Potters House brought practical assistance to the homes of widows of Appalachia, and conversely, volunteers from the center went to the streets of Harrisonburg to minister to prostitutes and the drug problem there in connection with a Teen Challenge Center there. The Potter's House did the work of an evangelist with a different twist. They took meals to the prostitutes.

At first people were reluctant to come to the food distribution point. They were wary. The area was not safe. So, the team began to deliver meals. They offered the gospel through song and word. Because the area was so rough, the police only tried to contain it at times without venturing inside the perimeters. Drug deals went down in plain sight with no fear of being apprehended, with no shame, with brazen and defiant actions. One of the team members, passing near the drug dealers overheard them say, "We might as well shut down. No one is going to buy with 'them' here." The presence of good had restrained evil, light had pushed out the darkness.

The team was emboldened. They added music, declaring the love of God to the whole area. Now, that area is a virtually drug and prostitution-free neighborhood. At least two prostitutes were saved and returned to their homes in neighboring counties. Another wanted so desperately to break free, but found herself paralyzed by a fear of her "pimps." She asked members of the team to help her return to her husband and family in another state.

This lady, once a Sunday School teacher in a Church of God congregation, had fallen into a deep trap of sin! She had a daughter who had become addicted to *Meth*, a street-term for *Methamphetamine*, a psycho stimulant that is most often illegally used to induce euphoria. It has a high potential for abuse and addiction due to the physio-psychological trigger of dopamine, norepinephrine and serotonin in the brain. It is sadly illicitly synthesized and then sold in a crystalline odorless, bitter-tasting crystal; thus the colloquial nickname *"crystal meth."* Heavy users experience a sensation known as "bingeing" lasting for days or even weeks, followed by a severe withdrawal experience that can last as long as 10 days. Bingeing can be accompanied by depression, fatigue, excessive sleeping and an increased appetite. Chronic users provoke prolonged psychiatric disorders, permanent cognitive impairment, and an increased risk of Parkinson's disease. Against major odds, both women were set free.

Poor ventilation in homes using solid fuels kills 1.5 million people each year, half of them under 5 years of age.

Beginning in the heart of West Virginia, and then reaching across the state, then across the nation to New Mexico, once again Michael was feeling stirred to reach out even further. This time it was to El Salvador. In a continued partnership with the Potters House Worship Center, they are in what is known as MIEPAN. In November, 2010, a crusade outreach drew more than 1,500 nightly, and saw 1,600 people come to Christ in 10 days, with 16,000 attending on the last night.

From the crusade, outreaches were launched into villages. At some locations, only a few heard the message. Each time, compassion and care were combined with the gospel. They ministered to felt needs. They gave toys to the children, along with hygiene items. In one small village in El Salvador, gang activity was very evident and distressingly real. A church service was conducted behind a wall in the yard of a pastor. Several children along with adults prayed that day, inviting Jesus Christ into their lives.

Suddenly, the unsettling cries of a small five-year old boy pierced the air. He was crying because he had not received a toy! Due to security concerns about gang intrusion, the gate had been closed on him. The translator asked for one more toy for the child, but there were none, only a pair of shoes. The translator told the young boy, there were no toys, only a pair of shoes, "What are shoes?" he asked. He had never had a pair of shoes. The team explained that shoes were to be worn on the feet as protection. To everyone's amazement, they were his perfect size. Joy filled his heart, and he wore them proudly.

Now, a second outreach is being conducted in South America, this time to Brazil. Each trip is calculated to minister to the needs of the community and also strengthen the local church there. Each year, one of the exciting moments is to see the growth of the young church, to see it advancing in the training of its leaders and the building of other churches. The key is creating congregations that see themselves as ministry teams to others that are not self-consumed and self-focused. "Often," Michael notes, "when one feels least equipped is when God uses them the most. It's the state of dependence on Him that allows the Holy Spirit to work mightily through all of us."

A Final Plea—The Sacrifice is Worth the Effort

"I challenge every pastor and leader, the elder and deacons, indeed, all Christians," Michael declares, "to look beyond the valley of despair in which you find yourself and see the needs of others. And feeling there is little to give, realize that the most effective and greatest work for God is done when you feel the least adequate, when finances are the most limited, and when all that is left is to depend on Him."

Ministry can be fulfilling, but Michael has learned it can also be taxing. With the expansion of the ministry across the continent to another hemisphere, he was at 33,000 feet aboard an airliner on Labor Day thinking about all the families that were having a good time, cooking out, and playing games. For a moment, he felt loss.

Then the Holy Spirit gave him comfort and the reassurance of his calling "But I have called you to go forth!" It was the gentle assurance he needed. Galatians came to mind, *"Remember that you can't ignore*

God ... You will always reap what you sow! Those that live only to satisfy their own desires will harvest the consequences ... those who live to please the Spirit will harvest everlasting life from the Spirit. So don't get tired of doing what is good. Don't get discouraged and give up ... Whenever we have the opportunity, we should do good ..." (NLT, Galatians 6:7-17).

The first years were fledging, tough and lean years. Moving from one facility to another. Would God provide? "Yes" faith answered, and He did! After years of ministry, thousands have been saved in the tenth year alone. There have been signs, wonders and miracles. One young man, Eddie, was in a prison in Honduras. En route from El Salvador to the facility in Honduras, Michael kept praying that God would show him what to preach. Prison preaching was new territory. An hour from the prison site, the Holy Spirit whispered, Isaiah 49:15-16:

> *Can a woman forget her sucking child, that she should not have compassion on the son of her womb? yea, they may forget, yet will I not forget thee. Behold, I have graven thee upon the palms of my hands; thy walls are continually before me. KJV*

The team arrived and was escorted into the prison yard. No cameras were allowed. Some 25 of the 100 inmates came to Christ that day. But as others were responding, Michael was drawn to one young

"Chainsaw"

Known only as "Chainsaw," Michael and his team found him living in a dwelling that was no more than a few pieces of roofing tin, cardboard and plastic. He battled the cold by burning tires and pieces of scrap wood. His dogs were his only true friends and companions.

Michael kept reaching out to Chainsaw, building bridges of trust. He finally convinced him to come to the Dream Center for hot meals. Little by little, Chainsaw allowed love to increase faith. He eventually moved into a camper purchased for him by another ministry, and he now lives on the property of the Appalachian Dream Center, and has done so for six years. He is an ever-present servant, at the young age of 82. A throw-away, rescued and given new hope and a sense of personal significance.

man the whole time he was preaching. He was at the end of the prison courtyard. Michael could see his face and his hands extended through the very narrow prison window. As the team was leaving, an inmate asked us if someone would talk to Eddie. It was Eddie that had been watching from the prison window.

The devious slogan of the New York State lottery is "All you need is a dollar and a dream."

The weather had changed, rain was falling, and Michael through an interpreter was engaged with Eddie, "Can your God love a man like me?" he asked. He was in prison for the rest of his life for murder, not of one man, but for multiple killings. "I heard the message but how can God love me?" Here was the Isaiah 49 moment in real time. God could not forget Eddie. He was engraved in the hands of Jesus! Standing in the rain, with water pouring down as if a sign from heaven, with clothes and Bibles wet in two kinds of rain, Eddie, the tough guy, was having a moment with God. His eyes were evidencing tears! He asked Jesus into his heart. As the team walked away, Eddie's eyes followed.

Later that night, at another service in the same city, Pastor Dan shared Eddie's story of conversion. "Did I hear you right?" a lady asked. She explained that Eddie had been raised on the streets of Honduras, an abandoned and hardened child, since he was eight years old. "He has killed both men and women, boys and girls, as if they were only mosquitoes. He was saved?"

Yes, Eddie was saved that day! It is a radical word– *saved.* The bread is only a metaphor for another kind of bread. The clothes are only symbols of another robe heaven offers. The housing is a temporary gift for a home in heaven. Michael declares, "I hope to see Eddie in heaven one day."

The world is full of people like Eddie. Every nation has them. Cities have them. Though some are in prison, others are not too far from the front doors of our church facilities. They will not be reached unless we answer the call. "I challenge you, even if you are in your own valley of despair, perhaps exhausted, give Jesus your five loaves and two fish," Michael urges. "If you 'send them away' so that you will remain comfortable, they will never know Jesus as their Savior."

All we are asked to do is to give what we have. No more. Above all, we cannot continue to send the needy away from our doorsteps. We cannot ignore them. Pray the prayer that Jesus taught us to prayer—pray it today, pray it verse by verse and let it speak to your heart. Even in your valley of despair, you can hear God call you to a higher level in your life. He has a ministry for you. He wants to love others through you.

> *After this manner therefore pray ye: Our Father which art in heaven, Hallowed be thy name. Thy kingdom come. Thy will be done in earth, as it is in heaven. Give us this day our daily bread. And forgive us our debts, as we forgive our debtors. And lead us not into temptation, but deliver us from evil: For thine is the kingdom, and the power, and the glory, for ever. Amen (Matthew 6:9-13 KJV)*

Discussion Guide

Big Ideas

- Michael Hartwell did not walk alone. "David Lorency," Michael noted, "gave us valuable teaching and assistance in helping expand and fulfill our vision."
- The "Christmas to Appalachia" program.
- Operation Compassion negotiated with the A. T. Massey Coal Company for the property now occupied by the Dream Center for Appalachia, a 40,000 square foot facility for ministry use.
- The Verdunville Church of God is the staging post for all of the benevolent ministries of the Appalachian Dream Center. "The church," Michael Hartwell declares, "is not a place 'to go to' but rather 'to go from!'"
- "At a time in my life when I wanted to curl up and quit, God was calling me and the church out of its self-preoccupation to engage a hurting and needy world," Michael recalls.

Notable Quotes

- ❖ Some 100,000 miners lost their lives in the last century due to accidents—an average of 1,000 per year.
- ❖ It was a faith walk. The small family lived in the basement of the church facility for several years and on poundings (food gifts) from the people who attended. The first Christmas was like those of his (Michael's) childhood—a hungry family with little food or means for provision. No one knew but God.
- ❖ The devious slogan of the New York State lottery is "All you need is a dollar and a dream."
- ❖ "Often," Michael notes, "when one feels least equipped is the time God uses us most. It's the state of dependence on Him that allows the Holy Spirit to work mightily through all of us."
- ❖ "The righteous care about justice for the poor, but the wicked have no such concern," Proverbs 29:7.

Questions for Consideration

1. Michael Hartwell was a "bus kid"—the product of an outreach popular a few decades ago. Ask if anyone in your group was saved by some similar outreach?
2. For years, Church of God congregations have had ministries to reach children—Sunday School, bus programs, Vacation Bible School, and more. Methods change with the culture, and so do needs. Now an entire generation of kids have been raised under the shadow of our steeples without hearing Bible stories, without exposure to the gospel, raised in schools where prayer and Bible-based morality are considered illegal. Do we have an obligation to reach them? How do we begin the process?
3. Would you be willing to give up your social/fellowship hall to minister to the poor?
4. Discuss the stories of rather radical conversions in this chapter—the prostitutes and Eddie in the prison. When has your church recently seen a radical conversion?
5. In these cases, the church had to go find the lost. In what ways is your church reaching out to lost people? How could you begin?

Baptists and Pentecostals Save A Children's Home

Ten years ago, the **Appalachian Children's Home** almost closed. Thousands were owed in debt and about a hundred thousand in unpaid payroll taxes. The government was preparing to foreclose. Only three children were housed at the home. Steve Yeary provided leadership and local churches—Baptist and Pentecostal—rallied to save the home. Some 50 churches now regularly interact with the home on some level. As a result of Steve's leadership and a proactive board of directors that saw the need and potential of the home, it was not only saved, it now has international accreditation, and is licensed for 52 children. It is typically at maximum capacity. About 100 are turned away each year.

In 1949, two children were found abandoned in a railroad car and the Appalachian Children's Home was founded by a group of concerned Christians and a collage of independent churches. Some things should bring us together. Some projects are bigger than a church, and they demand a community response. The Appalachian Children's Home survived its brush with death, and is now six decades old and sits on a sprawling 158 acre campus on the outskirts of Barbourville, Kentucky. The primary purpose of the home is to care for young people, typically between the ages of 10 and 18 years of age. The residential program focuses on kids from homes that are spiritually, emotionally, and financially impoverished.

Ordained Bishop, Pastor Sylvester Dunn, a former educator and now Vice Chairman of the board says, "Small miracles occur routinely when fear and want of young people in the midst of social and relational pain smile." At the home, he says, "We can calm a troubled heart taken by fear, doubt, grief, anger, and hate. Here, for the first time, they sense love and security. Unable to read and on a path that would have led to a life of destruction, they are redirected. Saved. Great things are now possible. Where only a nightmare existed before, dreams emerge."

Sixty staff members, most with college and master's degrees, serve an average of 40 to 52 young people. A collaborative effort with the Knox County Public School System allows for an on campus, technologically advanced school with five certified teachers and a Title One coordinator. Kids have been known to jump three grade-levels in testing when given personal attention and a disciplined learning environment they never knew before. Special Education services are offered with a certified Special Education teacher. Educational enhancement includes individual learning goals as well as music, horseback riding, water skiing, cooking and scrap booking. Instruments are provided for the students to practice and display their skills.

In the last decade, all buildings have been upgraded or replaced. Programs for abused children, alcohol and drug counseling have been added. The home is debt-free with a new housing facility recently completed through grants. The home has expanded its programs to touch retired ministers, mission endeavors, and widows. It offers community youth programs and provides food assistance to the needy. Each summer in July, some 500 kids flood onto the property for summer camp.

Established endowment scholarships at Eastern Kentucky University and Lincoln Memorial University allow the graduates of the home to better themselves with a college education. Tuition and book assistance is also offered to the staff to further their academic career. Kids at the home take frequent field trips for educational and recreational purposes to Washington, DC; to aquariums, and to historical sites.

There is every effort to make the atmosphere one of fervent faith. During the last week of June, the grounds host an annual "camp meeting." Baptists, Church of God, and non-denominational all come together for a community spiritual life week. These same pastors and churches connect regularly in the city for joint prayer. Frequent prayer meetings take place at the home with the staff. Area ministers come weekly to meet the spiritual needs of the children who attend some community church on Sunday, many at the Barbourville Church of God, where Sylvester Dunn, Vice Chairman and Secretary-Treasurer of the home, serves as pastor.

True ministry to the kids takes place daily through prayer, counseling, teaching and a caring staff. A large number of the children are introduced to Jesus Christ for the first time, and experience the love of God. It changes their lives completely. In the last 10 years alone, the home has served almost 1,000 kids. Many alumni live in the community, now married and successful. Some are now teachers, business owners and community leaders.

"Wealth is worthless in the day of wrath, but righteousness delivers from death."—Proverbs 11:4

"Do not wear yourself out to get rich; have the wisdom to show restraint. Cast but a glance at riches, and they are gone, for they will surely sprout wings and fly off to the sky like an eagle."—Proverbs 23:4-5

"Whoever loves money never has money enough; whoever loves wealth is never satisfied with his income. This too is meaningless."—Ecclesiastes 5:10

"A good name is more desirable than great riches; to be esteemed is better than silver or gold."—Proverbs 22:1

"He who is kind to the poor lends to the Lord, and He will reward him for what he has done."—Proverbs 19:17

"A rich man may be wise in his own eyes, but a poor man who has discernment sees through him."
—Proverbs 28:11

"The wealth of the rich is their fortified city; they imagine it an unscalable wall."
—Proverbs 18:11

And in that vicinity there were shepherds living [out under the open sky] in the field, watching [in shifts] over their flock by night. And behold an angel of the Lord stood by them, and the glory of the Lord flashed and shone all about them, and they were terribly frightened.
—Luke 2: 8 – 9, Amplified Version

The City of Refuge
Bruce Deel was assigned to an inner city church in Atlanta, and he faithfully went to fulfill his commission, which included closing the facility and merging members with another congregation, but God had other ideas. He now operates a mission ministry to the poor and homeless in a unique partnership with the city of Atlanta. Some 10,000 are served. Atlanta's respect for him was evident in his being chosen to represent the Braves at the MLB All-Star Game in the PEOPLE "All Stars Among Us" national campaign. He was honored at a Braves Game in Atlanta, GA; then again at the All Stars ceremony in Anaheim, CA, one of only 30 in the nation to receive such an honor. The budget for the ministry is now approaching $2 million annually

7

Just a Shepherd Boy

The shepherds around Bethlehem at the time of Christ seem a world and age away from downtown, inner city Atlanta. But there is a connection. Those shepherds were minding their own business when God's business interrupted the rhythm of their lives with flashes of God's glory. They were simply doing their job, but God wanted to include them in what He was doing. And he did.

Just Doing My Job

In 1997, Bruce Deel was *working* at a nice church in North Atlanta when the Church of God sent him on an unusual ministry mission to downtown Atlanta. The new assignment was, sadly enough, to close the doors of a small struggling church and sell the property. For Bruce, it was just a *job* given to him by people with spiritual authority over him, so he made the shift and began the task. Since it was only a drive of a few minutes to the facility from his home near Stone Mountain, he and his wife, Rhonda, decided to maintain their residence and commute to work and church. Their daughters continued to attend the same schools, play in the same sports leagues, and enjoy virtually the same lifestyle. Bruce admits, "I wasn't expecting God to do anything phenomenal—I was just *working*."

According to the US Department of Agriculture, 20% of America's food goes to waste annually, 130 pounds of food per person ends up in landfills, an annual value of $31 billion. Roughly 49 million people could have been fed by the lost resources.

His task was simple. Find a good real estate agent and list the property for sale, get the property ready to sell, continue to have services and ministry opportunities, all the while preparing the few remaining brethren for transition to other places of worship and ministry. He remembers, "I do not recall asking God to show up in miraculous ways or 'flash' in the night sky over the dying ministry." In that season, he was determined to remain faithful to the things to which he had been called.

As a boy of 16, he had acknowledged the call of God on his life. Most of his early years in ministry were founded on an expectation of the miraculous. He expected the youth group to explode into the hundreds, as a result of miracles of divine healing and deliverance. He anticipated unexplainable provision to show up in the mailbox. By 1997, his views had changed. He had concluded that ministry is mostly just plain work—getting up day after day and completing the tasks before you, remaining obedient to Kingdom assignments.

Flashes of Glory!

As Bruce plodded through the process of *working* at Midtown Mission, expecting it to be a short six months, he began to see flashes of God's glory. He wasn't really looking for such moments—they just showed up.

Pastor Deel now reflects, "I am really glad I never asked God to do things a certain way because He may have honored my requests and I would have missed seeing Him do things His way. I was busy cleaning out junk, negotiating with potential buyers, and preparing sermons, when a flash would occur. As flashes of God's glory should do, they caught my attention, and I was very thankful for the good things that were happening, but following each experience, I went *back to work.*"

Over 3 billion people live on less than $2.50 a day.

During one Sunday morning service, a young lady walked into the back of the sanctuary and took a seat. She listened intently and seemed moved by the worship environment. At the conclusion of the sermon, she came forward and asked for prayer. She was 32 years old and had been working as a prostitute for 14 years. That morning she prayed and was born into the Kingdom of God. That flash of God's glory was easily recognizable and one for which the church gave Him great praise. But on Monday morning, Bruce went *back to work*— cleaning, negotiating, and preparing to shut it all down.

On the following Sunday, the freshly converted young lady returned and brought with her a 55-year-old man—a person she described as "one of my former paying customers." Before the sermon was finished the man wanted prayer, interrupting the message. Obviously, he was not aware that the proper protocol for salvation in a church service is to wait until the sermon is finished and then come forward when the altar call is given. Quite the opposite happened. He was compelled by the Holy Spirit and could not wait. Bruce recalls, "I am very glad he responded to the Father's plan rather than following our order, or we may have missed another flash of glory." What a Sunday! Then again, on Monday morning, Pastor Bruce went *back to work.*

Redirection—A Dead Place Lives

At the end of six months, when the building should have been sold, the ministry should have been closed, and the few members transferred to the care of another shepherd, Bruce concluded that he *should not and could not* close the ministry and simply move on to the next assignment. The moments of divine interventions had become too numerous. "There was too much flashing going on to walk away from it all," he recalls.

By that time, the congregation of 20 folks had tripled and a vibrant after-school program for inner-city kids was just beginning to take shape in the basement. Meals to the poor were being distributed to the hungry from the church's small kitchen. There were the beginnings of a clothing closet starting to take shape. Bruce had backed into the will of God. He formed a corporation and founded the City of Refuge as an outreach arm of the congregation called "The Mission."

Outsiders were now taking an interest in what was happening on 14th Street. In addition, families were driving into the city from their suburban homes. The ministry was giving hope to families who had fathers and friends, husbands and brothers in prison. While they were still behind bars, inmates in Atlanta's jails and prisons were hearing about the hope their family members had gained from The Mission.

Isaiah 9:10 declared, "*The people in darkness have seen a great light.*" And they made their way to the "City of Refuge" upon release. Suddenly, the ministry was an employment agency and an advocate for the formerly imprisoned. Bruce remembers, "We *worked* to help them find jobs and places to live. We *worked* in cooperation with recovery programs and transitional living facilities to provide felons with a fresh start. We *worked* to secure our own properties where men and women could reside and be part of discipleship efforts. The flashes continued in regular succession, and with each one a little more of God's glory was revealed."

Still, Bruce did not lay expectations on the work. Each morning, he simply rose from his bed and went to *work*. But the work began to change—the tasks he was called to perform took on different shapes and soon the initial assignments faded into oblivion as Bruce and his small team plowed into the future with blind faith and increasing expectations, great expectations.

Now, the building that was to be liquidated needed to be treasured. They cleaned, painted, and worked on the roof of the old church building. They modified the basement to better accommodate groups of kids and homeless people for hot meals. One day, Rhonda, his partner and wife, surprised Bruce with an announcement. "If we are going to *work* in the city, I think we should live there." It was another flash, and before long Bruce and Rhonda were emptying their comfortable house in beautiful Stone Mountain and moving into the old church building on 14th Street. They were now missionaries to the city of Atlanta. They were no longer "missionizing" at a safe distance. They removed the protective barrier. They took the plunge. They joined the culture.

Moving Into the Mission

Living in the building gave Bruce more opportunities to *work*. He was only 25 steps from the third floor living quarters to his office. And then there was a regular flow of needy people who came to the church asking for assistance. "Believe me," Bruce remembers, "these people had little understanding of regular hours of operation." Suddenly life was disrupted with countless interruptions of family dinners, movies or ball games, and peaceful nights of sleep. It was clear, he and his family could not do this alone, and they needed a sanity barrier to protect the sanctity of private time.

Bruce began to bring on staff to help, and each one was quickly put to *work*. "I never hired a soul whose job it was to pray that God would do something miraculous. No one was given the assignment to stand in the parking lot and gaze into the sky with an expectation that God's glory might be revealed. No job description included a mandate to simply believe God for miracles," Bruce observed. "Oh, we prayed and regularly asked our Father for His guidance and that He would snatch us back into line if we ventured down paths of self-sufficiency. But mostly we just *worked* very hard at being obedient to the things He has commanded all believers to do—feed the hungry, give drink to the thirsty, clothe the naked, befriend prisoners, take care of widows and orphans, love other people as much as we love ourselves—all that kind of weird stuff that requires a little extra effort and omits most of the things that characterize modern day churches." Though the focus was on faithful obedience to what could be done, (not requests for God to lighten the load, create a shortcut, or alleviate a burden) the flashes of God's glory, the indisputable marks of divine intervention, continued to come. Crack addicts were set free from their addictions, prostitutes were redeemed and started new lives, homeless people emerged from under bridges realizing there was hope, and babies born into extremely chaotic situations were adopted by wonderful families. With each flash a bit more of the glory of God was revealed. And more importantly, following each extraordinary flash, Bruce simply went back to *work*.

Soon, months turned into years. Now, enough time had elapsed for a clear assessment of the work. The facts revealed that most of the people who came to The Mission for assistance were coming from a section of the city just west of their location—Bankhead, Simpson, or Martin Luther King, across Northside Drive, and then into the heart of Atlanta to find people with disposable dollars and organizations in the business of helping the poor. They came in search of food, clothes, assistance with utility bills, birth certificates and identifications, help getting into recovery programs, and a multitude of other things. Bruce realized he should relocate the center closer to the need.

Getting Closer to the Harvest

In 2003, he commissioned a real estate agent to find a suitable facility in an area called "The Bluff." That neighborhood had the reputation of being the worst in Atlanta for many reasons—crime, illegal drug activity, the high school dropout rate, the number of single parent households, etc. There were more inmates in Georgia's correctional facilities from that section of town than any other community in the entire state. This was a mission field. They needed a "City of Refuge."

While the agent looked for property, a new center location, Bruce continued to *work*. He remembered the season, "There were too many things to do to sit around hoping and dreaming." No one doubts the power of visions and dreams, but Bruce recognized that they also had the power of distraction. He could little afford to invest his limited time and energy into a potential dead-end street. He had been visited by more than one "visionary" who wanted to meet and talk about possibilities for the outreach. Along the way, Bruce had seen little come from such dreamers. And he increasingly allotted less time for such meetings. "I was duly busy doing the things about which Father had already given instruction. I already knew the heart of God toward the poor. He was just waiting for people like me to stop dreaming and start doing." Like Nehemiah, he was too busy to come down off the wall.

After a period of diligent searching, Rick, the real estate agent, returned with an amazing discovery—eight and a half acres of land on Simpson Road with two warehouses totaling 210,000 square feet of space. The property was surrounded by wrought iron fencing, complete with razor wire, and a post for an armed security guard at the gate. It was perfect! Bruce empowered Rick to negotiate terms with the owner. And he went back to *work* at The Mission on 14th Street. Rick returned with a full report on the property, and an asking price of 1.6 million dollars. Bruce made a proposal explaining, "We love the property and wish to have it, but do not have any money—not $1.6 million. The owner rejected the offer."

Rejection can be stunning. It has a way of stopping some people in their tracks. It is often a weapon that kills dreams and destroys potential. Many people have been cheated out of their purpose by allowing rejection to stop them from *working* toward their goals, causing them to give up. Marvelous inventions remain dormant thoughts because gifted inventors have allowed rejection to govern their efforts. Cures for horrible diseases may have gone unrealized because of the effects of rejection, and potential champions have likely gone uncrowned because they could not find the wherewithal to fight through rejection. When Rick brought the bad news that his proposal had been rejected, and that the owners were committed to $1.6 million, Bruce shrugged his shoulders and went back to *work*. "There was too much to do to spend time whining. After all, who really expects someone to sell you something so valuable for nothing!" he remembers.

Only a Miracle Will Do! But Don't Wait on One!

From time to time, as *work* at the Mission continued, conversations would occasionally arise about the property on Simpson. Bruce would ask Rick to check with the owner again, to see if things might have changed. Each time the answer was the same—$1.6 million. Months went by, and the ministry at The Mission continued to thrive.

One day, in the middle of a series of mundane tasks—meeting with children's ministry workers, planning summer camps and the next neighborhood Matthew Party, and then fixing a window broken during a recent burglary, Rick called with an unusual message. The property owner's attorney asked when they could meet to close on the Simpson Road property.

Confused, Bruce responded to Rick, "We do not have money for the purchase and we are not prepared to go that deeply in debt." Rick, as casually as if he was reciting the daily specials at the Silver Skillet, replied, "They want to give you the property."

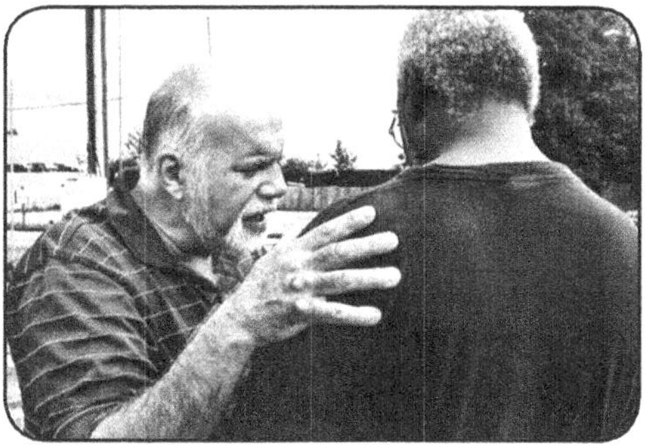

FLASH! A big flash of God's glory. Huge! Major!

Like the shepherds on a hillside "watching over their flock by night," Bruce spent his days (and nights, when necessary) making sure the details of his assignment were completed. Shepherds make sure sheep stay within protected boundaries, insuring that water and grass are readily accessible, keeping the campsite stocked and organized, moving the sheep when the time is right, and at times conducting business involved with shepherding. In the account recorded in Luke 2, the shepherds were doing nothing more than faithfully performing the duties associated with their jobs when the Creator of the universe showed up in a flash of glory, giving them a personal invitation to be the first outsiders to view the newly arrived Messiah. They were just "watching over their flock by night."

On that day, when the news came about the gift of the facility, in the face of that flash point, Bruce and his family and the whole staff, hooped and hollered, and high-fived each other. The donation of the property that day by Mr. Mimms was clearly a miracle, one of Biblical proportions, and there was a reason to celebrate. But when the fervor died down, the team rolled up their sleeves and went *back to work.*

Now there was much more to do than ever before. The newly acquired buildings were dark, dirty, cold and empty. They were faced with the task of moving an entire church to a new location, preparing the old building to sell, and making plans for the new facilities. The donation was a tremendous blessing, but it created far more work than Bruce and his team had ever known. One section of the warehouse was converted to offices. In another section, two basketball courts were installed along with a work-out gym in another. There was grass to cut and a huge parking lot to maintain. The fence needed repairs and *everything* had to be cleaned. But an even more haunting question had to be addressed. God had provided an enormous place. *Now what in the world would it be used for? What would the City of Refuge do with it?*

About 39% of adult clients served by Feeding America completed high school but have no further education.

The City of Refuge

Bruce remembers, "The gift of the building was anticipated, and yet still quite a surprise. I really did not know what to do or how to do it, so I just went to work every day and did the things set before me to do. I went to my pasture and cared for the sheep. I fed and watered, provided protection and direction, kept the place stocked and organized, moved the people along with me (spiritually) as the Holy Spirit led, and conducted the business of shepherding. I kept diligent watch over the given assignment, refusing to allow it to be manipulated or destroyed by figurative wolves and coyotes. I was keeping watch by day and night."

Not long after the basketball courts were completed, the ministry was asked if the *City of Refuge* would open a 30-bed cold weather shelter for homeless women. What an opportunity! Funding was promised if the *City of Refuge* would provide the facility. Bruce recalls, "I was under a mandate to care for the poor—as are all Christians, and for that matter, all humane humans. It was a no-brainer, an answer to prayer. In 2003, facing the winter, 30 beds were added in the north gym and the ministry provided warm beds and food to "the last, lost and least."

As more time passed and demands grew, the capacity was expanded to 50 beds. When winter evolved into spring, city officials asked The

Refuge to keep the shelter open just one more month, then another, then two more, and then year round. Another expansion took the facility to 80 beds—50 in the gym and 30 in another section of the building.

Some 58.6% of children under the age of six, living with a female householder and no husband present, are in poverty—more than five times the rate of dual parent homes.

Bruce reflects, "I realize more and more the Father is so blessed by our obedience to His instruction that He reveals His heart mostly in the process of our obedience. In other words, we are much more likely to hear from Him and grow in our understanding of His thoughts and ways when we are busy doing His work." Pastor Deel believes "Scripture is pretty clear on the things true sons and daughters of Yahweh are supposed to do. In Matthew 25, Jesus reveals the aforementioned list of actions on which we will ultimately be judged, and indicates the ministry of such actions to the poor and destitute is equal to ministry to Him. He paints a very clear word picture of judgment when He declares that sons who do these things will spend eternity with Him, and those who do not obey this very important instruction will not be recognized in the end as part of the family."

Most servants know faithful obedience is at the core of servant values, and there is very little glamour in service. Faithfulness amounts to putting one foot in front of the other and getting one's hands dirty. The bottom line? Service is the truest form of worship and nothing pleases the Father more than worshipful service. We are saved by faith, and not by works, and yet, we are saved by faith that works. True sons and daughters of God have a responsibility to the poor and needy, and to ignore them is to live in disobedience to some of the most important instructions God gives. Bruce believes, "It is *good* to pray and fast and beseech the Father to show us His plan and reveal His will. It is *better* to get up from our prayers and get busy doing the things He has already commanded we should do, for in our *doing,* He will reveal flashes of His glory and revelations of His will like we never imagined."

The City Turns to The Church

With 80 homeless women coming into the City of Refuge every evening, there is always plenty to do—meals to prepare in a very small space, linens to launder, bathrooms to clean and stock (women go through unbelievable amounts of tissue!), shopping to do, fights to break up, and on and on. Just when things seemed to settle into a nice routine, another call came from the Atlanta city government. "*Would you be willing to add another 50 beds to the shelter operation?*" The venture into housing for homeless women began with a partnership with the city that has grown over time.

More than a third of all client households served by Feeding America have had to choose between paying for food, or medicine, or medical care.

What an opportunity? What insanity? Another 50 beds? Another 50 women for dinner each evening? "Of course," but then counter arguments ensued. "The enclosed space is full. The kitchen, only eight by 14, is too small. Can the bare bones staff handle 50 more beds? But on the other hand, if there are 50 women still sleeping on sidewalks, under bridges, in abandoned apartments and houses, suffering from the cold, half-starving, scraping and scrounging for food, hoping to find help tomorrow, then maybe we can find room. What if we ... ? Of course, we can. We must. What if it were us? What if we knew one of the women? What if one was our mother, a sister, a daughter, a wife?"

Something had to be done, so Bruce went to *work* to find options. One of the men who was once part of The Mission family had left to organize his own ministry and was also reaching out to the homeless. He had acquired a spacious building only a few miles from the new location of The Refuge. Bruce approached him with a proposal. They formed a partnership. Bruce would provide the money to ready their place and purchase beds, if they would open their doors and provide shelter and meals to an additional 50 women who otherwise would sleep on the streets of Atlanta. His answer was, "Of course, we'll partner!" Fifty more women off the streets and placed in an environment of hope and healing—another "flash point" of God's glory!

The so-called "snowball effect" is the ideal metaphor to describe the City of Refuge operations for the past few years. In 2007, a 180 degree commercial kitchen and dining hall facility were completed—a gorgeous commercial facility accommodating more than 500 guests for meals. As the team faithfully *worked,* shepherding the sheep in their care, formulating plans and applying for grants, gifts started to pour in to pay for the new facility. The flash points were almost blinding—*Flash, Flash, Flash!* With the completion of the new section of the warehouse, the ministry could now realize another vision, a culinary training school for young adults as well as a catering business. With the new kitchen, the task of preparing several thousand meals per month was much easier.

As the 180 degree kitchen was being remolded, Bruce was in the midst of answering questions from plumbers, electricians, and painters. He was ordering tables and chairs for the dining hall, and meeting with the staff to formulate plans for its use. As he was *working* another call came from city officials.

This request was the biggest made to date. They asked if The Refuge would build a transitional living center for homeless women and children. The center would provide 42 individual living units with a capacity for 135 individuals. The program would include a full range of social services—free child care, mental and physical health assessments and treatment, career development and job networking, assistance with open legal, domestic violence, and Department for Child Services cases. At the end of the four-month program, the mothers and their children would transition into independent housing. The city would provide funding (1.5 million dollars) to build the center in a 40,000 square foot section of our warehouse, and would provide enough social workers to do the job, at a budget of $300,000 per year to pay their salaries.

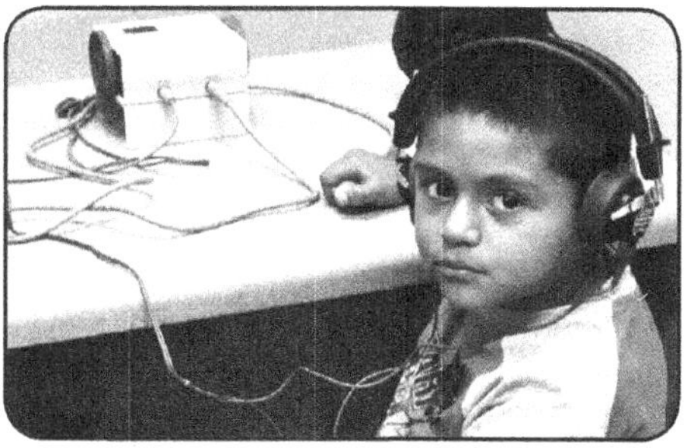

This Flash was almost blinding! Bruce was stunned. He recalls thinking, "To be chosen by God is an indescribable honor. The fact is, the Father has special assignments for each of us and loves to reveal them as we remain obedient to His instruction. Our best ideas cannot compare to His simple plan. Our greatest efforts are nothing more than wasted energy if not exercised within the framework He designs. We may accomplish things that are applauded by men; we may win fantastic awards and receive tremendous accolades; but without faith in Him our works are temporal and will fade away. He knows our hearts and if we follow His simple plan with great expectancy, from time to time He will show up in flashes of glory. He most definitely will."

In December of 2008, Eden Village was opened as a partnership between the City of Atlanta and The Refuge. It is a "Redemptive Housing Program" for women and children. Once again, job assignments morphed into new shapes unknown before. Staff members took on new elements and the whole enterprise required more than the level of service the ministry had offered before. More staff was hired. There were

Hunger Banquet

Consider holding a hunger banquet. Invite the church and their friends, but with a fair warning that the evening could be heart wrenching.

For every 20 tickets, make at least eight of them **black,** six of them **brown**, four of them **green**, and two of them **gold**. Have greeters meet those with **gold** tickets and take them to a table elaborately adorned. Feed them steak, lobster. Don't allow them to lack for anything. Station well-dressed waiters at their table. Ignore all others.

Point out neat, but not well-adorned and appointed tables for those with **green** tickets. Feed them a good, but less than scrumptious meal, cafeteria style.

Have those with **brown** tickets stand in line for a bowl of brown rice—no butter or salt. Allow them to sit anywhere, but at the green and gold tables.

Those with **black** tickets go hungry. They are given no place to sit.

suddenly 150 people living on campus 24/7 and that required a few additional hands. New programs needed to be implemented, new policies developed and enacted, facilities maintained, schedules set and observed, supplies ordered, and money raised. The list goes on and on. And the faithful work is sprinkled with regular and great times of corporate celebration. Bruce says, "We have lots of good reasons to sing, shout, dance, and otherwise offer gratitude to our Father, but mostly we make sure our daily *work* is seasoned with thankfulness for the opportunity to serve in the Kingdom of God. Each time a flash of His glory interrupts our routine, we feel more privileged than ever."

The wealthiest 20% of the world uses 76.6% of the resources, the poorest 20%, only 1.5%.

Bruce insists, "I am just a shepherd boy, but one who has seen brilliant revelations of the 'Peace, Power, Provision, and the Protection of the Creator.' I can relate to those simple men who sat on a Judean hillside on a clear night and had their plans interrupted by messengers from on high. In response to the call, I have journeyed to a nondescript place where I found the Spirit of Christ in the normalcy of servant-hood. The more I do what He says, the more of His heart and mind He reveals."

Soon after Eden Village opened, city officials asked The Refuge to build Eden II. So an additional 100 beds for homeless women were added. FLASH! That facility had barely opened when the call came to build a full-service medical clinic that would serve our community as well as overflow emergency room patients from Atlanta's notoriously over-crowded Grady Hospital. Clinic construction is now underway in another section of the warehouse. FLASH!

Tending sheep requires constant attention. Just as staff eyes begin to regain focus from the most recent "flash," another calls comes from Atlanta's Task Force for the Homeless to inquire if room could be found for 30 more ladies and kids. The weather in Atlanta is turning cold, and the city's Gateway Center is already overcrowded with lots of folks sleeping on the floor or even in chairs.

This is not a good thing! Quite the contrary, this is what the center is for, created to do. "In a way, I feel like a shepherd," Pastor Deel whispers, "like I have been to the stable one more time; leaned over and felt the breath of God on my cheek again; heard the angels sing in the star-laden night sky; and now I am on my way back to the hillside to make sure the most weak and vulnerable of God's creatures are not left unprotected."

Bruce Deel says he is just trying to be faithful. And God has done something rather fabulous. The hundreds of women who have found a safe haven at the City of Refuge will never forget it. Nor will the Lord. Many of those lives will be eternally changed.

Discussion Guide

Big Ideas

- Dominant in this chapter is a sense of faithfulness. Bruce did not go—he was sent. In the process of faithfulness, God worked. He went for a funeral, and God raised the dead.
- One section of the newly donated warehouse was converted to offices. In another section, two basketball courts were installed along with a workout gym for the inner city kids and the homeless. The cold weather shelter followed.
- Bruce created the corporation to serve the poor as a partner to the church and in doing so, he attracted support and entered into partnerships not possible prior to the new legal structure.
- His track record of service drew the attention of the city, and now, a formidable partnership exists between the City of Refuge and the City of Atlanta.
- The ministry is not merely passive. With the culinary training school and the catering business, Bruce is now providing tools for the poor to become productive.

Notable Quotes

- Bruce admits, "I wasn't expecting God to do anything phenomenal —I was just *working.*"
- By the time the congregation of 20 folks tripled and a vibrant after-school program for inner-city kids was beginning to take shape in the basement, meals to the poor and hungry were being distributed from the church's small kitchen. There were the beginnings of a

clothing closet starting to take shape. Bruce had backed into the will of God.

- ❖ He has commanded all believers to feed the hungry, give drink to the thirsty, clothe the naked, befriend prisoners, take care of widows and orphans, love other people as much as we love ourselves.
- ❖ "There were too many things to do to sit around hoping and dreaming."
- ❖ Faithfulness amounts to putting one foot in front of the other and getting one's hands dirty. The bottom line? Service is the truest form of worship and nothing pleases the Father more than worshipful service.

Questions for Consideration

1. Bruce chose the theme of the "shepherds" for this chapter. He wanted to emphasize the contrast between the unexceptional and exacting shepherding tasks with no glory, a tough and under appreciated vocation, caring for rather helpless sheep; and the portion of scripture we emphasize—the angel choir, the flashes of light in the darkness, messages from heaven. Talk about that perspective.

2. Bruce says "the flash" moments do occur, but only the faithful will see them. The real task is not gazing into the night sky, but getting a place ready—in his case, for the homeless, not knowing what they will need. Do you think the church shows up on Sunday looking for flashes of glory, and sometimes does little during the week to care for the hurting?

3. With only 60 people an after school program was started, meals for the poor distributed, and a clothing closet formed. Why do you think such a small group captured such a large vision? Could that happen to your church?

4. Some churches attempt to keep the neighborhood kids off of their property. Bruce built basketball courts to draw them. What is the difference in the underlying missional philosophies of these churches?

5. For many of us, the concept of church is quite narrow—a place we come to once or twice a week for worship. It is becoming clear that such a view is too culturally narrow to reach our communities, and may be too scripturally narrow to meet the criteria of Biblical mandates. Do you agree or disagree?

Milford Church of God: *Multiple Outreaches*

When you come to Hicks Road on the East-West Connector, northwest of Atlanta, you pass the handsome Milford Church of God. It looks like a typical suburban church facility, but the outreach endeavors are mind-boggling. They started in 1991 with their "Celebration of Christ" Christmas event. A second outreach began in 1994 with the "Back to School Backpack Give-away"—all the school supplies necessary to assist underprivileged kids at the start of the school year. That year, they served 350 kids at one school! This year, their "Give A Kid A Chance" program served 23,229 kids in 86 different schools in 14 states.

In addition to the kids, they are now providing help to the parents— often single moms—with job fairs, scholarships, aid and assistance, and spiritual, as well as moral support. Through a unique partnership with H&R Block and the Advanced School of Medical Transcription, they are providing scholarships to train single parents for new careers. At their job fairs, additional companies set up booths and recruit their clientele as prospective employees.

They also work to build healthy relationships between law enforcement and inner city kids, children in need, and those whose fathers are in prison. Their programs bring kids into contact with cops for child identity bracelets, a major help if the child ends up lost or abducted. And the officers educate the kids on safety issues, older kids on drug prevention. Fire fighters do demonstrations of fire safety and how to escape from a burning building. The red fire engine always gets a big welcome.

Medical teams provide exams as networked doctors, nurses, dentists, chiropractors, and audiologists are on hand. Eye exams are offered, a dental lab is on site, and hearing tests are offered. When a problem is found, local sources are explored to provide care—the "Help a Child Smile"'program, the health centers, and other help agencies.

Based in Georgia, their event sponsorships, in partnership with other churches, reach from Florida to Maine and from Michigan to Texas. At each event, the gospel is shared in a unique way—puppets, mime, skits. Hundreds of kids hear the gospel for the first time and pray to Jesus as Savior. Last year, they invested over $400,000 in the program. But through their unique partnerships, they delivered $2.4 million of services and goods to families in need.

The Milford church works to do more than provide immediate assistance to the poor through the "Free Indeed" endeavor. They developed educational programs to help families understand insurance issues, banking, bill-payment, budgeting, daycare alternatives, parenting, and an array of social education. They provide free haircuts, beauty salon hairdressers, and manicures—all to restore self-confidence, given as a gift of care and love, and to ready them to re-enter culture in a productive way.

They have a box truck and moving crew ready to assist a family with a housing crisis. There is a warehouse with furniture, clothes, and household supplies, including medical items and food. For poor families and single moms trying to squeeze a second 100,000 miles out of a car, critical to their income, they offer a car repair service. They change oil, replace belts and hoses, and even rebuilt an engine. Occasionally, when car repair is not an option, God assists with the miracle of car replacement. Their "Yokefellow Ministry" is a team that does home fix-ups as well.

At Christmas, when single moms and distressed families are worried about their children, their "Celebration for Christ" outreach is a blessing. This past year, it made a difference for over 1,000 families.

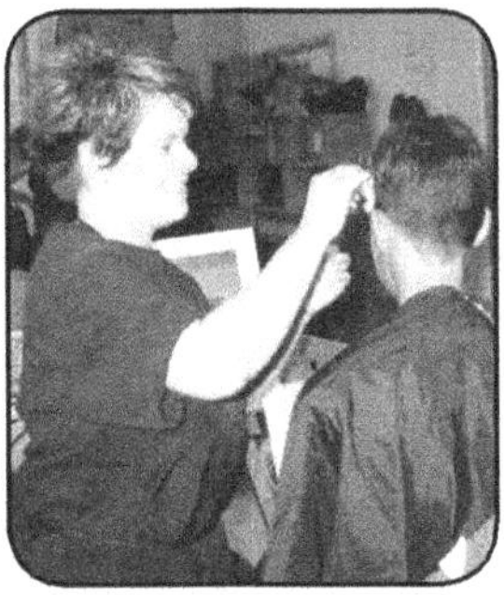

"Jacob's Well" is an outreach funded by a man who himself was not only delivered from drugs, but to incredible success. His deep regret is that his life was in great disarray when his son, Jacob, was small. As a way of giving back, he now wants to help others recover from addictions. Counseling, support groups, and on-going care are offered.. Currently, 24 men are in this program.

The partner to Jacob's Well is the "House of Ruth" which provides an orientation for social reentry in a 12-month residential program. Currently, 24 women and 14 men are in this program.

And there is more—the church has just opened a home for unwed mothers. The facility will house seven expectant mothers and has three residents now.

The church has a medical clinic that is staffed with 14 full-time doctors, pharmacists, dentists, physician's assistants, nurse practitioners, and support staff. Over 200 additional volunteers serve the clinic. Although 2.8 million dollars was needed to open the clinic, with the help of the community the Milford church raised 3.4 million, and the dream of a "free clinic" to serve the poor on the northwest side of Atlanta was born. When it opened in 2006, over 4,000 patients were treated. Last year, they topped 18,000. The clinic receives no government funds. It is supported completely by private donations and client contributions. Last year, they provided over eight million dollars in medical care.

In addition to the 400 medical volunteers, 250 "spiritual life" volunteers serve the clinic offering prayer and care support to the patients. The clinic has a prayer room where patients receive personal spiritual care. Last year, there were 145 conversions out of the clinic ministry. In a comparative study for private care in Cobb County, the clinic ranked number one out of a field of 151 other practices. By every indicator, in the delivery of services, they are ranked above the national average. For every $30 their patients invest in medical care, they receive the equivalent of $590 in comparable Cobb county care. For every $100 invested by private parties, the clinic delivers $1,600 in medical care. They also operate "Good News Counseling Center." There, individuals, families, couples, and kids can get encouragement and assistance.

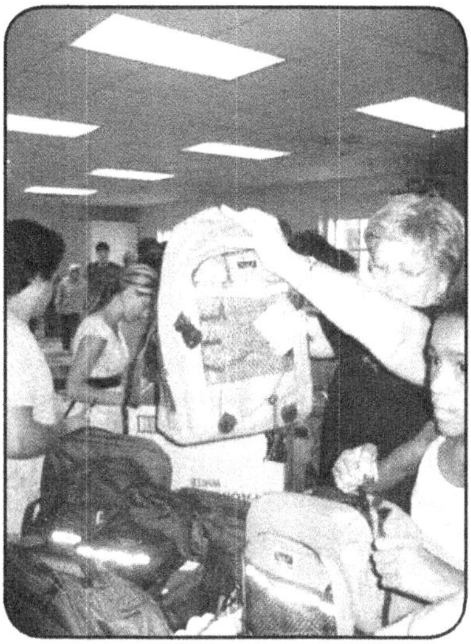

They go beyond recycled clothing by having their own clothing line dubbed *"OneNine"* (Joshua 1:9 named after their Youth Ministry) through an international partnership: jeans, shirts, blouses, and backpacks. The quality garments are used by individuals, inner-city uniform programs, and Christian schools.

Their weekly feeding program serves over 100 families. To support their work the Lord, through the graciousness of community businesses, has provided the use of two warehouses, one with more than 20,000 square feet.

Through the last few years, their benevolence ministry has soared. While they are persistently concerned about the nearby poor, they have not forgotten those that are distant. In 2009-2010 they rose to the coveted spot of number one in World Missions giving in North Georgia and number three in the denomination. Their light is bright both at home and abroad. That push to be more intentionally missional has been in a season of profound warfar. Brenda Gunter, the pastor's wife, brilliantly fought her war against cancer in this season. All the while, the missional endeavor of the church expanded. The church that grieved her loss, has determined to reach yet one more.

The driving force behind the outreach is Grant Cole, who Pastor Gunter calls his right arm. He is a brand plucked from the fire. A former addict and dealer, he had gone through six prisons during three different stretches behind bars. "It wasn't that I didn't want to quit. I couldn't quit." He was a graduate of five different treatment programs. During his second season in jail, he devoured self-help books. If the book involved behavior modification, he read it. He had determined to fix himself through cognitive therapy, through rigid self-control. It didn't work.

Landing in prison a third time, a victim of a unique three-strike law in Cobb County, he was facing life for his chronic drug use. All alone in a cell, he remembers crying out to God. He had only been to church once in his life. He knew no fundamentals of faith. He didn't know the gospel narrative, but if there was a God, that God was his only help. "Save me!" he virtually screamed. "I didn't even know what 'save me!' meant. It felt like I was drowning and I was going to die."

Suddenly, a deep sense of calm replaced his fear and desperation. "It was as if someone had wrapped me in a blanket of peace," he recalled. He opened his eyes. Beyond his bunk, in a pile of papers, he found a book buried, "Good News America: God Loves You!" It

was a *New Testament*. He had tried to read the Bible before, but it made no sense. Now he read it like a children's story. He had been delivered. He made a vow. "If you let me out of here, I'll go to church, and serve you."

On a Saturday night, a guard unlocked his cell, and he walked out a free man—a genuinely liberated man. He found himself telling his story in the very churches where he had done drug deals in the parking lots a few years before.

Now he, Pastor Gunter, and Milford's united Pastoral Team are

partnered and determined together to, one day at a time, make a difference—one kid at a time, one single parent home, one drug dealer, one expectant mother, one family below the poverty line in need of medical care. One, and then another, and then another. And it is happening. Their total outreach budget is now approaching a million dollars a year.

"Do not exploit the poor because they are poor and do not crush the needy in court, for the LORD will take up their case and will plunder those who plunder them."
—Proverbs 22:22-23

"There will always be poor people in the land. Therefore I command you to be openhanded toward your brothers and toward the poor and needy in your land."
—Deuteronomy 15:11

"You evildoers frustrate the plans of the poor, but the Lord is their refuge."
—Psalm 14:6

When the Son of Man comes in His glory, and all the angels with Him, He will sit on his throne in heavenly glory. All the nations will be gathered before Him, and He will separate the people one from another as a shepherd separates the sheep from the goats. He will put the sheep on his right and the goats on his left. Then the King will say to those on his right, "Come, you who are blessed by My Father; take your inheritance, the kingdom prepared for you since the creation of the world. For I was hungry and you gave Me something to eat, I was thirsty and you gave Me something to drink, I was a stranger and you invited Me in, I needed clothes and you clothed Me, I was sick and you looked after Me, I was in prison and you came to visit Me."

Then the righteous will answer him, "Lord, when did we see You hungry and feed You, or thirsty and give You something to drink? When did we see You a stranger and invite You in, or needing clothes and clothe You? When did we see You sick or in prison and go to visit You?"

The King will reply, "I tell you the truth, whatever you did for one of the least of these brothers of mine, you did for Me." "Then He will say to those on his left, "Depart from me, you who are cursed, into the eternal fire prepared for the devil and his angels. For I was hungry and you gave Me nothing to eat, I was thirsty and you gave Me nothing to drink, I was a stranger and you did not invite Me in, I needed clothes and you did not clothe Me, I was sick and in prison and you did not look after Me." "They also will answer, "Lord, when did we see You hungry or thirsty or a stranger or needing clothes or sick or in prison, and did not help You?" He will reply, "I tell you the truth, whatever you did not do for one of the least of these, you did not do for Me. Then they will go away to eternal punishment, but the righteous to eternal life."
Matthew 25:31-46

The Mission America Urban Outreach Center

Frank Allen began his ministry to the poor, one that now touches 26 nations of the world. For every donated dollar, through trusting relationships, he is able to serve the poor with almost seven dollars in goods and services. The amount of gifts he manages for the poor of the world is over 20 million dollars. Almost two dozen mission outreaches annually will involve hundreds of volunteers. And yet, he still serves the local poor with feeding programs, education, after-school care, summer camps, and more. He is a missionary to the poor who always puts his own salary last.

8 Missionary to the Poor

Frank Allen believes care for the poor is no mere peripheral matter. He boldly asserts that without care for the poor, a church is no church at all. For Frank Allen, the mandate to care for the poor is not satisfied by occasional giving or the involvement of a handful of parishioners who enjoy exotic work at a rescue mission. Far too few ministries focus on the poor. For Allen, this is no light thing. God has called every believer to care for the poor. He serves the *hard-core poor*—the term used to describe folks with complex needs who require a holistic ministry; folks who cannot fund the operation of a church, who do not fit into the typical church. These people need *whole man* ministry—body, soul and spirit. Few churches take on such a challenge, but Allen is one of them. The late Dr. John D. Nichols said of Frank's work, "Most churches have a ministry to the poor, but your ministry to the poor has a church." A church *for* the poor! And a church *of* the poor.

15.5 million or 20.7% of America's children under the age of 18 were in poverty.

The Early Days

When Frank Allen started preaching, he was full of zeal. He still is! He preached in parks and under gospel tents. He fed the hungry and worked in the inner city, "I thought this is what preachers did. If you didn't, you were not saved." He grew to understand the diversity of different gifts in the body of Christ, called to work up and down the social spectrum, but his passion for the poor remains and his perspective continues. All congregations and believers should bear a concern for the poor, and engage in a practical demonstration of God's love for the less fortunate.

Driven by Scripture and the example of Christ, his ministry is in the heart of the enemy's territory, behind the lines, in the cross hairs of spiritual warfare. He sees there the daily investment of Satan in lives. Every day, he observes the Dark Lord working to entice, entrap, and keep men and women bound in poverty. He is in the Devil's backyard, operating as a counter-agent, offering hope, setting captives free, and empowering people to find the abundant life. He says, "When you work with the poor and the oppressed, you hit the devil's bank account. He has spent trillions of dollars to entrap and imprison humanity."

It costs an average of $47,000.00 a year to keep a man in prison, even more for women and juveniles. The cost to prosecute a case is some $50,000. A drug habit is expensive, some addicts have a $1,000 a day habit—money that is acquired through robbery, theft and other exploitative means, and then put into the hands of socially lethal forces.

A teenager in the inner city without hope, without true friends, often without a father, without a faith is a generational project of the Evil One. He, too, has plans for lives—plans to do *no* good, plans to superficially prosper and permanently enslave, and plans to kill and destroy. Satan has worked to isolate the innocent inner-city teen. His mother is addicted and his father incarcerated. He has been formed as a weapon of darkness, unwittingly, unknowingly, through no fault of his own, abiding in the shadow of steeples whose buildings are only open for an hour on Sunday. Against such odds, the ministry to the poor works against the dark kingdom and the dark lord, Satan himself. It is more than food distribution. This is a battle for souls. This is a battle for the next generation, for the very soul of the nation.

3.4 million, some 8.9% of seniors 65 and older live in poverty.

Sadly, the investment by the kingdom of darkness is not being matched by the church. Many churches make no provision for the poor, outside of Christmas food baskets or a passing concern for a congregational member. Funds enhance the life of the parishioners, not the "least of these." According to Allen, we minister to Christ not in praise and worship, not in pious prayer or preaching, but through our care for the poor—"the least of these."

To the "Least of These"

Isaiah 58 and Matthew 25: 31-46 are the defining passages for Pastor Allen. The words of Jesus haunt him, "*Inasmuch as you have done it unto one of the least ... ye have done it unto Me.*" Christ came to the roughest of criminals, the nastiest of the homeless, and the craziest of the mentally ill. Everyone bears the image of God, not just the virtuous—everyone. All were created as His children, and though now estranged, God loves them.

Empathy is the wellspring of compassion. To care, you must allow yourself to feel the pain of another, to experience their reality, to stand in their shoes. "If my son became a criminal and harmed people, I would still want someone to be good to him, to feed and love him, to minister to him. God wants the same for His lost children, the very ones who have rejected Him, who have chosen prodigal paths, who have not accepted His love," Frank declares. Such a ministry stands in the gap, offering help and hope in the very stead of Christ Himself.

Infectious diseases blight the poor of the world. 40 million people have the HIV virus, with 3 million deaths annually. Every year, there are 350–500 million malaria cases with 1 million deaths. African account for 80% of the victims.

"The least of these" has become a blinding passage—a mandate for Frank. He isn't focused on homeless folks that have the greatest potential to climb out of poverty, or those whose conversions would demonstrate the effectiveness of his ministry. He wrestles with donors who are always looking for a return on their investment. Their giving is conditional. They want their donation converted into a reformed tithe paying member—a Christian like them.

In the US, out of 43.6 million people, 14.3% were in poverty.

Everyone wants success. Everyone rejoices when a lost person is found or a teen headed down the wrong path is redirected. Frank has seen disoriented souls saved, lives changed, converts now regarded as some companies' most respected employees. Some are in ministry. Some are in stable families and worship in suburban churches. They defeated despair and broke free by the power of grace from their shackles. They no longer find courage in a bottle or coping capacity in a pill. They are no longer so overwhelmed by life that they take flight from reality. They now face life's challenges with confidence in Christ.

Others, without a miracle, will die never experiencing success.

When Jesus says, "the least of these," does He mean the worst of the worst? The least prisoner? The deranged man who habitually strips himself naked? The person so bound that other street people view them as irredeemable and "the least" among them? Frank asks, "Could it mean the one who might never break free, who might never be able to *live right,* but with God's grace and our faithfulness, could *die right?* Do we have an obligation to them as well?"

33 million adults and 17.2 million children are food insecure, 14.7% of all US households.

Some people live in a constant grind of poverty, mental illness, addiction, and disabilities. Others live as undocumented aliens or unacceptable misfits. Some needs are met by various programs, but they need more than a social worker, a temporary bed, or a warm meal offered at an outreach center. Frank argues, "They need a pastor and a church family that is *their* church where they feel comfortable and own responsibility, where they do not attend as an object of ministry. They need to truly belong, to freely invite others, and in their fragile and less than perfect state, offer their gifts in service to Christ. They need a place where they find personal significance and opportunities for growth and development; a place where, through their unique gifts, despite past issues and current disadvantages, they can be recognized and legitimized."

Providing not only assistance *to* the poor, but a church *for* the poor is the life-calling of Frank Allen. He is a missionary to the poor. He says, "I am an ordained social worker that preaches a little–a social worker for the soul. God has called me to reach the hard core poor, who without a miracle will never have the capacity to become a working citizen or a tithe-paying member of a conventional church. As a missionary to the poor, this is who we are called to serve."

The Mission America Urban Outreach Center

In 1992, when Frank Allen felt God's call to serve the poor and outcast, he and his beautiful wife and baby boy moved from the suburbs into the inner city. Working with the Church of God in a pilot program, he started "Mission America Urban Outreach Center" in Norfolk, Virginia. He began by feeding the poor from the trunk of his car, grilling hot dogs, and turning jump rope for children from the projects. He worked at finding help networks, and then steering the disadvantaged into available services. It was his wife, their three-year-old son, and Frank.

When the winter came, they served hot soup and gave away coats, blankets, socks and hygiene packets on the same corners. When the crowd gathered, Frank preached from a milk crate. Churches learned of their efforts and provided support. Volunteers came. Donors surfaced. Local youth groups and inbound mission teams partnered with him.

A billion people entered the 21st century unable to read a book or sign their name.

At the center of their compassionate efforts is evangelism. "We are faithful to the evangelistic mandate, sharing the tangible gospel, evangelism with food, clothing, referrals and other resources. And without fail, at every program, we give an invitation to accept Christ. Sometimes," Frank says, "the same drunks, addicts, and mentally ill come to the altar crying and 'getting saved' time and time again." That doesn't discourage Frank. He is called "to the least of these," not merely to success stories.

Originally, he knew his role. Get down-and-outers up, get them saved, and transition them to local churches as productive members. Give the donors a return on their investment. But it didn't happen.

"We would get them saved and transition them, but assimilating them into the typical church was a challenge. A church van would pick them up, transport them to a facility, and provide a warm breakfast—just for them. When they walked into the sanctuary, everyone was friendly. People greeted and welcomed them every Sunday. But usually, they huddled together in some section of the auditorium as if wearing an invisible sign that said, 'Outsiders. From the projects. The mission group.' It just wasn't working."

Sunday after Sunday they remained the object of detailed attention, receiving the same visitor's handshake. It was always "the church folks" and the "poor homeless people." They were always being prayed for, but never asked to do the praying. They were always being taught, but never asked to teach, being served, but never asked to serve. It was never *their* church. It was someone else's church. The church was not at fault. They really cared. The poor felt welcomed, but the sociological distance, the cultural gap, the variance in needs left them with the sense that they did not fit. This wasn't home.

121 million children lack adequate education worldwide.

There, of course, was also occasional cultural resistance. A middle class family would express discomfort with an untidy and poorly dressed person. If they brought their affluent friend to a church social, hoping they might join, such a prosperous friend might not be impressed by the membership constituency. The new converts were also struggling to find an acceptable norm for social comfort with the middle-class members. The occasional scent of last night's alcohol wafting over an infant at a baby dedication, with extended family present, always broke the wagon down. It was just too much.

A Church *OF* the Poor

Jenny was a single mother, barely 20, with four children, all with different last names. Her reading skills were negligible, but improving. Still, she mispronounced simple words, but salvation had put a fire in her heart. She felt called to teach, and she wanted so much to contribute. Such a role was impossible in a typical suburban congregation, especially with her skill-set and checkered past. Most parents could not approve of her as a role model in Christian Education at any level, even though in the face of her unfortunate decisions, she had now assumed the huge responsibility for her children and, by the strength of God's grace, had experienced total life change.

Frank says, "As a missionary to the poor, you learn to work with imperfect people; not to throw them away when they fall off the wagon Saturday night and make it to church the next morning, hoping for new-found grace and a God who can give them strength to make the next week better than the last." People tell Frank, "You should not let those people into the church!" Others say, "You should use only the most dedicated people and certainly not that group." Frank's answer is, "We use what we have. We have to find Christ in 'the least of these' that we serve."

If you have food in the refrigerator, clothes on your back, a roof overhead, and a place to sleep tonight, you are among the top 75 percent of people on the planet in terms of comfort.

One winter, Frank had a fight break out every Sunday. Some resulted in police being called. Attendees would be handcuffed and driven off in police cars. One night, in a convenience store, he exchanged greetings with a police officer who winked and said, "See you in church on Sunday, Reverend!" Frank is a missionary to the poor. Sadly, in the midst of confusion and want, fear and uncertainty, conflict is inevitable.

He knows the challenge of having to carefully plan a baptism service to insure that HIV patients are baptized last. He knows the pain of losing a high dollar tither, who in the recent past was a broken soul, but now wants a better environment for their children. He knows the contradiction of people that come to serve the poor, then struggle with sharing a pew with a smelly homeless person. He knows the paradox of those ready to minister to the mentally ill, but who find actually worshiping and fellowshipping with them too much. The challenges of working with the poor are unique:

- One Sunday, in the middle of a sermon by a denomination official, in came ***Elaine*** who attended the mission and that day was in rare form—drunk, crazy, and dazed from her addictions. Elaine had an inoperable tumor of the brain that was neither malignant nor deadly. She is a victim of a system that did not have a category for her. She was not technically disabled, since medication made her capable of maintaining her cognitive equilibrium. But the side effects of the powerful medication made her too lethargic to consistently work. She was fired from her job, lost her insurance without which she could not afford the medication. Her behavior escalated from the eccentric to the bizarre. Out of control and antisocial at best, then disruptive at worst, she was often considered just plain crazy. She is one of untold numbers who slip through the cracks of the health care system. She has no family and in her present state, she does not have the capacity to successfully engage a complicated and vicious system that offers no reasonable choices or effective care. She is "the least of these" and one of far too many in the metropolitan regions. Where can Elaine go for help? To her church, of course! Yet not to a typical church. They can't assimilate her. She belongs to the church *of* the poor.

One of many children who grew up in a depressed community and a poor family, in childhood she was misunderstood, bullied, abused and molested, which only compounded her pain. Now she drank to numb herself and survive on the street.

This Sunday, she bounced into church to find a denominational official preaching. It wasn't his church—it was her church, and Elaine desperately needed church. She walked to the front, in the middle of the message, sat down on the altar and proceeded to offer loud "amen's." When the sermon was over, she was the first to respond. After the official prayed for her, she gave him an appreciation hug and kiss.

- ***Jena*** is an immensely gifted vocalist, so talented, but she also has a severe mental illness that affects her judgment. She sometimes responds inappropriately in public settings. In a really desperate situation, when basic provision—food and shelter—are at stake, she has turned back to an old habit, the quick money of prostitution. Then overcome by guilt, to silence the screams of shame associated with her dishonorable behavior, she compounds her backsliding by medicating herself with alcohol and illegal drugs.

Because of the abusive father figures of her past, she struggles to know God as a loving Father. So she comes back to him only as a last result, when life is spiraling out of control. Three of her children are already in foster care. Her youngest, a toddler, is still with her. In a recent season, she could have been working the streets or getting high in a crack house, but this Sunday, she is bathed and in a dated, but fresh, polyester dress from the ministry's center. She is on the positive side of a redemptive cycle.

Today, her testimony is, "Giving honor to the Bishop, the ministers and all the saints, thanking God on today, not yesterday, that the blood is running warm through my body. I am clothed and in my right mind . . ." Tomorrow, the cycle might turn, but today she is giving God praise for a liberation moment. Such moments can open up onto lifetimes and become doorways to a new way of living. Some people step from the back alleys of town, and walk into a bold new way of godliness.

❖ Carson lost his job and then hard times came fast. He could not find steady work. He fell into a terrible depression. His wife and daughter separated from him. He was suddenly homeless and soon addicted. Such a condition was unthinkable for him a few years before. His dependence on self-medication grew worse. He went from alcohol to cocaine. Crack in the daytime and alcohol as a sedative at night. He worked wherever he could as a day laborer, just trying to survive, moving from one soup kitchen to another, then one dumpster to another. He slept in vacant buildings, sometimes under shrubs or behind some church building. He was in and out of jail for petty larceny, vagrancy, using illegal substances and public intoxication. In this sad chapter of his life, he found Frank Allen's church and became a regular. He wanted to be better. He wanted his life to change. Each week he received a dose of hope and was told that God loved him. Each week someone hugged him and was genuinely glad to see him. That is no small thing for a street-person. The only consistent thing in his life were tears. Intoxicated or sober, he was crying. Frank saw his potential, how a good man, a decent man, had simply slipped and could not get up. He poured into him. Frank would find him intoxicated, take him into his own home, bathe him and dress him, arrange for a visitation appointment with his daughter or a job interview. He adopted Carson, "

Each week at church someone hugged him. That is no small thing for a street person.

He lived in our home, with our family, aggravating us and stealing from us. His changes would only last for days, and then he was drinking, drugging and crying. He would show up in the middle of the night."The ministry of a missionary to the poor, the oppressed, the brokenhearted and the bound is to liberate them from their invisible prison.
At the young age of 50, Carson died. The police called Frank and asked where they should send the body. Carson was such a perplexing case, a man with much promise, one who seemed to need only the right formula to find his way back to normalcy. And yet, he seemed to defy every attempt to fully rescue him. Now it was all over.

When Carson and Jenny, Elaine, or a hundred others are the focus of ministry, the lines are clear. But now, in the middle of the crisis over Carson, Frank was the one in trouble. He was the one needing ministry. Here is Frank's story, and the end of Carson's.

❖ ***Frank*** began to question his call and effectiveness. A sense of failure swept over him. All the investment in Carson, and still, he died without change. And he was just one, a sample, a symbol of the untold numbers with similar behavioral profiles. At this crisis point, Frank considered a vocational change. He prepared for Carson's funeral, viewing the man as a symbol of his own failure. He knew Carson's wife, daughter and brother would be present. Frank had pleaded with them more than once to "give Carson one more chance." He would say, "After much prayer, I believe that we have an intervention and program that will work." But it didn't.

Carson, who could not live right, nevertheless, learned to die right.

Now he faced them as a failure, a minister of a gospel that had not worked for this man. "What could I say?" he asked. "He ate in my soup kitchen and sat in gospel services. He cried at the altar. Days became years. But he never changed." Frank was wounded and angry. He chose a suit for Carson from the clothing closet, coordinated the funeral, arranged for a borrowed casket and free memorial service. At least the daughter's last memory of her daddy would be positive—he would be clean, dressed in a suit, groomed with his hair combed. He knew it would all end with a cheap cremation.

Praying and preparing, he determined this event would conclude his ministry to the poor. He was done. He had no exceptional success stories. He had Carson, a dead drug addict into whom he had invested so much. Carson, he believed, proved his ineffectiveness. And Carson was one of a hundred. There were just too many who had never learned to live for Christ.

Frank walked into the chapel, and Carson's wife and daughter were the only family members present. Across the aisle was a band of addicted and helpless friends, weeping.

Suddenly, a prostitute who had herself tried unsuccessfully to kick multiple habits leaped from her seat and unceremoniously fell around Frank's neck. Sobbing, she had a message she could barely share. She had been with Carson when he died. His last words were a prayer, "Lord Jesus, please have mercy. I am a sinner. I need You and I believe You are the Son of God; that You love me and You will save me. I have failed as a man, a husband and a father, and I need You to save me!" It was the message Frank needed, in fact, a revelation. "At that moment," he recalls, "the Lord revealed to me, that because of the traumas of life, Carson was not able to accept the grace to change his life and *live for Christ*, but because of our faithfulness, he was able to *die right* with God."

About 75% of runaways will become involved in theft, drugs or pornography. One out of every three teens on the street will be lured into prostitution within 48 hours of leaving home.

Frank Allen is no advocate for cheap grace, for salvation that does not inspire sanctified living, or for grace without truth. But he had experienced an epiphany, "During that season in my life, I realized that my call was not to judge people or question the effectiveness of the gospel I preached. My work was important." Frank considered all the people who were the opposite of Carson. Confessing salvation, they had no desire to actually change. Others have never learned how to call on Christ at the time of their death. Carson did. Frank could rest, "I have the assurance from God that Carson, who could not live right, nevertheless, learned to die right. At that moment, I had new peace and confidence about my work among the poor."

It's All about Relationships

In the early days, Frank lived in the suburbs, traveling into the city to touch the homeless, work at the soup kitchen, and do street preaching. He was a "do-gooder." The poor were grateful, but communication was limited to a "thank you" and passive nods of appreciation. When Frank moved into the neighborhood, he became a member of the community. Trust soared. Relationships and bonds were formed. He was more than a preacher; he was one of them.

12% of the world uses 85% of its water.

Soon a larger facility was available. With more space, growth accelerated. New workers joined the effort. Support increased. Some donors demanded measurable outcomes—changed lives. To assure funding, the ministry began to profile "clients" who were, without a miracle, the least likely to change. Some were resistant to change, others virtually incapable. And which clients could be empowered to change with the least investment of time, resources or energy? Different intake processes were developed to differentiate those with the most immediate change potential, who with a dose of hope or mild remediation could become a contributing member of the community, and a poster child of success. Donors were less interested it seemed in "the least of these."

A significant number of street people suffered from some degree of mental illness or had a history of self-medication with alcohol or drugs, combined with an abusive past, and scarred with traumatic life experiences, none of which they had signed up for. The streets had become home. Facing the constant grind of hard core poverty and homelessness, without a real miracle, there was little hope. That was not good news for donors. It was a tough decision, "We decided we were called to work with people, not profiles. We had to help the 'least of these,' not 'the most likely to change." But transformations did come, and they brought hope.

- In that season, God gave us ***Pete***, an alcoholic. He had lost his license and could not legally drive. He owed court costs and fines with a healthy rap sheet. He became a gleaming success story. God delivered him. He now works at a public job every day. He provides lawn care at the church he now attends. He also drives their outreach ministry box truck and handles their weekly food distribution. He is still a bit ragged around the edges, but he has come a long way. He reads his Bible and prays daily. He can be trusted with money and resources. He is no screen test model, not on the most handsome list, but he has a bright toothy smile and is on the road to renewal.

- For ***Elwood***, Frank prayed, "God, if you will clean this fellow up and get him off the corner, I could really use him to do Your work." But Elwood was a significant challenge, and Frank had almost exhausted his supply of patience. "When people hear God, they usually need their medications adjusted," Frank mused. "But one day, God really spoke to me, 'If you will give *my son* (Elwood, a man Frank was about to confront with an ultimatum) something to do and give him the opportunity to rise up, he will.'

  Frank began to meet with Elwood and pray with him. He challenged him to accept serious responsibilities. Elwood began to weep. By the next day, he had lost his taste for alcohol and had no desire for other drugs. Tearfully, he began to confess that this was the only positive thing in his life. Frank committed to disciple him. An affluent Anglican Church, along with a Lutheran Church, learned about his transition. They knew his past, saw hopeful changes, and agreed to sponsor him in his new position.

Someone from a poor or disadvantaged environment has to be twice as successful as their suburban counterparts to succeed. But, if the children in "the 'hood" can be exposed to positive things, given early chances, envisioned and mentored, they will out-achieve middle and upper class kids because they have a survival instinct. They have had to learn to be street smart and tough, but they need exposure to positive adults, technology, and professional mentors who have achieved success.

And Then There Are the Children

Many children in the projects come from multiple generations who have only known public housing, some for as long as public housing has existed, four generations. Frank has found 13 family members in a two bedroom apartment, none of whom ever finished school. No one in the family has steady work. To survive, they have learned to push and shove, curse and fight.

When Christian youth groups come to serve, Frank immediately notices a positive vocabulary and elevated ambition in the children. First and second graders suddenly stop talking about gangs, making gang signs and began talking about college. These inner city kids have never known their father. Their mother is in prison, and they are often being raised by a grandmother. All the men meant to be in their life are either dead, incarcerated, selling or doing drugs. The child, who a few days ago, was talking about drive-by shootings, is now talking about going to college. They don't even know what college is, but they are now convinced that they are going, simply because they met someone from that college on a mission trip. They have hope, a goal, something to talk about, other than getting ahead through crime and violence.

Most young girls dream of growing up and getting married. But in the projects, getting a "baby's daddy" is sadly perceived as the first step out. Attention from a man, a welfare check, and assistance comes with a baby. It is a twisted and contradictory system. It devalues the child, making them a chip with which to barter. Such children have little hope.

The Liberated Leave

Some who receive ministry die violently and in sin. Some, despite all efforts, end up in prison. Others are successful, and they escape sin and the slums. One of the harsh realities of success is that your spiritual children outgrow the inner city ministry. After pouring in love, resources and influence, you watch them rise. They emerge as hard workers, earn the respect of others, act responsibly, and develop as leaders. They understand the vision. They have passion. They grew up as a child, and the ministry reached them, spared them from tragic outcomes, and now they are reaching out to others. They are the measurable outcome desired by donors. They can preach and teach. With them, the ministry can soar to the next level. But then they leave. They want a better life for their families than the slums offer.

Government anti-poverty programs fail because persistent poverty is not primarily material. It's about relationships and behavior. Even in good times, fatherlessness and joblessness, trap the underclass.

- ***Ray*** was a drug addict who came to the ministry with phenomenal talents, and the habits of a con-man extraordinaire. As we worked with him, he continued to deceive, steal, and abuse our trust. Finally, his life completely changed. He relocated to a nearby resort, and got a job. He called one day weeping, "Pastor, I had to call you and thank you. If it were not for you, I would be dead. I have been clean for three years. I have a good job. I am now married. I drive a new car and am buying a house. I am in a church and serving as a volunteer." Ray is now a transformed contributing member—in another church. He is the pastor's helper, serving and contributing. Some plant. Some water. Some reap. God gives the increase.

- The ***Sasser*** family came to the ministry. With Frank's help, they worked through all of their debilitating problems. They were young, and nearly shipwrecked. But God gave grace, and they were redeemed, their marriage saved, their home kept intact, and they rebounded wonderfully—then left to serve at a suburban church. Just a few years later, they appeared at an international convention, and then were engaged in a national tour featuring ministry success.

When folks like Ray and the Sasser's leave, Frank Allen goes back to the trenches to find more who might, with God's grace, become like them. He writes letters to prisoners who were once teenagers in his group home. He is a regular in court, advocating for some soul who fell off the wagon. He takes risks. He believes in people. His first full-time staff member wrestled with the effects of a fetal narcotic syndrome. He was emotionally and intellectually challenged, struggled with schizophrenia and bipolar disorder, but the ministry took a chance with him. He, along with three widows and six senior citizens, became the backbone of the outreach.

Now the outreach staff has grown to about 45 persons, including part-timers and an extensive volunteer force. Yet the congregation itself is less than a hundred. The finances are stronger, but the needs multiply as well. Frank Allen has made his salary the first thing cut and the last thing paid. The faces of street kids, the sea of needs around him, still move him to sacrificial compassion.

First in Portsmouth and Then into All the World

The humble effort has become an international ministry with a full-time outreach center in Portsmouth and a full-time staff in Jamaica. It reaches across the United States and beyond into 26 third world countries through a network of companion ministries. Dozens of tractor-trailer size loads of relief reach across the North American continent and to disadvantaged nations.

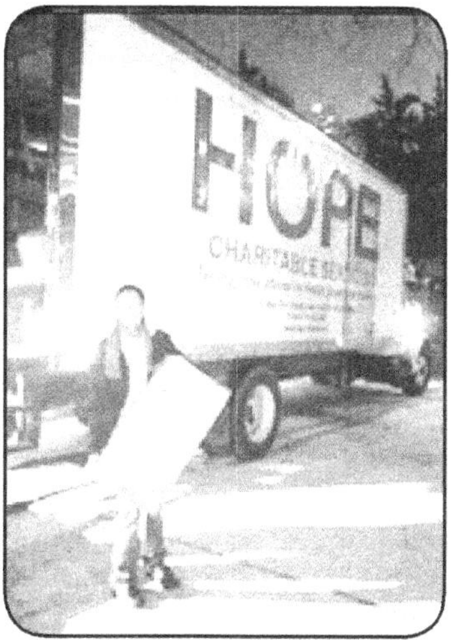

In the early days, Frank contacted local grocery stores for dented cans and expired products. Food drives in churches supported the work. When grocers discovered the legitimacy of his work, they offered more assistance and spread the word to suppliers with larger volumes. Frank graduated from buggies full of single items, to pallets of surplus goods, then to tractor trailer loads. Soon, abundance transformed him into a supplier to partner ministries.

Their international relief work began in 1997. A distributor in California called and suddenly he had two tractor-trailer loads of designer vitamins valued at a million dollars. The vitamin labels had the wrong colors. It was cheaper to donate the vitamins than repackage them. But, the supplier required the goods to go overseas. Frank quickly found a home for them.

In the early days, when internal strife surfaced, a larger vision and an external focus was often the cure. Power struggles were expressed as, "We are the workers; you are the needy." In such an environment, the needy could not transition into the ranks of workers any better than they had previously at suburban churches. Those from "the 'hood'" felt that suburban helpers who drove in to assist with the ministry "fed them with a long spoon." They did not want to mingle. It was the empowered ministering to the unempowered, the strong to the weak. Such dynamics blind-side us. They are often so subtle.

If you have money in the bank, in your wallet, and spare change in your pocket, you are among the top 8 percent of the world's wealthy.

Frank's solution was an external focus. He offered a mission experience to his inner city congregation. His wanted to get the "drive in" constituents and the "live in" folks on the same team ministering to others. The theme of the trip was "from the guttermost to the uttermost!" Fourteen team members went into deep rural Jamaica. A donor financed the trip after a season of prayer and fasting. They purchased 40,000 pounds of rice, 10,000 pounds of beans, flour and cornmeal. They shipped three 40-foot containers with relief supplies. They provided 4,000 families with a month's supply of groceries, treated people in their mobile medical clinics, conducted Kids Krusades in the daylight hours, and Gospel Crusades at night. They had 1,270 converts.

The team came back unified. Mission trips increased. The next phase was sending teams to build churches for the converts. God spoke to Frank, "If you build people, they will build the church!" So they began to partner with Jamaican churches through more *Invasion of Hope* mission trips. They fed the hungry, clothed the poor, built houses for the homeless, treated the sick in medical and dental clinics, all around evangelistic crusades for children and adults. Thousands have now been saved and added to the churches in Jamaica. Thirty-three mission teams have now gone to Jamaica involving more than a thousand short-term missionaries, many of whom had themselves been a brand plucked from the burning, right off the streets of Portsmouth.

Most Jamaicans live in abject poverty and suffer from poor nutrition, improper sanitation, a lack of education, and a broken social system. The children run barefoot with ragged clothes and are often hungry. They suffer from treatable sicknesses, inadequate nutrition, inferior housing, and no education. They live in a sea of poverty in the shadow of five-star resorts enjoyed by American tourists.

Teen prostitution and the sexual exploitation of children is a growing problem in the US. The age of newly recruited prostitutes is only 13. The majority of teen prostitutes are runaways from poor, inner-city neighborhoods, the number from upper-middle class homes is rising.

Jamaicans who work at such resorts are exploited by low wages, even as they serve visitors from wealthy nations. At the end of the day, they often leave plush resorts and return to a small, overcrowded shack, without sanitation or electricity. They may have earned eight dollars for the day. As an import society, Jamaicans need the same basic supplies as Americans, but import fees and taxes make the price of the same goods higher. Electricity, fuel and household supplies are almost a third higher than in the USA, with wages of only $40 a week.

Out of these mission trips, there are now Jamaican medical and dental clinics that have treated thousands. They have remodeled orphanages, schools, and nursing homes. They have built 63 *Homes of Hope* for poor families. Each day, as a part of their crusade ministry, they serve hot meals to poor children and distribute thousands of assorted food parcels, clothing, and shoes to the poorest of the poor across the island.

In 1995, he led a tour to Israel. He saw the typical sites and walked where Christ walked. At Aboud, visiting the mission station of the veteran, Margaret Gaines, located in Palestinian Territory, he met an Arab Christian family. The ethnic tensions in Israel are particularly harsh on Arab Christians. Israelis treat them like terrorists, and the Muslims as enemies. Some of these Christian families can trace their ancestry to

Payday Loans

A Baptist Press report says that Texas has more payday-lending outlets than it has McDonald's and What-A-Burger restaurants combined. Pastors are calling for more education on handling finances. Others are calling the payday establishments a social justice issue. Texas Appleseed, an advocacy group for low-income families, showed most payday-loan borrowers earned $30,000 or less and used the loans for recurring expenses of basic needs like rent, utilities and food.

"The loan is born out of desperation," he said. "Without having a reasonable answer, what do you do? It's hard to tell people that are poor not to use payday loans without having some other alternative to meet their needs. Without filling the need, it becomes an intellectual conversation."

Arkansas recently shut down payday-lending businesses. "Michael Novak says our economy rests on a three-legged stool comprised of political freedom, economic freedom, and moral restraint." Without all three, the economy collapses.

In December, Brownsville, Texas, placed a six-month moratorium barring new payday lenders from opening any new stores in town. One Texas mayor declared, "Our most vulnerable citizens are easy prey for these legal loan sharks, and we want to protect our citizens by regulating them."

Mesquite Mayor John Monaco said, "Any business that depends on people who are desperate and preys on them has no place in my community."

Some organizations are beginning to create payday loan alternatives. Loans Plus offers small-dollar loans that function similarly to payday loans, but with an interest rate of between 12 and 15 percent. Customers fill out a spreadsheet with an adviser, establish a budget, and get a mini-financial education. Loans Plus offers no roll-over payment plans. It does offer 90 day notes. It has a 70% approval rate. Customers not approved are directed to crisis help. The Loans Plus product is designed to get people out of a crisis rather than entrap them.

"Parishes and churches are beginning to ask themselves, 'How do we proactively offer alternatives to payday loans?'" Adapted from an article by Amy Wiles, a student at Austin Presbyterian Theological Seminary, "Culture of Debt: Churches can help poor avoid predatory-lending trap," (Baptist Press, Sunday, April 11, 2010).

the early church. Their forefathers were the Arabians converted when Peter preached in Acts 2. They are peace-loving Christians caught in an unholy situation. Some are starving, suffering, and in dire need. Those two days in Aboud opened another ministry venue, one very unique. Frank now partners with Christian churches in the Holy Land, recently sending a 40-foot container valued at more than $300,000 in relief goods. Their *"Hope for the Holy Land"* project has also supplied relief goods for families, orphanages, schools, and hospitals. They are exploring other opportunities to help the poor Christians of the Holy Land.

We'll Keep the Light On!

The light shining brightly abroad does so because it shines brightest at home. The inner city work in the Portsmouth-Norfolk area continues with the support of churches, businesses, and individuals. Frank Allen is a missionary to the poor. The Sanctuary of Hope is a beacon to the poorest of the poor, the church where the lame, maim, and crazy can feel at home.

- **After School Hot Meal Program**—At Portsmouth, 70 children are served a daily hot meal they might not otherwise get in the after school program. And they are tutored in reading, math, homework and the computer labs. Their character is developed by mentors and life-skills are taught. They learn about Christ in the Chapel. Their confidence is bolstered as they participate in the performing arts offerings, and their culture is expanded through field trips.

- **Summer Children's Program**—During the summer, the number of children served breakfast and lunch doubles everyday, all day, all summer long. Mission teams assist with chapel, academic refreshers, field trips, mentoring, performing arts, sports and recreation. Not only are the lives of poor children changed, but also that of the participating mission team members.

- **The Family Services**—The soup kitchen serves hundreds of hot meals per sitting. The outreach team distributes groceries, clothing, household goods, and schools supplies to more than 300 families each month. In addition, medical, dental and social/psychological services are provided for the poor. And the good news of God's love is shared.

- **Hope Charitable Services**—The charitable warehouse, called "Hope Charitable Services," receives, sorts, stores, distributes and ships hundreds of truck loads of valuable, life-essential relief goods to inner cities and rural poverty pockets such as Appalachia and the Native American Reservations, as well as Immigrant Camps. Almost 10,000 individuals in more than 3,200 homes in the Tidewater region are touched each month through the efforts of the ministry. Relief goods go regularly to 26 poor countries around the world.
- **Charitable Supply Chain**—Through the "Charitable Supply Chain" Frank partners with churches across the nation, providing goods to assist them in their ministry to the poor. They assist major charities and organizations in international shipping. They do logistical consultation. They become a critical link in times of national disaster to provide poverty and disaster relief. They are the link between suppliers with excess food and commodities, and the poor across the nations.

It isn't the numbers that drives Frank Allen. It is still "the least of these"—the worst and most hardened, the throw-aways, the ones maddened by mental illness, the smelly ones stripped naked by drug addiction and alcohol. It is the hungry human, a mere shadow of humanity, starving most for love and trust, combative due to constant abuse and neglect. It is the poorest of the poor, the least of the least, and the worst of the worst. Christ came to save them. And Frank Allen wants to assist in that Matthew 25 mission.

Discussion Guide

Big Ideas

- "A church *for* the poor! And a church *of* the poor." A church that is contextualized.
- The "Mission American Urban Outreach Center"—a hub for an international compassion outreach.
- The ministry runs an after-school program, a summer program, family services, charitable services including food and commodities, clothing and various other needs of families. They also are the hub of an international charitable outreach distribution network.
- The *hard-core poor* is a term used to describe folks with complex needs who require a holistic ministry, folks who cannot fit into

the operation of a typical church. These people need *whole man* ministry—body, soul and spirit.

- Frank began working out of his trunk, grilling hot dogs on a corner, and skipping rope for the project kids.

Notable Quotes

- It costs an average of $47,000.00 a year to keep a man in prison, even more for women and juveniles.
- The cost of a trial to prosecute a case is around $50,000.
- "We would 'get them saved' and transition them, but assimilating them into the typical church was a challenge.
- "At that moment," he recalls, "the Lord revealed to me, that because of the traumas of life, Carson was not able to accept the grace to change his life and *live for Christ*, but because of our faithfulness, he was able to *die right* with God."
- Frank believes, "If you build people, they will build the church!"

Questions for Consideration

1. Talk about assimilation issues, particularly Frank's statement, "They (the poor) were always being taught, but never asked to teach; being served, but never asked to serve. It was never *their* church. It was someone else's church. The church was not at fault; they really cared. The poor felt welcomed, but the sociological distance, the cultural gap, the variance in needs, left them with the sense, they did not fit." Do you think people feel the same way when they come to your church?
2. Discuss the profiles—Elaine, Jena, and Carson (all real people with fictitious names). How typical do you think their stories are?
3. Could your church minister to them? Do we need to create a church alongside our Sunday church to reach such people? A kind of bridge?
4. What about the idea—if the children in "the 'hood" can be exposed to positive things, given early chances, envisioned and mentored, they will then out-achieve middle and upper class kids, because they have a survival instinct. They have had to learn to be street smart and tough, but they need exposure to positive adults, technology, and professional mentors who have achieved success. Agree or disagree?
5. Who are the poor around you? Does your church have an obligation to them? And if so, if Frank Allen is right, what will you do about it?

Campus Prayer Ministry

"Need Prayer?" The sign said it all. It first appeared on the University of Tennessee, Knoxville Campus, in the fall of 1999. It was the place at which the Church of God Christian Connection campus ministry could touch students. The prayer booth sat on the main student thoroughfare, the University Center Plaza. Once a week, every Tuesday, the portable prayer tent was a campus feature.

The goal was not to solicit prayer needs, but to offer students the opportunity to stop by and share their needs. John Unthank whose passion to reach university students spans decades says, "Workers met them with a smile, a nod, or a warm welcome with a lot of love."

Each Tuesday, hundreds of students pass by and over the years, thousands have shared their needs, relieved their hearts, and returned to share testimonies about answers to those same prayers. For students wanting to take the next steps, the Prayer Booth provides Bibles and other resources for growth in the Christian walk. Not only do students stop by for prayer, but staff, faculty, and even members of the administration have all been beneficiaries of the Prayer Booth.

John Unthank, Director of the Church of God Campus Christian Connection ministry, says the stories of lives impacted are heart-touching. So often, the transition to college is the point of complete disconnect from faith and Christian community. John and his comrades work on 83 university or college campuses across the nation. Some of these learning islands are larger than a small city—tens of thousands of students huddle together, adjacent to and in the middle of major cities. Many have little or no Christian witness.

Any major spiritual awakening that fails to reach university campuses will simply fail. Today, for the first time in more than a century, a spiritual stirring is occurring on college campuses.

Rick Bradbury, a local pastor, volunteered at the booth. "We would stand at the edge of the sidewalk and watch students approach with a wary eye. You could see the skepticism as they read the sign – 'Need Prayer?'" Rick would offer a stick of gum or a piece of candy, something to slow them down for a moment. "Could we pray with you about anything?" he would ask.

"No, I gave up on that when I left home," they would profess. Life on campus tends to be hostile to fragile faith, and peer pressure is bent almost exclusively against conservative Christians.

"Is your school bill paid?" Rick would ask. An awkward smile would often break out on their face. "Can we pray about that?" Rick inquired.

At some points, there would still be declared resistance mixed with intrigue. "I don't really believe in that anymore." Rick would smile and say, "You don't, but I do. After all, what will it hurt?" And with that he would pray a brief, heartfelt prayer for the student's need. Sometimes it was financial. At other times it involved not hearing from their parents. On occasion, relationship issues were the focus of prayer. Some students were never seen again. Others bounded by the booth in the next few weeks, some with a telling smile, others with a puzzled expression. "You won't believe what happened after we prayed," they would report. The simple answer to prayer was for some enough to jump-start a renewal to their faith. For others, it forced them to reexamine issues they thought they had neatly folded away with other childish notions, only to discover a God who was not a fantasy, but alive in a very personal way.

Such moments are doorways to change.

Not long after the Prayer Booth was set up, a young atheist stopped by. John Unthank remembers. "He stated emphatically that as an atheist, he did not believe in prayer." But here he was—at the prayer booth. The inner conflict was obvious. John waited. There was no arguing. No persuasive arm twisting. Then, with equal passion, he explained, "I have a friend in New York, a close friend, who is dying. I don't believe in prayer but would you pray for him."

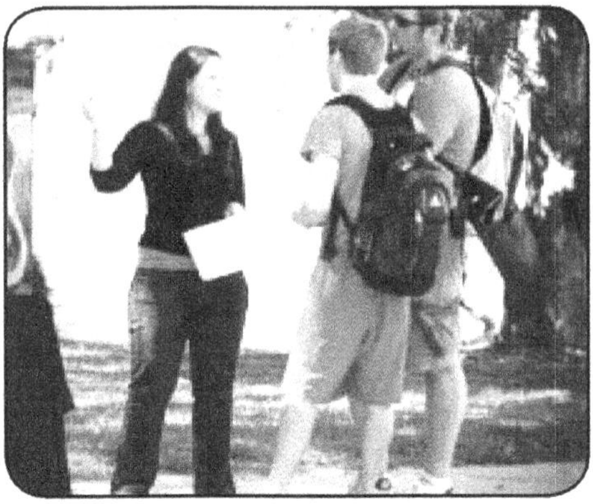

Such moments reveal that even among those whose attitudes are hardening, at the core of their being, when faced with mortality, a hunger for faith explodes on the inside. Such people will rarely make the trip to church. We must make the trip to them. Prayer was offered on the spot. John recalls, "He thanked me. I knew God was dealing with him."

Not only do declared atheists stop by the Prayer Booth, there are other surprising customers as well. University campuses are breeding grounds for the bizarre. Christianity is the official enemy of modernism and its secular intellectualism, but the faith vacuum creates a vulnerability that makes the atmosphere ripe for diverse types of cult followers. The students that fall prey to the campus cults do so because they are hungry for God, searching for answers. John notes, "Many times these students stop by the Prayer Booth. They don't come in antagonism or hostility. They come searching, asking many questions."

On one occasion John was approached by a man dressed in his Satanic robes, "I am a Satanist and what is this?" John patiently explained the purpose of the prayer booth. The young man declared that he and John had nothing in common. John offered to pray for him, "Even if you do pray, it will not help me," he emphatically declared. John refused to argue. Instead, he confessed that he was deeply committed to Christ, and a believer in Scripture. John thanked him for stopping by, and assumed he would never see him again. Surprisingly, he became a regular at the prayer booth. Each visit was another opportunity to demonstrate the love of Christ. At first, he talked casually about campus life and his needs. Then he began to confess his loneliness and isolation. Love and acceptance kept drawing him back, time after time. "I was able to share with him an openness of love that touched him. He knew we were praying for him and cared for Him," John recalls. Who knows what might come of such seeds.

Sometimes the prayer booth gets busy, and more than one student stops by for prayer at the same time. Praying for a young lady, John noticed one day that another girl was standing behind her, waiting her turn for prayer. Her head was down. As John finished praying with the first student, she came toward the booth, but did not look

up. "I am a Wiccan," she professed. John asked how she was doing. What followed was telling. The cult to which she had devoted herself was not meeting her inner needs. She poured out a confession of her loneliness and isolation. As John shared, he noticed her eyes searching over the scripture-based literature he had available. He placed materials in her hand that pointed her to Christ.

Every January, the Prayer Booth promotes the Right to Life cause. That is just one hot-potato issue on campus, and the Prayer Booth is a beachhead to sound forth Christian views on social and moral issues. Not only is the Right to Life cause noted, but the corollary issues are addressed as well—abortion, forgiveness, and sexual purity. Christian students bombarded by secular views often stop by to find resources and resolve to hold on to their convictions. John says, "They are assaulted in the classroom and on campus about the politically correct views. The Prayer Booth is a special place where they are reassured in their convictions." Suddenly, they no longer feel alone. They have found an ally on campus.

During February, resource materials on Biblical creation are on display. It is during this season, that the university sponsors "Darwin Days" and the entire student body is baptized in evolutionary thought. Some years, the Prayer Booth and the Darwin Days booth stand side by side. Christian students find a place that openly affirms their belief in divine creation.

The requests of students cover the gamut—personal needs, healing, relationships, family stress, academic and financial stress. John observes, "One of the greatest needs is for spiritual strength to stand on campus." The prayer requests are shared with Church of God congregations in the Knoxville area. "There have been so many students who have returned to give praise to God and thanks to our intercessors for the answers they have received," John reports.

The Prayer Booth is now in its second decade and is known on campus, and recognized for its consistent campus presence in offering prayer. John serves as the Chair of the Campus Ministers Council. In that position, the administration asked him to give a campus ministries tour for the Head Chaplain from the U.S. Naval Department in Washington. John remembers the moment, "At the end of the tour, as we were walking across the pedestrian plaza, a young man called out. "Aren't you the one who prays for people?" It was the Chaplain who heard the young man and stopped John to respond." The student was sick with the flu and needed relief. "Would you please pray for me," he humbly asked. "I am going to a class I cannot miss. I need help." On the spot, John and the Chief Army Chaplain of the nation prayed. Two weeks later, he stopped by and thanked John for the prayer.

The campus is a busy place, like a colony of ants. Students are coming and going from classes. Staff and faculty are moving about to lunch and to meetings. Demonstrations. Speeches. Rallies. Petition drives. The pace is quick. Sometimes you get used to seeing faces, John observes, but, never meet the people. "I noticed one lady, every week we had the tent up, who would walk by, smile and say, 'Hello,' and then always touch the tent." Even when the Prayer Booth was moved inside, she found it, and came by just long enough to brush by it. Then one day she stopped and explained that the Prayer Booth was a spiritual connection point for her. She told John she knew that he and other volunteers were praying for her and for the spiritual needs of the campus, especially the students.

One philosophy student stopped by the booth one day. A fellow student was a member of her project team and had boldly proclaimed his agnostic status. He did not need or want anything to do with God. As a Christian, she became very burdened for him. She consistently let her life and attitude be her witness to him. She prayed and she asked the Prayer Booth workers to pray with her. Suddenly, she noticed a change. It was visible, evident. She asked what had happened to him. He quickly confessed that he had been saved. He was now attending church. His disposition was one of joy. She then confided that she had been praying for him and asked what had changed his mind about God and Christ. "It was that Prayer Booth and the man who is there every week. Every time I would walk by, he would smile at me. And I would see that sign— 'Need Prayer?' I would hear a voice in my heart 'What are you going to do with God?' Over and over, week after week, the same voice. I never actually stopped at the Prayer Booth, but God pursued me, and He won. I surrendered to Him."

The contemporary church is in retreat. We must again find a way to the marketplace of souls. Just our presence is a powerful witness that will bring change to lives. "Tell the Prayer Booth guy to never stop the ministry, because the Holy Spirit was speaking to me. I know His voice was sounding out loud and clear to everyone who came by."

"No one can serve two masters. For you will hate one and love the other; you will be devoted to one and despise the other. You cannot serve both God and money."
—Matthew 6:24 (NLT)

"People who want to get rich fall into temptation and a trap and into many foolish and harmful desires that plunge men into ruin and destruction. For the love of money is a root of all kinds of evil. Some people, eager for money, have wandered from the faith and pierced themselves with many griefs." —1 Timothy 6:9-10

"Keep your lives free from the love of money and be content with what you have." —Hebrews 13:5

"Remember this: Whoever sows sparingly will also reap sparingly, and whoever sows generously will also reap generously. Each man should give what he has decided in his heart to give, not reluctantly or under compulsion, for God loves a cheerful giver. And God is able to make all grace abound to you, so that in all things at all times, having all that you need, you will abound in every good work. As it is written: 'He has scattered abroad His gifts to the poor; his righteousness endures forever.'" —2 Corinthians 9:6-9

"If you really change your ways and your actions and deal with each other justly, if you do not oppress the alien, the fatherless or the widow and do not shed innocent blood in this place, and if you do not follow other gods to your own harm, then I will let you live in this place, in the land I gave your forefathers for ever and ever." —Jeremiah 7:5-7

Princeton Pike Church of God

Barry Clardy assumed the leadership of a great revival center church - the Princeton Pike Church of God. Soon thereafter, God met him and began a change in his own heart and he has now called the church to trade titles for towels. He represents the challenge of turning a church without a tradition of service, toward mission and community sensitivity. His story is compelling. He and the congregation are in the middle of a journey. Here is a snapshot of their transition.

9 Trading Your Title for a Towel

Discovering the Joy of Great Commission Living

When you walk through the doors of the Princeton Pike Church the first thing you see is a sign that reads, "Making Ministry Our Mission, and People Our Purpose." It is not so much how it reads, but rather how it is being lived out that is transforming the church and, in return, touching the personal lives of people both locally and around the world.

Change Begins with a Pastor

Most pastors struggle with the temptation of borrowed programs and settle for short-term excitement with little or no long-term results from the impact of transfused, passionate people. Pastor Barry Clardy tells his people. "Passion is what you feel when you see a need; compassion is what you do with that passion." In his second year of pastoring "the Pike," Barry had become inwardly discontented with ministry and burdened by a church culture that settled for the experience of "having church" while acting confused about the behavioral profile of "being the church."

For centuries the poor have been *the object* of help and almsgiving, but they have never been *the subject* of decisions and thinking by the church or its leadership.

Pastor Barry remembers the moment, "I knew there had to be more to it than this—going through ministry motions, saying all the right things, without doing the right things. Talk without action. After months of growing inwardly empty and being unfulfilled, I embarked on a personal journey produced by a passionate desire and hunger to find out if there was more to ministry than what we have experienced within the walls of the church; and on a personal note of what I was experiencing as a pastor."

He plowed into a reading marathon, a small library of inspirational "how to" books loaded with "this is how we did it" examples on being effective and fruitful in ministry. This occurred during an uncharted, unscheduled three-day personal prayer sabbatical. The spiritual trek was a journey for only two—Barry and God. Surrounded with resources designed to inspire him out of his condition, it became clear something had to change. At that moment, the Lord touched his heart and spoke to him, "There is *nothing* you have brought into this room that I want more than you, and when you want Me more than all the 'things' you brought into this room with you, I will speak to your heart." The invitation was one he could not refuse.

Barry was at the same intersection at which so many pastors arrive in moments of challenge. Sadly, when pastors feel they are missing something, they conclude, "Maybe I need to move. Relocate. Go to another church." Such moments are loaded with missed messages from God saying, "*You* need to change." It is not a call to change locations, but a call to a change of heart and approach. At that moment, Barry was compelled to put aside all the "things" he had brought into the room. He picked up the Word of God and began to read the Gospel of John. When he came to John 13:15-17, he read it as if for the very first time. Jesus had just washed the feet of the disciples and then He said:

About 790 million people in the world are chronically undernourished, two-thirds of them in Asia and the Pacific.

> *For I have given YOU an example that YOU should do as I have done to you. Verily, verily I say unto YOU, the servant is not greater than his lord: neither he that is sent greater than he who sent him. If YOU know these things, happy are YOU if YOU do them.*

The word *you* leaped off the page as if God were saying, "I am talking *to you,* Barry!" It became very personal. He asked God, "How can You use me to change the church?" God spoke again, "There is nothing that I can use you *to do for me* unless you first allow *change in you.*" It wasn't the message he wanted to hear. But suddenly the principle was clear—"If you want something you've never had, you have to be willing to do something you've never done." It was both a demanding challenge and a delightful relief—God would lead, he would only have to follow. God would be the prototype, he would be the reflection. Pastor Clardy recalls, "Reading that verse was like drinking cool refreshing water. For a pastor in a dry desert, desperately needing direction on how to lead a congregation to a lifestyle change that would mirror the reality of John chapter 13, it was revolutionary." That day, he began to seek God in a new and fresh way.

Change Comes from God

Comfort creatures resist change, especially when change affects personal lifestyles. Being effective, efficient, and fruitful requires a people who are willing to change, as clay changes in the hands of the potter. Someone has said, "Change is tough, but the key to change is in knowing *when* to change *before* you *have* to change." Proactive change is better than compulsory change required by the moment or some misfortune. Free change is better than forced change. Either way, you cannot taste the fruit of positive change without paying the price of change, and experiencing the effects of change. Our cultural desire for the fruit of change, without the rigorous demands of change, is both irrational and contradictory. And if we persist in such contradiction, we sabotage our own quest for change. We become our own victims. And the positive outcomes we desire are forfeited by our insistence that everything else changes but us.

> **In 1820, the distance between the richest and poorest nations was three-to-one. Now it has exceeded 72-1.**

"There is nothing I can use you to do *for me* unless you first allow me *to change you.*" There are moments with God that are so profound they mark our lives forever. That moment, that Divine response, became the motivational force, the grace point for personal redirection of Barry, and then for the church. The moment became the wellspring of catalytic change that moved the pastor and church toward transformation of both life and ministry.

That moment changed the way Barry viewed people. He began to offer ministry to them, laced with care and compassion, and offered in the spirit of Christ with the heart of a servant. That profound personal transformation continues to give personal, pastoral direction and motivation. It is a daily reminder that there is "more" to ministry than programs and events, both of which are helpful tools, but alone provide only short-term impact. Ministry is more than the routine of "having church" rather than "being the church," all the while wondering why so many people are content with business as usual; more than the activity of personal ministry without results, without progress, and without fulfillment. Ministry is *more than this!*

In four decades, the wealth gap has more than doubled. The top 20% in rich nations had 30 times more income than the poorest 20% in 1960. By 1997, the gap widened 74 times as much.

Sometimes even gracious acts of care and compassion are swallowed up and their meaning lost because they are more connected to "what we do" than "who we are." We adopt actions and programs, and we learn *to perform* both services and ministries because they are expected of us. We do our duty, rather than joyfully serving as an expression of who we are, and doing so out being as a "gift" sacrificially, freely given to God. Such a shift is seismic. It transforms the people and the atmosphere of the church itself. It is the difference between "have to"and "want to." The inner force of grace motivates instead of the outer force of guilt. And the inner attitude that blossoms into fresh ministry action is evidence of the inward change.

Pastor Clardy continued his reading in the Book of Acts, but he was reading through new eyes, from the perspective of a servant, a subordinate ready to receive orders. He was looking less at the action of the text, and more at its relational core. Suddenly, he saw a different church than he had ever seen before. It was not merely a busy church, but a growing church—one that was thriving, living with excitement, and with a kingdom purpose. He saw a church whose faith, focus, passion, and commitment had become their lifestyle. He suddenly realized that he had always read about "the acts" of the disciples and had preached about them, but there was not a ready parallel to such acts in his own life. He was not living "the acts" of the disciples. He was convicted, caught up short. Admitting that he was not living out principles and practices he readily preached was a moment of conviction over the open Bible, and an uncomfortable one.

Change Affects the Culture of a Church

Street children live in junk boxes, parks or on the street itself.

As he continued to read, the differences between the church in Acts and the lifestyle of the contemporary church, his church, were far too striking to ignore. The church in Acts, beyond Chapter 10, was not preoccupied with the class and kind of people. The outpouring of the Spirit on the Samaritans and the Gentiles had removed grounds for any ethnic prejudice. They knew their call was to engage all people, all nations, tongues, and tribes for Christ.

Out of the three days of personal prayer, came a renewed sense of purpose. More importantly, there also came a new awareness of identity in Christ, of who he was in Christ, what he had been created for, and what God wanted from every person who would follow Him in discipleship. The three days of prayer were only a doorway, a life-changing challenge, and an invitation to an exciting journey. Pastor Barry Clardy walked through that door and continues to enjoy the journey today. It all begin with his own change within. "Barry," the Lord challenged him, "if you want to be fulfilled in ministry and live out what you have read in John chapter 13 and in the book of Acts, then be inwardly content with *trading your title for the towel* of a servant—living and serving me, through loving and serving people—all people."

There would no longer be an exclusively congregational focus. The words "all people" were wildly inclusive. Genuine love for "all people"was mandated. Intentional expressions of love to "all people"are the evidences of our love for God and his unconditional love for us. Our commitment to the Great Commission demands that we reach the whole man, and different kinds of men who live throughout the whole world, without which we become a whole failure.

Suddenly the Great Commission was also seen from a fresh perspective, one that left Pastor Clardy changed, challenged, and committed to living out the example of Jesus. He was committed to inviting others to experience with him the power of trading titles for the towel of servant-living, and experiencing the authentic joy of living the lifestyle of the Great Commission.

Jesus said, *"All power is given unto me in heaven and in earth."* And He added,

> *Go ye therefore, and teach all nations, baptizing them in the name of the Father, and of the Son, and of the Holy Ghost. Teaching them to observe all things, whatsoever, I have commanded you: and lo, I am with you always, even unto the end of the world. (Matthew 28:18-2)*

Before the Culture Changes—the Church Must Change

> **Suicides among young people in the US have increased dramatically. Each year, about 5,000 teens commit suicide, triple the number from the 1960s. Suicide now is the sixth leading cause of death among children aged 5-14, third among people age 14-24, and second among college students.**

The Great Commission is not an option for the believer, but a command. And this command is not to reach "some" of the world, but the "whole" world. Barry is one of the pastors across the nation who has realized that the "tactical" alone is an add-on, a mere supplement to congregational activities. What is needed is more than superficial tactical tools—ideas merely borrowed, shared information gleaned from what another church is doing, and a deluge of resources are only more "things" that have no lasting impact, even if they are good things. The change must come to hearts; it must affect the culture of the church; and it must fuse hungry hearts together in a response to their own personal call. If the change is only programmatic, it will fail. A new vision is needed along with strategic, not merely tactical changes.

What is happening at Princeton Pike is an attempt to grapple with the more important foundational issues, the necessity of a primary and unifying vision that realigns the church in a strategic way, including its resources, all to reach a different harvest. We serve churches living with a 50's mentality, and are not poised to reach our neighbors now living in a post-modern age. We are in denial. The church is our escape to the safe past.

UNICEF guesstimates that 100 million children around the world are in some stage of homelessness. India has 11 million, Egypt 1.5 million, Pakistan 1.5 million, and the USA 750,000.

Sadly, in an era when the church needs to be strong enough to give, to engage the culture in positive and creative, yet challenging ways, to be shining lights in the midst of the darkness—missionaries, we are passive. The people of faith gather to be ministered to, to be served. The church is there "for them." They are preached at, sung to, prayed for, propped up, and encouraged. A transformation of the church itself is needed, from being merely recipients of grace, to becoming transformation agents of grace. To add an array of compassion tactics to the evangelism ministry only joins the fad, the "add-on" makes such actions optional and superficial. What is needed and necessary is a more profound change. We must reassess the identity of the church itself, and out of her identity, our fundamental function.

The three "C's"—*Change, Challenge,* and *Commitment*—are the core of the Princeton Pike philosophy. They are corporate goals, and yet they must be owned personally by each member and family. This road map is providing understanding to Princeton Pike in fulfilling Christ's commands and following His example.

The lessons continue. Learning is a lifelong excursion and humility invites diverse and various teachers, students with hungry hearts, and ready hands whose desire to do more fuels the need to know more. Methods and approaches vary, but the fundamentals of servant-hood, the spirit, the ethos, and certain principles for engaging the world and doing it effectively, remain the same.

Helpers and Healers—All

"Find a need and Fill it; Find a Hurt and Heal it" is a simple slogan. This is a constant message to both the people and the pastor at Princeton Pike, and the daily objective is to fulfill the example of Christ's service and ministry to a lost world, doing so with care and compassion. Princeton Pike has found God's creative power at work among them. And God's plan is being played out in the same, yet variant ways, through different lives. Each is the same story, and yet each is a unique and personal story—a testimony of compassion and care, personalized. The goal is the whole body touching the whole city, making a Christ difference in the community and the world, but doing so out of lifestyle changes, not merely programs and events!

The World Health Organization says the causes of the phenomenon of child homelessness are the family breakdown, armed conflict and poverty.

Sadly, the church has grown used to presenting ministry opportunities to people and encouraging someone to step forward and volunteer. Dutiful members usually do, but something always seems to be missing in the end. The ministry opportunities appear in the buffet of an "event" mentality, and do not rise out of the transformed lives of people eager to find a role in fulfilling the Great Commission. The mission to which we are called will never be fulfilled by a program, not even a noble program. It will only be accomplished when believers embrace the call of Christ to personal ministry as a lifestyle.

Institutionally framed opportunities for ministry are important when the need requires the mobilization of a group or team, but even then, if someone with a fire in their belly is not leading the effort, it languishes. Ministry is born of the Spirit. Callings are personal matters, affirmed by the church, offered as extensions and arms of its outreach, integral to the soul of the institution, and yet a burden of the Lord born by some humble and godly man or woman. Such ministry becomes a part of the fabric of someone's life. It is what they live and breathe. It is an intentional matter with them. And so it has to be with the whole church.

Our obligation to the Great Commission, to make disciples, must become a native thing. It demands more than words; it requires the music—lives of care and compassion. It cannot be practiced occasionally; it must be constant daily. Great Commission action demands Great Commandment love—and love is spelled *care* and *compassion*. It is a lifestyle every believer should embrace with passion. It requires word and deed. As a "minister" of Jesus Christ, we must "serve"— serving is what ministers do. And all of us are called to be servants.

There are about a half-a-million children in the foster care system. Of those, 118,000 are currently available for adoption.

The Mission, the Message, the Methods

The vision is the whole world reached with the gospel. The mission is "the Great Commission." The message is Jesus, the good news, God has come. Once core values (vision and mission) are owned and hearts transformed, methods come easily. It's getting ownership of the mission at the heart level, and reinforcing the central message of Scripture that is the difficult hurdle. The values are constant and the transformation on-going. However, the various methods of caring and expressing compassion in ways that live out the implications of the Great Commission change, both in relationship to time and culture, to people groups and situations. The message remains the same, though the methods, the cultural mediums of expression, may vary. At Princeton Pike, they use the term "Operation Great Commission." That expression is code for the care and compassion used to touch the needs of the local community.

Using a combination of prayer and research, church leaders discovered and verified needs in the church, the community, and the region. Looking past superficial similarities, they found profound differences. Then they chose specific targeted areas to engage in missional ways. Their action profile was simple, "Find needs to fill, and hurts to heal." They instituted a card ministry, one of encouragement to engage people and teach the power of encouragement. Kids in the youth ministry would occasionally take rolls of quarters to area laundromats and look for single mothers. They would ask for the privilege of paying for

their wash and entertaining their children. Their purpose was to share the love of Christ. At restaurants, church members were encouraged to purchase the meals of someone who might need a blessing. They sent "ambassadors of care" to the homes of those imprisoned by a health issue and helped them get to church.

As creative ministry ideas are acted out sincerely, more are spontaneously born. These are more than cute and sweet ideas. Their purpose is to engage the church in reaching out and touching, in meeting felt needs as an expression of the love of Christ in a non-threatening, natural way. They are offered as a knock on the door of some lost heart. The work of the Spirit is critical. Kindness alone will not save. But that catalytic moment when light engages the darkness and hope meets hurt could echo for a lifetime.

The testimonies of lives impacted, of personal transformation, of conversion and life change through these "acts of care and compassion" inspire multiplied similar actions. They edify the believer and motivate the entire congregation to wild acts of grace. Not only are sinners changed, the church by obedience, by its missional activity, is changed. Pastor Clardy believes that such actions bring pleasure to the heart of God.

No 'Risk-Free' Change

The change at Princeton Pike has involved risks. It required moving from trusting programs to trusting people. That is a major modification. It demanded a shift from orchestrated and staff-driven outreach to body-ministry, without which the lost world around us would not be engaged. It required a critical change from programmed care to compassionate, Spirit-energized care. It required people be trusted. Led, but not driven. Inspired by example, but not coerced. It required the abandonment of certain church patterns and standards that had been rooted in traditional approaches, but did not reach beyond the church walls.

The GDP (Gross Domestic Product) of the 41 most heavily indebted nations with 567 million people is less than the wealth of the world's 7 richest people combined.

The folks at The Pike feel they are now beginning to experience results. Engaging the church in an expectation of "Great Commission living" is more complex than recruiting volunteers to execute mere programs, but it has exponentially more promise. The greater reward always demands a greater risk. It also enlarges vision. Programs tend to be narrow, but our mission is global, cosmic. God is calling us to something much bigger than we have been offering. It is more than a few good deeds in our community. We have been given the world as our harvest field, both at home and abroad—every unreached home, every hamlet and village, every teeming slum, and every little child yet to hear.

The Pike has adopted mission efforts in Haiti and Chile, and many other parts of the world, with the same attitude and approach, the same passion. Money and men alone are not enough. No more mission-tourism. They have chosen a compassion-based approach that is also strategic, not a short-term tactical mission jaunt. They are studying generational outcomes. What will their efforts look like in 20 years? And if a given change is desired, what steps are necessary to get there?

They are taking a relational perspective, asking how they might be involved in the lives of people who are the focus of their missional efforts—and for a lifetime. It is no longer enough to feed them for a day. The whole person must be considered, the needs not only of the soul, but of the whole person—education, medical, family, empowerment, and more. Each convert must be develop as a disciple, grow to spiritual maturity, experience the joy of innate potential, and experientially know the wholeness of Christ and His plan for them. The acts of compassion are merely step-by-step building blocks, ministry avenues focused on meeting the immediate need, but there is a higher goal—the transformation of the whole individual. The folks at The Pike are challenged to see people in Southern Ohio and South America change, one at a time. Then become agents of change in their own communities and villages until whole regions are impacted for God's glory.

Tent cities are springing up from coast to coast as the unemployed lose their homes and apartments.

In some areas, the church has partnered in building schools, but the building is only the beginning. They continue to be engaged, watching the fruit of their commitment blossom, caring for its developmental needs. To the school is added an orphanage, and then training centers for older children and adults. With such strategies, the witness of the church multiplies through many varied avenues of care and compassion. Such relationships cannot be terminal. The engagement in the mission is not merely tactical, but strategic and generational. The immediate needs are considered but with the transformational vision of the end in mind. What is the ultimate outcome desired?

A Corporate Mission—A Personal Commission

The joy of giving, sharing, and being an avenue of care and compassion must begin with the right motive, one of "giving to *be* a blessing." The acts of service must be *personalized.* Barry believes that relieving social pain in some section of the city or some region, or a mere reaction to some personal or social pain, is not the answer and not a wise strategy. From the beginning, the effort must be seen with the goal of ministering to the whole person. If the efforts of care and compassion enable the problem, they are wasted. They may temporarily relieve some pain, but profoundly aggravate the problem and deepen dependence. Success is measured by changed lives.

The church, through an organized group effort, or the spontaneous actions of its members, finds creative ideas and special occasions to touch human needs with the whole person in mind, not a slice of the individual. Meeting some immediate need is easy—paying a light bill, giving away food, providing transportation. These are all important, but ultimately superficial. Underneath the immediate pain are other needs, perhaps unconsciously held, not even clearly perceived. Destructive habit patterns drive cycles of dependence and create a stream of continual needs.

51% percent of the world's 100 hundred wealthiest bodies are not nations, but corporations.

The goal, the proof of success, is seeing people come to Christ for salvation, become disciples, and then develop into ministers to others out of the wellspring of personal joy—the joy of knowing what God did for them and seeing the same thing happen in the lives of their friends. This is fulfillment of not just seeing compassion as an event, but as a lifestyle. Compassion cannot be housed in the church. It is not an institutional commodity. The church is compassionate because its people are compassionate. It must be personalized, and then actualized, and only then will the world have a real chance at being evangelized.

No effective evangelism? No transformation in the lives of Christians? No actualization of the incarnational Christ? Walk and talk not congruent? No living reality of Christ in the lives of Christians? No personalization of faith, prayer, and passion? No concern for a lost world? No personal gifts given to be used in ministry? Only when mission is personalized will it become transformational. And when it does, it becomes contagious!

1.6 billion people, 25% of humanity, live without electricity. Almost a billion are in South and East Asia.

Princeton Pike embraced the reality that behind every need is a person with more fundamental needs. The presenting needs can be met, but dealing with the debilitating cycles engendering the chronic need state is more difficult. Throwing food and money at the immediate need without investing the compassion and care to understand the deeper and ongoing need of the person was not adequate.

The guiding philosophy is now gauged at four basic need-state levels that govern lives, whether locally or on a distant mission field. The basic model transcends the boundaries of style, ethnicity and cultural diversity, while respecting diversity and uniqueness. The four spheres are common to every human being and are used to assess basic God-given needs.

1. **Spiritual**—the need for a relationship with God through Christ.
2. **Relational**— the need for relationships with one another.
3. **Purpose**—the need to be needed.
4. **Affirmation**—the need to be valued and celebrated.

Pastor Clardy believes these need states are a part of our divine design. We are not needy as an indication of imperfection, but because we are not complete outside of our relationship with God. The Redemptive God that creates supply is the same Creator God that created in us a need for Him and one another! *"But my God shall supply all your need according to His riches in glory by Christ Jesus."* (Philippians 4:19).

Mission efforts must address these deeper needs, instead of merely focusing on the immediate and transient needs. The "presenting need" is often a clue to the more "profound need" lurking under the surface. Ask, "Why do these immediate needs exist in such abundance, in this person or family?" Meet the immediate need, but strategically assess, and develop a more holistic plan to address the whole need, the deeper need. This is a more challenging approach, and yet, infinitely more exciting, thrilling, and motivating than temporarily responding with a quick hand of compassion.

Currently, 10% more food is produced in the world than is needed. The problem is not supply, but distribution. Nevertheless, 35,000 children die every day of hunger.

The greater sense of fulfillment is in being intentional and creatively working toward short and long-term goals with the ultimate transformational end in mind. Seeing an individual personally changed, and their chronic need state addressed, is the objective. It also means that the four fundamental needs must be kept in view, and attention and compassion rallied to meet such needs. Whatever help is given will be short-circuited by a person's greater need, one that is connected to one of these four fundamental areas, until profound change comes by the Spirit.

When Jesus fed hungry people, He gave them literal food for their body, but in that moment, He also spoke of "living bread" that fulfilled their deeper spiritual need. To the woman at the well who came in need of water, He offered "living water." He demonstrated that we are called to meet the most obvious needs with compassion, but also be an instrument in meeting the greater need, one that produces life change. He said to the thirsty woman at the well, "You will never thirst again." He was speaking to her spiritual need.

Care and compassion can, of course, feed the addiction for comfort, and fuel me-first, "feel good" experiences. The occasion of care must engage the whole need of the whole person. What is happening in some care and compassion ministries is the mere exchange of commodities, of superficial assistance. To touch a community, change a nation, and create life-giving ministries, more than commodities must be exchanged. Personal change is needed. Of course, this, too, is an exchange—the exchanged life of the sinner with Christ. When a person is genuinely changed, the need state itself changes. The impoverished person experiences abundant life in Christ. They grow from someone with a need for ministry to someone who ministers to needs. From one who gets, to one who gives. From weakness, to strength.

This happens, one person at time, one family at a time, one church at a time, one city or region at a time. We must move from merely meeting needs to planting the internal seeds which contain the life-giving quality and ability to become reproductive. The trainees become trainers. They reach others, offer sustaining help, bring life-transformation through the power of Jesus Christ. Barry often asks, "What good is a full stomach, if at the end of the day, they still have an empty soul?" We may be sincere, but sincerely wrong. And we can't afford to be wrong, not if we are going to effectively share God's care and compassion. Waste is unacceptable—lost time, resources, and most importantly, lost souls are the expense of our errors.

For centuries the poor have been the object of help and almsgiving, but they have never been the subject of decisions and thinking by the church or its leadership.

The Pike realized they could no longer call mere actions of compassion success. Constant fishing and empty nets were not adequate. It was not the number of boat trips, the sum total of the times the net was cast, the commodities distributed—it was people they were after. That demanded a new equation. A *person* had to go into the place a *number* had gone before. And then, there needed to be a willingness to walk with that person.

Conversion was the event. Discipleship was the process. Maturity (Christ-likeness) was the goal. The fish, now a fisher of men, was the result. That demanded a commitment to move the person to wholeness. The church specializes in meeting spiritual needs. We compartmentalize humans. It is a part of our call to pour into other areas of a person's need. We lead a person to Christ. We celebrate the fact that they are now a follower of Christ. But then we relinquish the commitment to

Churches Open Credit Unions to Help Poor

The Church of God Credit Union, not affiliated with the Church of God (Cleveland, TN), offers financial as well as spiritual help. LeAne Cloud is president of the Wichita, Kansas, based institution. It is one of about 500 faith-based credit unions across the nation, created to help members and people in need. They are set up in church basements, donated office space, and staffed mostly by volunteers. Most, though affiliated with churches, are in low-income neighborhoods. Due to legal codes, they are operated independently of their parent churches, but require a federal charter and are monitored as are the more traditional credit unions.

As a group, they have more than $2 billion in assets. According to the National Credit Union Administration, they represent a variety of faiths and denominations—Protestant, Catholic and Muslim. Some offer services to people outside the church's community, though they are set up primarily to help members invest their money according to their religious values. Most see their financial services as an extension of their ministry's efforts to help the poor and needy.

"We were started in the church and we go by Christian principles of helping people who need our help," says Rita Haynes, the treasurer and manager of Cleveland's 50-year-old Faith Community United Credit Union, one of the oldest faith-based credit unions in the country. Even with 4,000, that credit union has only five paid employees. The Alexandria Federal Credit, created by Shiloh Baptist Church, has no full-time staff. The three loan officers are deacons. The Credit Union offers secured and unsecured loans for cars and other purchases, and plans to add credit cards and mortgages to the menu soon. They educate clients, "We tell them what a checking account is, compound interest is, major banks won't do that."

The National Credit Union Administration has turned deacons and pastors into successful credit union directors. Government officials note that the faith-based credit unions have low default rates and report a lower percentage of problem loans. The Credit Unions operate as a business, but not without a heart. One manager confessed that some clients paid slower, but did pay, and they did save. Churches are using the faith-based credit unions to reach out to poor people in ways that other financial institutions cannot. Some offer only limited services and are restricted to members, but others cite their call to serve the poor. Unique? The church-based credit unions can probably go where virtually no other similar institution can." (Adapted from an ABC News Story, September 10, 2010).

continue the journey of care and compassion, meeting the next obvious need – for example, the need for healthy and affirming relationships, "iron sharpening iron."

If a person is being fulfilled both spiritually and relationally, the "alone factor" erased, and vigorous and wholesome friendships cultivated that both stretch and sustain, they are more likely to address the third level of need. That is the area of "purpose" —the need to be needed. Recruiting people to become compassionate care givers and world changers will not occur by emotional pleas for volunteers. They will rise from the ranks of those who themselves have been moved from the state need-deficit, to that of being fulfilled, one person at a time. Having experienced such healing, they are now ready to do something out of the overflow of their life.

Empty people have nothing to give. One cannot give what is not possessed. Can you imagine a church where the helping ranks of compassion ministries that make a difference are not made up of the same 20% who respond to pastoral pleas for workers, but rather, where compassion, care and the Great Commission is the lifestyle of each member and the church at large?

Barry Clardy believes such a church is possible! It's do-able! He believes that it is the heartbeat of God. He also believes church members are more ready to be led into meaningful service than ever before. "Issue the challenge. What you will find are people with a servant-heart who are eager to trade their title for a towel and step into the footsteps of Jesus."

The journey has endless possibilities, beginning with reaching a community and then reaching out to touch the world. In the process, God profoundly touches such a servant people. Their church is completely changed. "Go ahead; drink in the water of compassion. Let it become personal through a lifestyle of prayer and brokenness that will give birth to the most exciting journey in which you and those you influence can know the joy of Great Commission living."

Discussion Guide

Big Ideas

- Their slogan is "Making Ministry Our Mission, and People Our Purpose."
- Princeton Pike sends out "ambassadors of care" to the homes of those imprisoned by a health issue and serves them, helps them get to church, etc.
- The church is attempting to move from "trusting programs" to "trusting people."
- Acts of service must be personalized—not merely the response of programs or merely institutional responses.
- Once core values (vision and mission) are owned, and hearts are transformed, methods come easily.

Notable Quotes

- "Passion is what you feel when you see a need; compassion is what you do with that passion."
- "There is nothing I can use you to do for me unless you first allow change in you."
- Ministry is more than the routine of "having church," but rather "being the church," all the while wondering why so many people are content with business as usual; more than the activity of personal ministry without results, without progress, and without fulfillment. Ministry is more than this!

- "Find a need and Fill it; Find a Hurt and Heal it" is a constant message at Princeton Pike. Their daily objective is to fulfill the example of Christ's service and ministry to a lost world, doing so with care and compassion.
- Compassion cannot be housed in the church. It is not an institutional commodity. The church is compassionate because its people are compassionate. It must be personalized, and then actualized. Only then will the world have a real chance at being evangelized.

Questions for Consideration

1. Discuss the four spheres used to assess needs: ***Spiritual***—the need for a relationship with God through Christ; ***Relational***— the need for relationships with one another; ***Purpose***—the need to be needed; ***Affirmation***—the need to be valued and celebrated. How does your church strive to address these needs?
2. Discuss the transition of a congregation from an inward focus to an external, missional focus? Where is the focus in your church? Could it change? If the Great Commission is not an option, what is your church willing to do to obey the final command of Christ?
3. "Comfort creatures resist change." That being the case, how do you navigate the change necessary to reach the culture and revive a missional church? 'The Pike" emphasizes missions at home and abroad, near and far? Does your church do that?
4. Barry talks about "free" change and "forced" change. What do you think he means? When and how would a church be "forced" to change? What are the "forces" that would demand change? Cultural? Economic? Lagging attendance?
5. "Conversion was the event. Discipleship the process. Maturity (Christ-likeness) the goal." Does your church see enough converts? Do you have a process to disciple the converts? Is the goal Christ-likeness? Is the relentless pursuit of the members Christ-likeness—models of devotion to be emulated?

Prayer Station Ministry

Praise Cathedral, led by Bishop Jerry Madden, in Greer, South Carolina, sets up a Prayer Station at the local flea market. The stand is portable, supported by a PVC frame that displays a red banner that reads simply – "Prayer Station." A small team offers prayer for people passing through the market. On a typical Saturday, as many as 50 people stop for prayer. The needs range from terminal illness to life issues, from divorce and custody battles to life choices. People come to Christ. Literature is available. The goal is to promote Christ – and yet the people always want to know, "What church are you from?"

The gift of prayer is so powerful when combined with unconditional love. Those who pass through the flea market and receive prayer often return with amazing stories of God's intervention. Suddenly, they are awake to the reality of God. Prayer is a gateway to knowing God. We invite people to unlock the door that begins the possibility of a transforming relationship with Jesus Christ when we give them the gift of prayer.

The "Prayer Station" ministry began in 1992 in preparation for a New Year's Eve Outreach in New York. A Youth with a Mission (YWAM) group was asking God for an evangelism strategy. They heard God say, "Pray for people on the street". They set up the first "Prayer Station." From the first day, people warmly responded and many were ready to receive prayer for needs and subsequently open their hearts to the message of the gospel. This strategy has proved itself to be one of the most effective, powerful and disarming street evangelism methods we have ever been involved in.

Examine the model of Jesus. He often first prayed for a person's felt need and then addressed the need of their eternal soul. This was also common in the ministry of Paul, Peter and the other apostles of the first century church. In Acts chapter 3, Peter and John prayed for the healing of the crippled man at the Beautiful Gate of the Temple. The man is healed and as a result the whole city is impacted with the gospel and the power of God.

Praying for people in the market place was an everyday practice of the first century church. The miracles and healings that resulted were used of God to draw attention to the message of the gospel and the real need of the people - their need of a relationship with Jesus. People today have very real needs they want help with - a healing, a job, a place to live, problems at home, a family member or friend. By believing God to meet their need, their hearts are warmed and opened to hear the gospel and respond.

Praying for people at a Prayer Station is not a gimmick. In the gospels and the book of Acts, the prayers prayed for the unconverted were powerful. They were answered and needs met. Christians that participate in Prayer Evangelism need to be prepared to believe God for the miraculous. Here you pray not merely for the lost, but with the lost Every Christian can practice Prayer Evangelism. We are simply giving to others the special gift given to us through Christ—ACCESS WITH GOD!

The Basic Strategy

The Prayer Station provides an opportunity to pray for people who have a variety of needs, believing that God will hear that prayer and act. Our prayer of faith becomes a starting point for their faith, and often a doorway to share our faith.

We begin with the temporal and move to the eternal. A full prayer station including a prayer station training video is available to equip you and your church in this evangelistic effort. When you order a Prayer Station, you will receive everything you need to hit the streets the very next day, including a 5' folding table, a Prayer Station banner, 10 Prayer Station aprons, contact cards, all necessary hardware, and a bag and cart for easy transporting of your Prayer Station. Now, a new portable free-standing Prayer Station banner stand is also available. It is very compact and the entire kit folds up into a carry bag. It is complete with a small literature rack built in.

The Prayer Station Training Kit includes a training video and an audiotape giving the full history of Prayer Stations along with a detailed manual. The price for the Prayer Station, including the Training Kit, is $495 plus shipping. If you are familiar with Prayer Stations and do not need the Training Kit, total cost is $470 plus shipping. If you have access to a Prayer Station in your area, and would only like to purchase the Training Kit, it is available for $30, shipping included.

Prayer Station Kits
YWAM Metro New York
70 New York Ave.
Smithtown, NY 11787 516-366-4826

And he said: "I tell you the truth, unless you change and become like little children, you will never enter the kingdom of heaven. Mt. 18:3 (NIV)

Brothers, stop thinking like children. In regard to evil be infants, but in your thinking be adults. I Corinthians 14:20 (NIV)

Like newborn babies, crave pure spiritual milk, so that by it you may grow up in your salvation, I Peter 2:2 (NIV)

I beseech you therefore, brethren, by the mercies of God, that you present your bodies a living sacrifice, holy, acceptable to God, which is your reasonable service. And do not be conformed to this world, but be transformed by the renewing of your mind, that you may prove what is that good and acceptable and perfect will of God. Romans 12:1-2

Now the Lord is the Spirit; and where the Spirit of the Lord is, there is liberty. But we all, with unveiled face, beholding as in a mirror the glory of the Lord, are being transformed into the same image from glory to glory, just as by the Spirit of the Lord. II Corinthians 3:17-18.

Hold fast the pattern of sound words which you have heard from me, in faith and love which are in Christ Jesus. That good thing which was committed to you, keep by the Holy Spirit who dwells in us. II Timothy 1:13-14.

And the things that you have heard from me among many witnesses, commit these to faithful men who will be able to teach others also. You therefore must endure[a] hardship as a good soldier of Jesus Christ. II Timothy 2:2-3

K.I.D.S

Chris Blake is Vice President of K.I.D.S., a ministry that has provided over 65 million underprivileged and disaster-struck children with nearly one billion dollars of new clothing, toys, basic necessities, juvenile products, books, and more, through a network of 1,000 affiliate social agencies. US efforts garner 85% of their support, and 15% helps international children. They are rated as one of America's most efficient charities. Nearly $90 million of commodities were distributed in 2009 to children in poverty, homeless, domestically abused, with low literacy, with a military service family, major illness, and incarcerated family members.

10

Qualities of Change Agents

Our nation and world is in trouble. Christians and atheists. Democrats and Republicans. Young and old. All agree that things can't continue as they are now. The problem is bigger than fiscal responsibility; balancing the budget or homeland security;

stopping terrorism or educational reforms for our children. The world system polarizes us with either-or paradigms. The solution is not so simple. We are beyond the moment in which the mere management of complicated problems or evasive solutions can change our dilemmas.

Surprisingly, Christianity isn't a mere answer to the complex questions. It is not a "patch" to a torn social or economic garment. It demands that the garment itself be changed. It presents a whole entirely alternative "way." "True compassion is more than flinging a coin to a beggar; it comes to see that a system that produces beggars needs restructuring." (Martin Luther King Jr.)

Couples living together without marriage have more illness, conflict and violence than married couples. A woman is 62 times—that is 6,200%—more likely to be beaten by a boyfriend than by a husband! Wives are respected more than girlfriends.

Pastoring an inner city church has its struggles and victories. Visitors come to New York City and feel overwhelmed by the sheer volume of sin and violence. Chris is often asked, "Can a pastor of an inner city really make a difference?" He is living in the middle of a city with people who feel hopeless. In a sea of people, a dense concentration of humans, they feel lonely. Cities change one person at a time. And Chris has seen changed lives.

In Numbers 16, the Israelites were grumbling against Moses and Aaron and, as a result, they faced the judgment of God. Since leaving Egypt, the grievances and protests had escalated. They moaned about water and the lack of their favorite delicacies. They objected to the route, to manna, and then to quail. Finally, God threatened their very existence (16:45). If He had acted, the greater portion of the Old Testament would have disappeared. And were He to act today with retribution against murmuring and dissident folk, a lot of churches would be without members.

The plague that rippled through the Israelite encampment was a tsunami of death sweeping through the camp—1,000, 2,000, 5,000,

10,000 died before Moses. Aaron took fire from the brass altar, fire that had fallen from heaven, fire that had consumed the sacrifice months earlier, and he ran through the middle of the camp. What a sight that must have been! Aaron ran, drawing a line between sin and death. Aaron stood, acting in a priestly manner, reconciling men to God and God to men. One person, in the middle of a national calamity, recovered fire from the altar, and took it into the middle of the plague. He stood with fire from the altar, a representative of the people before God. He stood with fire from the altar, a reminder of the fire that must quench sin. Where he stood, death stopped. His position marked the line between the living and the dead (Numbers 16:47-48).

Last year, poverty in America grew more than in the 51 years that the government has tracked the poor. The total climbed by 3 million to nearly 44 million -- or one in seven Americans.

The aged Aaron was well into his 80's at the time of this incident, but the Bible declares that he ran to the altar. It was a time for urgency. And unction enabled the elderly high priest to run. To change our world, to stop the plague of killing and violence, to end the unnecessary dying, the surrender to the status quo, an urgency is needed. We can no longer take lightly the social and moral condition of the nation. Our comfort zone can no longer define our service level. Imagination is needed. And isn't it amazing, how we exceed common knowledge limitations and transcend native abilities when we are forced into dependence on God? With God, all things are possible.

Here's the best part! Aaron was the High Priest and his actions typified those of Christ, who came to stop the plague of sin. Where He hung, the line of death stopped. And now, following the prototype of both Aaron and Christ, we must stand among the people of our cities, with fire from the altar, and stop the plague. Aaron, fraught with flaws, was nevertheless capable, through the grace of the extraordinary. The dying victims all around—dozens, hundreds, thousand's—motivated him with urgency. Had he not fulfilled his priestly duties, the entire nation might have perished. Some 14,700 died. It was not Aaron that stopped the plague. Nor was it merely his passionate action. It was the fire of the altar. One person can make a difference. Aaron stood between the living and the dead.

Waiting until marriage to have children is the second of three "golden rules" for avoiding poverty that researchers identified over the years: (1) Graduate from high school; (2) Marry before having children; and (3) Get a job.

Does it take an extraordinary person to make a difference? Two things seem to converge—an overwhelming awareness of crises and the fiery altar. Both Aaron and Christ allowed themselves to be thrust into the uncomfortable middle between God and hopeless men and women. Too many Christians live sheltered lives, away from any disaster, any pain, any plague. But when we are caught between the difficult awfulness of this world and divine answers, sometimes quite ordinary people act in extraordinary ways.

Are you that someone? Are you witnessing some urgency? Are you in a place that is in desperate need of change? Then, run to the altar. Go, and stand between the living and the dead. It starts with prayer. Like Aaron, where you stand, invite God to act, and death to stop.

A parishioner in the church Chris serves in New York City was unable to speak English. She was a recent immigrant from South America. Her desire was to be involved in children's ministry which was quite a problem, given the language gap. She assumed that the church leadership would say she wasn't qualified. Chris told her, "God is not looking for ability, but availability. That's all you need." She was asked if she would be willing to sit with some of the more troubled children. She loved her new ministry assignment. In a short time, she learned two simple phrases in English, "I love you" and "Jesus loves you." With two phrases in her arsenal, she began a "preaching-teaching" ministry to those same troubled children. When one of the more challenging kids acted up, she whispered to them, "I love you! And Jesus loves you!" into the child's ear.

"Aging Out" at Age 18

Jack was a foster child in Seattle until he turned 18 years old. On that day, he aged out of the foster care system only a few weeks from his high school graduation date. With $100, a bag of clothes, and a few personal toys, he was on his own. An adult, according to the state, he was now to care for himself. For a few weeks, a friend's couch was his home. But that was short-term. "I'm gonna be homeless," he told a reporter.

He is only one of about 500 kids that annually "age-out" of the social services system in the state of Washington alone. As if the ride in the government-run social system has not been rough enough to this point, at 18, it runs out of pavement altogether. "There's a real cliff between the child and adult serving systems in this country," says Mark Courtney, Director of Partners for our Children, a foster children advocate group. "A place to live, food, someone who's looking after them on a day-to-day basis, access to health care. All of those things are there for them, and then a day later, they're not."

Courtney has tracking the "age-out'" victims for years. Here is what he has discovered. By the age of 24, only 6% had completed college. Less than 50% had a job. Nearly 40% had been homeless or had couch-surfed for years. Of the girls, 75% were on public assistance. Almost 60% of the young men had been convicted of a crime. One young man saw it coming at age 16. He confessed, "Turning 18 is the scariest thing that is going to happen to me."

Research at the New York University School of Social Work discovered that 28% of the children in that state had been abused while in the system. In Maryland, another study found substantiated allegations of sexual abuse in foster care are four times higher than found among the general population. In one report, 21% of abuse or neglect cases involved foster homes. In 2002, approximately 896,000 children were found to be victims of child abuse or neglect.

Steve is a shy young man from the West Coast of Tampa. He has lived in 14 different group homes in the last two years. That is a different home every 51 days. He was removed from his mother's care because of her drug use. Now he is 18, and like 30,000 other foster teens across the nation this year, he is on his own. These kids go from foster care, where they might handle a few bucks a week, to full self-responsibility. Sometimes, when the last foster care subsidy arrives,

"Aging Out" Cont'd

they are given a plastic bag for their few belongings and taken to the nearest homeless shelter. The number of children who "age out" of the system has increased by nearly 64%. In the last decade, more than a quarter of a million have hit the streets, the government having intervened and severed parental ties, is only one more player in the process of their abandonment. Since 1999, approximately 228,000 youth have "aged out." Foster care alumni do not fare very well—25% do not collect a high school diploma or a GED. Less than two percent finish college. Half experience an episode of homelessness. Nearly 30 percent end up in jail.

One particular child was especially difficult. He came from a very abusive home. Chris and his team were working with Child Services to find better living conditions for him, but after each outreach session, they were still forced to send him back into the same toxic environment. At the end of yet one more children's ministry session, an amazing thing happened. He turned to the volunteer who had been whispering love with her limited vocabulary and simply said, "I love you ,too." What a breakthrough. For once in his life, he felt loved. And for once in his life, he had the security to express love. A bond had occurred. A miracle occurred in a little heart that had only known hopelessness.

That moment transpired at 2:30 on a Sunday afternoon. Four hours later, his little body was found dead in a garbage bag. His foster mother had beaten him to death. With only a few words, two phrases, an immigrant had become a missionary to a child from the projects.

David Bornstein, in his book, *How to Change the World, Social Entrepreneurs and the Power of New Ideas,* says that social entrepreneurs are "transformative forces: people with new ideas to address major problems who are relentless in their pursuit of their visions, people who will not take "No!" for an answer, who will not give up until they have spread their ideas as far as they possibly can." Although Bornstein is not referring to Christians, he nevertheless describes how Christians must think in order to change the world.

Six Qualities of a World Changer

The greatest leader in history, the one who changed the world more than any other, is of course, Jesus Christ. In his short earthly life of only 33 years, He could only claim a handful of followers. He never wrote a book or taught in a proper institution. His public ministry lasted only three years. He left behind a rag-tag group of disciples and prayed to the Father to send the Holy Spirit to help them remember what he had said and to empower them to change the world.

A few years after His death, there were thousands of people who would be called "people of the way," and eventually, derisively, "Christians." Across the Roman Empire they trekked, to the ends of known civilization, spreading the gospel, the good news. They turned the world upside down. They impacted cities. Within five generations, there were millions of followers.

Two thousand years later there are more than one billion people who claim Jesus as their Savior, and millions more join every year. The organization he founded, the Church, has branches in every country on earth. How did He accomplish this? What key principles did He follow? By following these same principles, can we become world changers as well?

1. A High Calling

It is sometimes assumed that the more highly successful a person is the more naturally confident and persistent they have been. Among pastors, missionaries, and Christian workers, that will certainly not account for all of their success. There are plenty of overtly confident, charismatic and knowledgeable Christian leaders, but there is another difference—the sense of a divine call. Ultimately, among true Christian leaders, it is not merely the person themselves that is persistent, but the call. It moves one to search for solutions, seize opportunities, anticipate obstacles, monitor results, and envision a future. Technology and modernization can never replace the call. It makes a divine difference. Neither a seminary degree nor organizational ordination can replace a divine call. Computer software is a great source for study, but it is the call that causes a message to burn in the heart until it is delivered with the aid of the Spirit. A calling gives assurance. It enables persistence and makes it impossible for true men of God to quit.

Changing the world begins with a unique calling. It is insurance against worldly distractions. It is a constant beacon calling us back to faithfulness to God and onward to a demonstration to the world of His Kingdom. It is more than obedience to rules and regulations. It is a call to participate in the "*Missio Dei*" (God sending missionaries into the world). We are to call people, human systems, and organizations into harmony with God's Kingdom principles. These principles become a sign and a foretaste of the coming Kingdom, now breaking into this "present evil age" and one day experienced in fullness.

First, the church must change in order to become the foundation, the sending and equipping center, enabling us to effectively impact our world. We must change before we can change the world. George Barna in his book, *Revolution,* says our "primary emphasis is not salvation among the unrepentant but the personal renewal and commitment of the believers. The dominant catalyst is people's desperation for genuine relationship with God." Or as Acts 1:8 says, "*You will receive power when the Holy Spirit comes on you; and you will be my witnesses, first in Jerusalem, and then in all Judea and Samaria, and then to the ends of the earth.*"

The worldly pressure on the church and our ministries is constant, yet subtle and incremental. Like the proverbial frog in the pot, the change occurs imperceptibly. Pastor Blake urges, "Guard your calling. Treasure it. Weave it into your sermons. Talk about it. Make yourself accountable to others for it. It is easy to be influenced by the world away from your high calling. The high calling, the clear and compelling sense of divine call, is the driving force that emanates outward, influencing the world rather than being the influenced."

Pastor Chris sees a whole new generation of Christians determined to live according to that higher calling. Barna agrees, "Millions of devout followers of Jesus Christ are repudiating tepid systems and practices of the Christian faith, and introducing a wholesale shift in how faith is understood, integrated, and influences the world."

2. A Genuine Gospel and Authentic Presenters

For far too long, our evangelism mode has been a monologue. It has been content proclaimed, rather than a lifestyle demonstrated. One zealous man tried an experiment. He sat down at a coffee shop counter with a sign that offered to buy anyone a cup of coffee if they would listen to his story. He got no takers. Then he changed his sign, offering a cup of coffee to anyone who would tell him their story. A line formed. Talking about love and care proved less effective than demonstrating care by being a compassionate listener.

Some 60% of US children, by age 18, will live in a household with only one parent. This cultural achievement is a calamity that is only recently yielding its devastating results.

To reach this culture demands a different evangelism model, one that embodies the gospel in a lifestyle; one that reveals by choices the superiority of living by kingdom principles. Arguing individuals into submission to our superior claims and reasons-to-believe rarely works in a post-modern culture. The switch for the light in the head of mankind is in his heart. Humility always has a better chance at flipping that switch than superior debating techniques. Even if one agrees with the rational argument, his heart must be changed, and that is a work of the Spirit.

This generation is wary of truth claims. And they have learned that every sales pitch has a hook. To them, the gospel is the product of big business religion. What they need is exposure to authentic Christ followers. Appealing to their self-interest is defeating, They need a radical call to take up the cross. More importantly, they need to see others on the costly path of discipleship. Meeting felt needs will only produce more needy people. Seeker-sensitive appeals will fail if there is bait-and-switch perception when the true cost of discipleship is unwrapped.

Caring people will produce caring converts. We must live in ways we want converts to model. That means we have to walk our neighborhoods, taste the pain around us, pray for people, visibly demonstrate Christ's compassion and justice.

About 1.05 million children a year are victims of their parent's divorce. Another 1.26 million are born to never-married mothers.

It is not the culture that will move toward us. We must move toward society, the city, and the community around us. Our churches have developed a culture in which we are comfortable, but visitors are not. We speak church-ease. The language gap is now so profound, words and phrases so common to us are like foreign terms to the neighbors living next door. It is not enough to continue to preach to the choir.

Our theological terms must be interpreted for the common man, the untaught, the searching sinner. This is not a dumbing down of the essence of the gospel, but the cultural translation of the good news. As someone has reminded us, "In the beginning, the Word became flesh, and moved into the neighborhood." If we are going to truly change the world, our preaching should evoke a consciousness about the culture around us. And it must connect with our neighbors.

3. A Sacrificed Life

In the 1990's, AIDS was ravaging communities in New York City. Chris and his church had a ministry to the "boarder babies" at Woodhull Hospital. Church volunteers went to hold and cuddle infants who had acquired the disease from their mothers. Chris remembers one story particularly.

At Woodhull, church volunteers met a mother who was dying of the AIDS virus. She implored them to somehow provide a home for her baby, Alyssa, also afflicted with AIDS. The infant had been born to a crack-addicted, HIV mother, also hospitalized. After prayer and consultation with mentors, Chris decided to bring Alyssa home with him. He was certified as a foster parent, and it didn't take long to get permission from New York's ACS (Administration for Children's Services). The decision was difficult, and taking care of the infant was even more challenging.

Doctors anticipated the infant to live no longer than six months. In addition to AIDS and the crack issue, there were also serious physical and developmental complications. Regular doctor visits didn't seem to help the child's progress. Even the church's prayers weren't making an apparent difference. Chris was soon at the end of his rope. Then one day, the doctor mysteriously ordered more tests. And then more tests. Chris assumed that the disease was progressing more rapidly than anticipated. He expected Alyssa to be back in the hospital at any point.

God had other plans. The doctor confided that extra tests were needed because he was no longer able to find any trace of the HIV virus in her little body. Alyssa had been healed of AIDS. Her condition changed. She began to thrive. She gained weight. Her T-cell count steadily increased. Chris held her up in front of the congregation as proof of a God who still works miracles. Alyssa is now 16 years of age, in junior high school. Chris would say, "She changed my life. She is my everyday miracle. In all, it taught me that miracles still happen to those willing to take a step of faith and live a life of personal sacrifice."

But miracles don't come easy. There is a prayer, heartache and struggle behind each one. Sacrifice and surrender are the missing links keeping Christians from experiencing the world changing power of Jesus Christ. Chris believes, "The willingness to sacrifice is directly related to the ability and capacity to change the world. Comfortable people don't need miracles. Comfortable people don't want change. It's only in the midst of heartache and suffering, or 'putting oneself in the urgency,' that you truly experience the moving of God's hand."

4. A Disregard for Failure

Hundreds of children on the streets of New York live in broken families where love has been lost. These families, torn apart by sin and heartbreak, are difficult to reach. David was only three when Chris first met him. He had been left in his crib with his legs sticking through the slats. His out-of-control mother, under the influence of alcohol, became upset with his chronic crying. In her frustration and anger, she repeatedly slammed the moveable crib-side down on his tiny legs until they were broken multiple times. Although doctors were able to patch up his legs, he would forever walk with a limp.

When David was seven, he came to church for the very first time. He, like many other inner city kids, was rebellious and had learned to act up for attention and control. But David was a master at manipulation and his behavior was dangerous. Volunteers feared that he presented a hazard to others. They thought it best if he wasn't allowed to return.

But one of the volunteers named Laura intervened. She agreed to take personal responsibility and give David the special care for which he was crying out. David had other ideas. He didn't respond to Laura. Her efforts did not seem to phase him. She failed. They all failed. But Laura refused to give up on David. This was not a short-term commitment. Throughout his teen years, David continued to get into trouble, but Laura demonstrated unconditional concern. His failures did not shake Laura's faith that God was working in his life.

David eventually married one of the girls in the church youth group. He graduated from school and went to seminary. Soon, there were three—the couple had a daughter. They have now moved from New York and David is serving as the pastor of a church in the Midwest. David may touch thousands because Laura touched one. She had a complete disregard for failure even when it looked like David was a lost cause.

Measurable outcomes is the mantra. Churches define success by numbers—church attendance, conversions, baptism, and new members. Chris believes the attention to superficial numbers, even to the initial decision to follow Christ, and not to discipleship, has led to a diminished quality of disciples serving our ministries. "Too much attention can be given to numerical growth, efficiency, and the salvation decision. Mega-church conferences have introduced the concept of an "economies of scale" approach. How can we deliver a better quality of religious goods, programs, and services that more are more effective and easily adaptable by ministry teams, and can deliver the most impact to people? The idea sounds reasonable. Who could object?"

But Chris worries that mere numerical "effectiveness" is used as the bottom line. He sees the focus shifting to ecclesiastical business techniques and cost effectiveness—higher numbers at a lower per person cost. Sunday productions may attract new attendees, but what relationship do they have to the prophetic message of the church in today's chaotic culture? With such approaches, Chis contends that "we are merely reinforcing the cultural idols of consumerism and individualism." He is reexamining the entire active-passive, performers-spectators model we call church. Paid staff, charged with a weekly quality religious experience for consumers, is not producing disciples.

5. A New Thinking

Thomas Edison once said, "If we all did the things we are capable of doing, we would literally astound ourselves." Changing our world requires new vision. We must see the world, not only as it is, but also as it could be. That requires a new way of thinking.

Jesus, as a prophet, was a visionary, a seer, who painted pictures of life as it should be. Through Him, we have a new avenue of interacting with the Father, God, and with the world. Jesus painted a radically different picture of the world. As a result of His teaching and values, the whole world is now affected.

His new world envisioned a loyal people, free from the religious tyranny of the state, *"Render therefore to Caesar the things that are Caesar's, and to God the things that are God's"* (Matthew 22:21). It envisioned people loving their enemies (Matthew 5:44). It disposed of racial stereotypes used to marginalize people based on their ancestry. The vision rooted in the story of the 'Good Samaritan' (Luke 10:25-37) towers above all others models as Ethic of Reciprocity (the Golden Rule).

But Jesus intended more than good ideas. He inspired by example.

Yet, His radical but benevolent ideals led to His crucifixion. At the moment of His lynching, the disciples were scattered, depressed and momentarily lost to the global mission. They did not fit the profile of world changers.

But after the resurrection, ascension ,and descent of the Spirit, the disciples were not only capable of changing the world, they turned it upside down. They almost appear as two different groups. What made them so bold? What transformed them into change agents? Brueggemann, the writer and theologian observes, "The resurrection of Jesus is the ultimate energizing for the new future. The wrenching of Friday had left only the despair of Saturday (Luke 24:21) and the disciples had no reason to expect Sunday after that Friday. The resurrection cannot be explained on the basis of the previously existing reality. The resurrection can only be received and affirmed and celebrated as the new action of God, whose province is to create new futures for people and to let them be amazed in the midst of despair." [4]

6. A Commitment to the Long Haul

The book, *Salvation in the Slums, Evangelical Social Work, 1865-1920,* tells the story of Charles Nelson Crittenton. Before the days when William Booth entered the slums of East London, Charles was a wealthy New York City businessman, and a Christian. In 1882, he lost his four-year-old daughter, Florence, to scarlet fever. The tragedy became the inspiration for philanthropic work and he started the Florence Night Mission in New York, a safe haven for "lost and fallen" women.

During the first year, the home received 176 women and was soon overcrowded. Crittendon spent the next six years supervising the activities of the Bleeker Street Home, which eventually became the "mother mission" of a large group of such institutions. From there, he traveled across the country by railroad, stopping all along the way, and donating $500 to each town willing to start a home for young women and children in need. Seventy homes sprung up across the nation.

Consider living like members of a third world nation overnight or for a weekend. No lights. No car. No TV. Rationed food. Do it as a family adventure. Camp out in the backyard or in a lean-to. Cook over an open fire. Randomly choose one person to live in the house with all the privileges thereof. After the experience, draw comparisons between you and the unreached. Pray for the power of the Holy Spirit to enable you to do the impossible—reach the world. Choose one action step you can do as a family to fulfill the Great Commission.

Charles worked tirelessly for the cause of young women in need until his death in 1909. It was said that no other man had done as much in rescue work for women. For more than a century, the 27 members of the Crittenton family have operated a string of care agencies in 24 states, almost half the nation. They provide innovative, comprehensive, strength-based gender and culturally responsive, trauma-informed services grounded in research, respect and results.

There is a special connection to the century-old work of the Crittenton family with Pastor Chis Blake. He reflects, "It was in the Florence Crittenton Home in Washington, DC in 1964, that my own biological mom put me up for adoption, allowing me to be adopted by Charles and Doris Blake." Crittendon was committed to changing the world that he saw, that he felt in the loss of his own daughter. "His work was not a fleeting reaction, not a flashy and temporal response. He made a commitment to the long-haul. And he has offered hope to hundreds of thousands of lives, mine included," Pastor Blake acknowledges.

According to one strand of Jewish theology, when God created the universe, He left a portion undone—the component needed for a world of justice and peace. That portion God entrusted to us, the Bible being its blueprint. Whether such Jewish ideas are true or not is now mute. We, in a fallen world, are now called to bring positive world change, social and moral transformation, to guard and nurture, as in Genesis. Jesus gave us the same command to multiply, to make disciples of the nations, to pray for the kingdom of God to come into this world, for the will of God to be done on earth as it is in heaven.

Six qualities, according to Chris Blake, are the marks of a world changer: "A High Calling; A Genuine Presentation of the Gospel; A Sacrificed Life; A Disregard for Failure; A New Way of Thinking; and A Commitment to the Long Haul. These qualities will lead to a significant spiritual breakthrough that will transform your life and ministry. You will never be the same again. These six qualities will redefine who you are at a fundamental level. Along with a fire that you get from the altar, they will also open the door to a radically different world."

Chris is waiting and believing that he and those who work with him can change, no, radically change the world.

Discussion Guide

Big Ideas

- Surprisingly, Christianity isn't a mere answer to complex questions. It is not a "patch" to a torn social or economic garment. It demands that the garment itself be changed. It presents a whole, entirely alternative "way."
- Couples living together without marriage have more illness, conflict, and violence than married couples.
- A woman is 62 times—that is, 6,200 percent—more likely to be beaten by a boyfriend than by a husband! Wives are respected more than girlfriends.
- First, the church must change in order to become the foundation, the sending and equipping center, enabling us to effectively impact our world. We must change before we can change the world.

- For far too long, our evangelism mode has been a monologue. It has been content proclaimed, rather than a lifestyle demonstrated. One zealous man tried an experiment. He sat down at a coffee shop counter with a sign that offered to buy anyone a cup of coffee if they would listen to his story. He got no takers.

Notable Quotes

- Last year, poverty in America grew more than in the last 51 years that the government has tracked the poor. The total climbed by 3 million to nearly 44 million-- or one in seven Americans.
- David Bornstein, in his book, *How to Change the World, Social Entrepreneurs and the Power of New Ideas*, says that social entrepreneurs are "transformative forces: people with new ideas to address major problems who are relentless in their pursuit of their visions, people who will not take 'No!' for an answer, who will not give up until they have spread their ideas as far as they possibly can."
- "Millions of devout followers of Jesus Christ are repudiating tepid systems and practices of the Christian faith, and introducing a wholesale shift in how faith is understood, integrated, and influences the world."
- Thomas Edison once said, "If we all did the things we are capable of doing, we would literally astound ourselves."
- Since 1999, approximately 228,000 youth have "aged out" of foster care.

Questions for Consideration

1. Should we, as Pastor Chris suggests, reexamine the active-passive, performer-spectator model of church we currently have? Are we merely attempting to produce a "quality religious experience for consumers" that has little possibility of transforming them, or the culture?
2. Using the image of Aaron, is there a place where the church needs to stand to stay the plague? Do we believe, that in prayer, we could stay the decaying power of sin and death to any degree?
3. Discuss the six traits of a world changer.
4. Chris asks the question, "Does it take an extraordinary person to make a difference?"
5. Talk about the adoption of Alyssa. What an example!

Central Parkway Goes Back to the Future

In 1923, in an old pool hall on Broadway Avenue in Cincinnati, Ohio,, a missionary-pastor named J. H. Ingram started what became the Central Parkway Church of God. Ingram went from Cincinnati to a ministry reaching around the world. Many refer to him as a Father of Church of God World Missions. At one point, he was credited with bringing more people into alignment with the denomination than any other pastor or leader.

In time, Central Parkway grew to have national prominence, an upstanding reputation, a congregation with prestige, and some would argue, one without the missional edge that they had at their launch. Their early years were marked by frequent prayer meetings and mighty moves of God. Their meetings were electric, with demonstrations of the Spirit.

But they were also full of trials and persecution. Services were interrupted by drunks. Neighbors resented the Pentecostal believers. Disruptions became so frequent that Pastor Ingram sought the protection of the City Police. But instead of giving protection, they began to raid church services, harassing attendees, and on at least two occasions, arresting and jailing members.

On one occasion, the police came to raid a service, but found the people in prayer. New converts were fervently praying at the altar. Several had just been filled with the Holy Spirit and were speaking in tongues. The police rounded up attendees, but they did not interfere with those at the altar, lost in the presence of the Spirit, speaking in tongues. Observers recalled, "It was as if there was a wall of protection around them."

Still, police harassment intensified until it became necessary that the governor of Ohio issued an order of protection. When the city police ignored the order, the governor threatened to send the State Patrol. The difficult days only deepened the resolve of the church that is now 87 years strong. Some families in the congregation are now fourth generation.

Ron Martin, the present pastor, was raised in the Central Parkway church. His goal has been to help the church recover the mission of those early years when the hand of God extended to a lost and hurting world, bringing healing, hope, and a future which God intended.

Their benevolence ministry is not self-serving; it touches multiple partner congregations. Their women's shelter has served prostitutes, drug addicts, and rescued homeless ladies from the streets. They have a center that offers clothing and shoes. But, Pastor Martin insists, "We are not a benevolence agency, not a homeless shelter, not a thrift store. We are the church of Jesus Christ, finding a need and meeting it, finding a hurt and healing it, ultimately fulfilling the mission of Jesus Christ."

Pastor Martin has struggled, like most pastors who lead strong historic churches, with becoming institutionalized and internally focused. "God has placed us here to win the city to Him," he tells his people. Cincinnati is changing. The population of the city has decreased and the demographic has shifted. Pastor Martin says, "We have learned to concentrate on those moving into the city. We now have over 100 Spanish speaking members. We have over 20 nations represented in the congregation on any given Sunday."

Central Parkway offers a rich worship experience, a "place to find the love of God, feel the care of God, and experience the power of God!" Pastor Martin is attempting to create a place where people up and down the social continuum are welcome, "Whether you laid your head on a plush pillow in a comfortable home, or slept under a bridge or in a shelter, we are your church."

When Lee Ann showed up at the church, she appeared lost. Without funds, she had been released from the hospital the day before and had gone home to a homemade wooden bed alongside I-75 in the middle of downtown Cincinnati. She had numbed her pain with alcohol, and awakened to a strange sound and smell. Two men stood over her, futilely attempting to light a match. Smelling gas, she suddenly realized they had doused her with gasoline and were trying to set her on fire. For three years, this primitive place had been her home, but that would now end. The men wanted her space.

Miraculously spared by God, she believed, she jumped to her feet and ran to the top of a nearby hill, but the men pursued and caught her. They beat her and abandoned her. At the hospital, Lee Ann realized she had to change, "If you'll help me, I'll follow You." She got out of the hospital, walked down a hill, and suddenly saw Central Parkway. There she found God's love and care, along with a new life.

The Central Parkway Church has 47 different ministries. They have learned that ministries are for seasons, but the mission and call is enduring.

And no one puts new wine into old wineskins. For the old skins would burst from the pressure, spilling the wine and ruining the skins. New wine is stored in new wineskins so that both are preserved (Matthew 9:17 - NLT).

I will shake all the nations, and the one whom all the nations desire will come. Then I will fill this house with glory, says the LORD of Armies (Haggai 2:7 - GWT).

hear in heaven Your dwelling place, and do according to all for which the foreigner calls to You, in order that all the peoples of the earth may know Your name, to fear You, as do Your people Israel, and that they may know that this house which I have built is called by Your name. (I Kings 8:43 - NASB)

When He approached Jerusalem, He saw the city and wept over it, (Luke 19:41 - NASB)

They forced the poor to cry out to him, and he hears the cry of those who suffer. (Job 34:28 - GWT)

Project Pray

P. Douglas Small serves as a catalyst for prayer - but more importantly, prayer that is linked to mission and has a Great Awakening cultural focus. For more than a dozen years, he was involved in the city-reaching movement as a prayer mobilizer, casting vision for collaborative city-wide efforts that demonstrated the love of God, and created public space for witness. He conducts Schools of Prayer, as the foundational piece of transformation. His passion is a church that exists for kingdom purposes, that lives beyond itself, and touches a world near and far. He is President of Alive Ministries: PROJECT PRAY.

11

The Call to Be a Missional Church

Part 1

Jesus was a missionary! His entire life was mission. God wondered, Isaiah 59:16 said, surveying the earth, "that there was no intercessor," no one in the middle, no one standing between heaven and earth as an advocate for dying humanity enslaved by sin, victims of Lucifer's rebellion. Therefore His own arm worked salvation." God Himself came to the earth on a mission. He came to pray—to pray as a man on behalf of men; to confront on every hand sin and Satan; to proclaim the good news of an alternative kingdom; to offer healing for broken hearts; and to release captives and set free those in bondage (Isaiah 61).In effect, to declare the one year Israel never fully observed—"the Year of Jubilee."

That year, to be celebrated every 50 years, once in the lifetime of every generation, was to re-calibrate the social sphere of the entire culture. It cancelled debts, a symbol of sin. It restored lands that had been lost, providing the opportunity for new beginnings. The land was to lay fallow. The entire year was one of celebration and reconciliation, of giving and reordering, of the rich sharing with the poor, the advantaged with the disadvantaged. It leveled the economic playing field with the aim of keeping the nation a single class—not one with rich, land-owning aristocrats that exploited the poor, and not a pauper class of victims and debtor slaves. Such a notion is radical.

So Israel never celebrated a "Year of Jubilee." Thus God, in Christ, came to proclaim it— not as a geopolitical endeavor with the force of the State, but as a spiritual and relational revolution with the force of a servant-hearted and anointed, priestly people.

The mission is still not complete. We have been redeemed and called to the same extreme enterprise. We often see prayer as a personal and private matter, a sweet exercise in the cool of the day that adds value to our lives. In truth, though, prayer immeasurably enriches our personal lives. It is a radical practice. Jesus taught us to pray, *"Thy Kingdom come, Thy will be done on earth as in heaven."* Such a plea for the in-breaking kingdom of God is anything but docile and tame. It is the cry of our hearts to join the mission.

Prayer and mission are bound together. In Jesus, they are incarnated and bound together. Jesus came to the earth to pray—and out of that dependence on the Father, through the communion of the Spirit, he moved to complete God's mission in the earth.

The State of Things

William Van Dusen Wishard observed, "All the major currents of the 20th-century intellectual thought have now dried up. Marxism has collapsed. Socialism is vanishing. Totalitarianism is discredited. Even the French are losing faith in rationalism. Liberalism inspires few hearts and little action ... Modernism has deconstructed. While science continues unabated, few believe that the objectivity of science provides ultimate meaning in life."[5]

If the whole world were a village of 100, there would be 42 radios, 24 televisions, 14 telephones, and 7 computers, but they would not be equally distributed. Only 7 would own an automobile. Five, only five people, would possess 32 percent of the entire village's wealth, all from North America. You would be one of them. The poorest one-third, many in the 10/40 window, almost all non-Christians, would receive only 3 percent of the total income of the village.

Divorce rates have more than doubled since 1960. The teen suicide rate has tripled. Births by unwed mothers have risen from five-percent of all births to 30 percent—and that rate is much higher in cities. The home, meant as a safe haven, has become a brutal place for some children. Sexual and physical abuse rates have tripled in the last 20 years alone. The number of homeless children in the US is now some three-quarters of a million. Some are on the streets all alone, finding the insecure streets safer than "home."[6]

Black families have fared much worse. Black America is in a state of poverty with unabated crime, drugs, and relational disarray. The infant mortality rate among black children is double that in white families and the children who survive are three times more likely to live in single-parent homes. Almost half, 43 percent of black children live in poverty.

"Possibly no other generation of young people in an affluent country has been made so vulnerable to social and psychological risks associated with having parents who are dysfunctional, divorced, or simply disinterested."[7] Sixty-eight percent of children are now born to father-absent homes. Even those born to two-parent homes are usually in double-career households. The relationship between crime and one-parent homes is so strong, no other indicator comes close—neither race nor low income compares as a determining factor. And the absent parent is typically the father.[8]

In the 2000 USA census, 45 million people said the language spoken in their home was something other than English. Some 311 different languages are spoken throughout the USA. 29.1 million speak Spanish, 2 million speak Chinese, 1.2 million Tagalog Filipino, 1 million Vietnamese, 700,000 Russian, and 600,000 Arabic.

Per capita spending for prisons is up 400 percent. In the 1980's, the US spent 30 billion dollars to double the nation's prison capacity. One-million citizens are now behind bars, more than any other nation on the earth. Only South Africa and the former Soviet Union are close.[9] The "lock 'em up!" solution has failed. The prisons are now becoming educational centers for Islam.

Across the nation, there is an escalating hopelessness shared by governors, mayors, police chiefs, and other law enforcement officers. Additional money or even men is not adequate to stop the rising tide of crime and lawlessness. Gangs increase. New drugs appear and new distribution networks spontaneously form. Liberal thinking has assumed that crime is driven by poverty— increase wealth, raise the minimum wage, redistribute wealth and the problem will be solved. And yet, other nations, with deeper poverty pockets than America, do not suffer from the same lawlessness. [10]

James O. Wilson is an expert on the roots of crime. He has scrutinized possible connections between felonious behavior and financial hardship. In three seasons of economic dislocation, he found that crime rates fell, rather than rose as is popularly believed, including the Great Depression. Wilson says crime is not driven by economic considerations. It is not a function of money, but of morality. Crime, he believes, will not abate until faith and values are instilled, character is imparted, and self-restraint is inculcated. Those changes intersect at one juncture—they demand stronger families.[11]

In the last 50 years, economic and social forces have reshaped family function and form. Other forces have been at work as well. Liberals have exacerbated family definition issues and advocated for alternative family forms as being healthy and functionally equivalent to the nuclear family.

The very nature of the family has been transformed. A bit more than a century ago, farm families and semi-rural families were units of production. They worked as a team. They had a mutual purpose—to survive and thrive, to save the farm. Their efforts produced tangible and measurable outcomes. The corn they planted and the livestock they raised were now on their table. The watched the crops grow. They saw hail, wind and water damage. They sat up with a newborn calf, and cried when the family horse died.

The modern family is no longer a unit of production, but one of consumption. The opportunities to invest labor and talent, resulting in team outcome and feeling useful, have been replaced by the opposite dynamic. Now kids petition parents for allowance money, often tied to no social responsibility or contribution to family life. The funds are spent on some material prize or pleasurable moment—usually with friends, not family. Money has become an entitlement rather than a reward for hard work. Independence, rather than, interdependence is the new value. Individualism triumphs over community. The cultural forces pull us apart rather than move us together.[12] The home is now merely a house where things are stored.

Idolatry is not primarily a matter of sacred statues scattered here and there. It is the ideology behind the idol that entraps. American idolatry may be the most potent and subtle form of paganism in history. The material objects are not in the form of idols, but they are more seductive and addictive.

For almost 100 years we have battled secular religions that do not present themselves as religions, but have the same effect. They are world views that shape culture. They guide behavior. They inform values. The unholy trinity against which we struggle is "Enlightenment,

Socialism (Marxism), and Scientism."

Man, in the image of God, though fallen, is called to be a noble creator, guarding and caring for the creation. Now he is seen as "little more than a chance deposit on the surface of the world, carelessly thrown up between two ice ages by the same forces that rust iron and ripen corn, a sentient organism endowed by some happy or unhappy accident with intelligence indeed, but with an intelligence that is conditioned by the very forces it seeks to understand and control. [24]

"Such a view is utterly nihilistic. It spawns expedient values. It engenders existentialism. It offers no motivation to care for self or others. In the community of faith it is birthed as 'the doctrine of instant satisfaction." Richard Foster begins his classic book on *Spiritual Disciplines* with the declaration, "Superficiality is the curse of our age ... the desperate need today is not for a greater number of intelligent people or gifted people, but for deep people." [25]

Buddhist, Hindu and Islamic countries are home to 85 percent of the world's poorest nations. It is the Protestant world that has flourished in the last 500 years. Is that merely a coincidence? The second most prosperous nations are those that are predominately Catholic.[26] Is that a mere coincidence? And yet we are turning our back on the root source of the values that have made us strong, believing that cut flowers can still sustain their beauty and offer their fragrance without a grounding and nurturing root system.

A Single Dimensional Gospel

A great tragedy occurred early in the last century. German theologians had convinced much of Europe, and subsequently Americans, that the miracles of the Bible were not true. Rationalism was in full bloom. The Scriptures were stripped of anything supernatural. There was suddenly no virgin birth, no literal resurrection, no blind eyes opened, and no little boy's lunch phenomenally multiplied. Jesus was celebrated as a great moral teacher, a framer of an incredible ethical system. His values were to be lauded and commended to all. But he was not God.

Half the church clung to the loving principles of Christ and abandoned the mind-boggling miracles. Genesis was allegorical. The credibility of the Bible was doubtful. Sin became failure. Satan was a myth. The blood had only symbolic power. The new birth was merely new resolve. Death remained. Eschatology was cloudy. Hope was confined to how we all chose to treat one another. All that was left of Christianity was the remarkable love of God, now to be translated into loving deeds toward others. It was half the gospel. And it came to be known as "the social gospel." Influential preachers publically backed away from rudimentary and foundational theologies— the virgin birth, the vicarious atonement, the literal resurrection, the second coming. At the same time, the nation was riveted with the Scopes trial on evolution. Conservative Christians reacted and gave birth to the fundamentalist movement.

An additional 6 billion dollars would fund education for every child on the planet, less than 1% of what is spent on global weapons annually.

Half the church, the conservatives, refused to relinquish their grasp of the fundamentals, the core of theological truth. Half the church, the liberals, laid hold of love, began to preach the social gospel, emphasized love and kindness, and gave up on absolute truth, including Biblical truth. Those who came to advocate love and kindness to all, charitable works for the good of mankind as the new work of the church, spurned rigid doctrines.

And those who preached the uncompromised truth did not intend to pollute the purity of their doctrine by being confused with the "good works" crowd. Liberals did good deeds without a call to repentance. They conveyed the message of God's merciful love. He had no special children, did not punish sin (mistakes), and laid no requirement on us for repentance or contrition. Fundamentalists, the conservatives, reacted with doctrine. They strengthened their hold on truth. Salvation was by "faith alone"—and not by works. Not by good deeds. The church had split the gospel. The divide persisted through most of the last century.

When Jesus spoke of salvation to a Jewish audience, they heard the term in the light of the Old Testament framework, which held no division between the material and the spiritual, the individual and the social, or between righteousness as a personal condition and justice in the social sphere. The concept was holistic. Today, our concept of salvation is personal and individualistic, lacking corporate and social implications. It is experiential, without an adequate relational emphasis. It is an event, instead of a journey. It is the one soul, as if he were an island apart from community. It is a call to personal ethics without the corollary injunction to the collective good of the city or nation. It is without the justice dimension almost altogether.

If we persist in preaching a one-dimensional gospel, compartmentalizing faith as a cure for the spirit and soul, excluding our social responsibility for the poor and the oppressed, the imprisoned and those in bondage, we will continue our drift away from the center of the greatest opportunity we have to reengage a disinterested culture. Yet, the move to be a demonstrably compassionate people must be genuine, not merely a posture we assume. This means, that to authentically serve, we must be genuinely transformed from the self-interested faith system we have created.

For Wesley and Whitefield, revival and social reform were companions.[27] Finney, a prominent figure in the second Great Awakening, believed the church was called to advocate both soul and social reform. Out of the Second Great Awakening came an army of young people who advocated for social transformation, including the abolition of slavery.

Some 1,200 passages in the Scriptures deal with the poor, the downtrodden, the oppressed, and those who discriminate against them.[28] The word, *just* or *justice* (*mispat*) occurs more than 400 times in the Old Testament. It means "doing what is right or just." It is often used as the force of a judicial ruling. Another term, sadaq, references the moral and ethical norms that guide just actions. It implies that a just or righteous people act in harmony with such principles. When we do not, injustice occurs.[29]

The Truth Love Divide

"Our society finds truth too strong a medicine to digest undiluted.

In its purest form truth is not a polite tap on the shoulder; it is a howling reproach," declared anchorman Ted Koppel.[30] The gospel is love and truth, not one without the other. A church that preaches truth without love misses the greatest truth of all—that God is love and His love is unconditional. Yet, it is not love, but truth, that "sets us free." It is truth that transforms. It is truth that cures our crooked souls. Love makes the medicine of truth go down. Love is the motivator for change— not guilt, not our wrong, not our bent and fallen condition, but love.

The cross was the love of God revealed. But, it was simultaneously a note of zero tolerance for sin. For, when sin was found "on," not "in" Christ, my sin and your sin, the connection between heaven and earth was momentarily interrupted. "My God, why have you forsaken me?" Jesus in that moment "had become sin," the one "who knew no sin" that we might stand in the righteousness of God. At the cross, God judged sin. He was true to truth. We discovered through the cross that "the wages of sin are death." And yet, we simultaneously saw God's mystifying love in action as He took our judgment on Himself.

The mission is clear. We identify with sin and sinners. We pray "Father, forgive them." We do not dismiss their guilt or the standard they violated. We bend no rules. We honor the holiness of God. Standing stanchly for truth, we love unconditionally. Instead of mastering the tension between love and truth, the church tends to one extreme or the other, offering less than a whole gospel. It preaches truth, but without love. Or, it preaches love, and it muzzles truth lest it offend someone's sensibilities. Who wants truth without love? And who wants love without truth? It is so subtle. The very term *rationalization* suggests the reasonableness of the distortion. It is a half-gospel and the lie is believable. More than a decade ago, the Barna Research group discovered that four out of 10 people who described themselves as "born again" did not believe in absolute truth.[31]

The Long Road Back

Reinhold Niebuhr, a theological moralist, observed, "Nothing that is worth doing can be achieved in our lifetime; there we must be saved by hope. Nothing which is true or beautiful or good makes complete sense in any immediate context of history; therefore we must be saved by faith. Nothing we do, however virtuous, can be accomplished alone; therefore, we are saved by love. No virtuous act is quite as virtuous from the standpoint of our friend or foe as it is from our standpoint. Therefore we must be saved by the final form of love which is forgiveness."[32] The fix will not be easy. It is not just the society that needs to be transformed—the instrument that God uses to fix the culture, the Church, is itself in need of transformation.

The problem is, in part as Richard Neuhaus says, evangelicals play "defensive offense."[33] For example, conservatives continue to react to the 50-year-old battle over the removal of prayer from public school and the war on any public display of faith. The liberals use conservative frustration and powerlessness to further marginalize Christians, and the faith and values they advocate. The problem is partly exacerbated by the misplaced goal of conservatives; namely, merely restoring rights that were lost—prayer in schools, the posting of the Ten Commandments.

The preoccupation with this superficial fix has paralyzed us. It is deeply flawed. Sadly, creativity for public policy, the art of dialogue, the discovery of common ground with community leaders for the good of all, and joint efforts with unbelievers to care for the poor and the marginalized, are not considered. Neuhaus says, "By separating public argument from private belief, by building a wall of strict separatism between faith and reason, fundamentalist religion ratifies and reinforces the conclusions of militant secularism."[34]

And there is a deeper problem. The church not only lacks intellectual respect among the cultural elite and the liberal, it lacks moral credibility. The world recoils at the rebuke of the church with the stinging words, "Physician, heal thyself." The self-serving record of the church, our moral chaos, is constantly paraded by the media in front of the whole culture—embezzlements, fraud, sexual scandals, and gold-plated toys. It is all too much. As someone has said, "If the gospel is to be believable, the church has to be more believable."

The late Dr. Joe Aldrich, a leader in the pastoral prayer movement and president of Multnomah, was fond of saying, "The gospel rides on the back of the transformed church. We don't have the message. We are the message." What we proclaim we must incarnate. Walk and talk must be congruent. We have a problem. And the problem is us. "If the church does not assert custody over the inner life of believers, it cannot hope to assert influence over the outer life of society."[35]

Sadly, as one pastor observed, "Shallow repentance leads to shallow healing."[36] The new birth experience we offer is no longer connected to restitution or, for that matter, deep repentance. There is little godly sorrow. Salvation is a ticket to paradise with an inconsequential notice of past sins as deadly behaviors—they are merely failures. And Christ is the key to abundant life. Salvation is an additive to enrich the life, not a call to die. Repentance without restitution is no repentance at all. Forgiveness without reconciliation is only half the cure, with the relationship still distant and sickness remaining in one or both souls. Love, without the recognition of the truth that has been trampled on, is cheap love, and in the end, no love at all.

The church not only lacks intellectual respect among the cultural elite and the liberal, it lacks moral credibility.

Love without truth is only a wrapping for a lie. It is only in the face of truth's glaring light, a revelation of holiness, that calls me up short, that I am stunned to discover a God that deeply loves me. Gazing compassionately at me over the dead body of His only begotten Son, who was slain for my iniquities, the Father loves. And that love is what we offer a world in transgression. We offer such love in the full light of sin and failures. Our love should be shocking. And yet, it is no endorsement of the behavior. Rather, it is the one thing that empowers the transformation of the behavior. Cheap salvation produces people who cannot love across such moral divides because they never experienced the reach of

God across such a divide to rescue them.

We must cease to view conversion as a terminal event or as a detached "forever" experience. Conversion is not an end, but a beginning. It is a doorway to a whole new way of living. John Stott empathizes with the current plight, "We bewail the world's deteriorating standards ... we criticize its violence, dishonesty, immorality, disregard for human life, and materialistic greed." Despite the deterioration, there is also a record of renewal "through the courageous and sacrificial service by Spirit-led reformers." [37]

If you woke up this morning healthy, be grateful. One million will not survive the week due to some contracted disease or illness for which they have no funds for medical care. Ninety percent of the world would be willing to live in your garage. It is better than the house they now have. If you can read this, consider yourself blessed. Two billion people in the world have never been taught to read at all.

In the late 19th century, urban conditions were deployable. Thousands of abandoned orphans roamed the streets of New York. Infant mortality rates were 10 times those of our day. Prostitutes and opium slaves lined the streets. The transformation of the city was not led by government sources, but by the church. A movement of compassion swept through the city, led by caring Christians, individuals and groups. In a short period of time, 4,500 families were lifted from poverty levels. Sixty thousand children were taken from the streets. Churches served meals and offered basic skills training and lodging, in some cases. Abortion was higher, on a per capita basis than now. It was radically reduced by social, rather than legislative strategies. [38]

In 1881, Paris could have been renamed Sodom or Gomorrah. It was certainly no place for a 21-year-old girl and two teenage companions not initiated to sin and worldly ways. Crime was high. Disease was rampant. Alcoholism was common. And there was a veritable hatred of Christianity. But the 21-year-old Catherine Booth was no pushover. She didn't wait for sinners to come to her. She went to them. She waded into bars and café's to preach. Wearing her bonnet, men would grab it from behind in an attempt to strangle her. When outright rejection of her message and methods didn't seem adequate to dissuade her, cobblestones were hurled at her. She and her little team were both physically and verbally abused. Her tenacity grew, and so did her little Salvation Army band.

Five years into their crusade, 200 of her comrades had been injured, 175 arrested, and one martyred. But Booth never balked. She had preached her first sermon at the age of 14. Her commanding way earned her the nickname, la Capitaine, and soon, la Marechale, the Field Marshall. Eventually, the nation that had first rejected her, would embrace her because of her love for France. Though she was a fierce champion of righteousness, she was simultaneously an advocate for the poor (justice). It was said that she manifested love and respect for every person she met. [39] Could that be said of you? Of your congregation?

Discussion Guide

Big Ideas

- Jesus was a missionary.
- Prayer and mission are bound together.
- The number of homeless children in the USA is now three-quarters of a million.
- Thirty-two percent of all children (one-in-three) are born to unmarried women. In the African-American community, the number is 68%. Where are the fathers?
- James O. Wilson has scrutinized connections between felonious behavior and financial hardship. In seasons of economic dislocation, crime rates fell, rather than rose. Wilson says crime is not a function of money, but of morality. Crime will not abate until faith and values are instilled, and character is imparted - that demands stronger families.

Notable Quotes

- "Possibly no other generation of young people in an affluent country has been made so vulnerable to social and psychological risks associated with having parents who are dysfunctional, divorced, or simply disinterested."
- Idolatry is not primarily a matter of sacred statues scattered here

and there. It is the ideology behind the idol that entraps. American idolatry may be the most potent and subtle form of paganism in history. The material objects are not in the form of idols, but they are more seductive and addictive.

- Richard Foster begins his classic book on Spiritual Disciplines with the declaration, "Superficiality is the curse of our age ... the desperate need today is not for a greater number of intelligent people or gifted people, but for deep people.
- When Jesus spoke of salvation to a Jewish audience, they heard the term in the light of the Old Testament framework, which held no division between the material and the spiritual, the individual and the social, or between righteousness as a personal condition and justice in the social sphere. The concept was holistic.
- "Our society finds truth too strong a medicine to digest undiluted. In its purest form truth is not a polite tap on the shoulder; it is a howling reproach," declared anchorman Ted Koppel.

Questions for Discussion

1. Talk about the "Year of Jubilee" and how the year that Israel never celebrated, would have leveled the social-economic playing field — redemption of lost family lands, debt cancellation, release of prisoners, a Sabbath year of spiritual celebration. Why did Israel never celebrate such a year? Why did Jesus come to proclaim one? And what are the implications for us?
2. The very nature of the family has been transformed. A century ago, families worked as a team. Efforts produced tangible and measurable outcomes. They were a unit of production rather than one of consumption. Can such a team spirit be recaptured?
3. What do you think about the idea that the church—liberal and conservative—split the gospel, the liberals abandoning absolute truth and clinging to love, and by extension, good works; and the conservatives, grasping truth and defending the faith, without an adequate emphasis on compassionate deeds?
4. What is the difference between a faith that emphasizes personal holiness and righteousness, and one that emphasizes social justice? Do we need both?
5. Is the call to care for the poor, the orphan and widow, the outcast and needy, our best opportunity to engage this culture? Are we now preaching a "soul-spirit" gospel that is too narrow? Are our churches consumed more with the needs of members, than the mandate of Christ?

Prayer Box Ministry

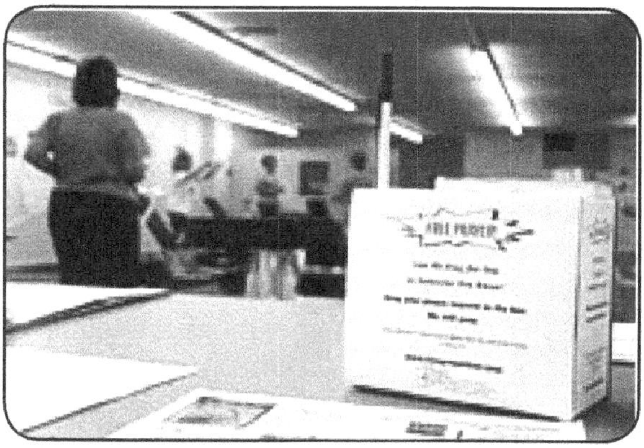

In December 2001, Molly Saunders placed a homemade prayer box in a Hardee's restaurant in Mount Vernon, Ohio. It was a great idea and bit "out there" for most people. She wanted to pray for the needs of customers and employees of the local Hardee's. Soon other Christians who saw the box wanted to put them in other businesses. Molly Saunders and a group of volunteers began to make homemade prayer boxes. In a little more than a hundred days, prayer boxes were in over 100 businesses in Knox County, Ohio. The ministry spread to Charleston, West Virginia, where in a short time, there were over 200 homemade prayer boxes in that city.

A group of Christian businessmen saw the larger vision and arranged for boxes to be produced professionally—pre-cut and printed. Less than a year later, the prayer boxes were in nearly every state in the US and almost 20 nations. To order the boxes in Spanish, go to www.oramosporti.org. Folks in the UK can go to www.freeprayerbox.co.uk. The USA contact is www.freeprayerbox.com.

Businesses are incredibly open to the idea. Prayer requests are harvested at least one time each week. The weekly connection with the business owner is often as powerful as personal connections with people in need, who leave not only their request, but also their contact information. The action of people who take a moment and fill out their need, stuff it back into the box, is a demonstration of hunger for prayer, often by people who don't attend church regularly. Prayer Boxes are in hospital and doctor waiting rooms, a variety of lobbies, cafes and grocery stores, bars and banks.

One pastor dropped by a bar to collect prayer needs by bar patrons that had accumulated over a few days. A man approached him. "Are you the prayer man?" The man was planning to get married. He had no pastor, no church. Now he does.

Marketplace Chaplains

Lee Kelly is a pastor's wife and a member of the Ohio Prayer Commission. And she is also a chaplain to an area corporation. Once a week, she makes a trip to the company location. She is visible and available. She connects with managers and employees. She is on call to talk to any and all, to care, to pray, to share. She is affiliated with Marketplace Chaplains.

Founded in Dallas, Texas, in 1984, the ministry has expanded every year for the past 20 years. It has chaplain affiliates in 44 states and over 850 cities. Some companies have multiple locations and use a diverse group of chaplains at each of their sites. Marketplace Chaplains USA is the longest and largest continuing provider of workplace chaplains to corporate America today. Over 2,400 chaplains serve from California to Massachusetts, providing personal care for over 500,000 employees and family members who work in 65 different industries. Almost one-third of the chaplains are females, many are couples. Almost 700 are minority chaplains. Among some of the clients are the Biltmore, McDonalds, Taco Bell, companies that employ tens of thousands, or only a handful.

Their mission is to "share God's love … in the workplace by an Employee Care Service …" What companies in your area could your church serve by appointing a retired minister or a lay-leader with a heart for ministry? What a way to expand the borders of the church.

The Employee Care Service offers professional training and experienced chaplains to directly serve employees and corporate clients. Each approved chaplain applicant brings extensive experience in caring for people. Technical training, significant care-giving experience, and mature and proven character are essential qualities. The ministry provides specific orientation and training on the issues faced in the workplace, including ethical and legal constraints and how to relate to company management. Training and guidelines to help employees resolve workplace conflicts is also emphasized. Continuing education is also provided.

In addition, each chaplain is supported and supervised by a veteran in chaplaincy and administration. Go to www.mchapusa.com for more information.

12

The Call to Be a Missional Church

Part 2

The City

In the New Testament alone, there are 160 occurrences of the word city. In the Old Testament, the number of mentions is 1,090—a total of some 1,250 times in Scripture. Great Biblical themes are mentioned only a fraction of this total. Some 142 different cities are mentioned. Jerusalem is mentioned the most, accounting for about half of all citations. And 51 times the city of Sodom is mentioned. It is a city that won't go away. God cannot forget it, and he doesn't want us to forget it either. [29] In Genesis 18:20-21, the Lord told Abraham that he was going to Sodom and Gomorrah "*because the cry*" of the city was great. Whose cry? "*I will go down and see whether they have done altogether according to the cry of it, which is come unto me ...*"

God listens to the cries coming from the city—cries of abuse, cries of oppression, cries of victimization, cries of immorality, and cries of injustice. The cries of the city call to Him. And He investigates. Do we hear the cries of the city? And when we do, should we investigate? The word cry (*zaaq*) means to scream from threat or torment. It is a cry of fear and vulnerability, of helplessness and danger. The cities are now crying. They are the mission fields of America, as unreached as the nations on the other side of the earth.

People from 63 different nations were living in the same square mile in Chicago.

Ray Bakke, the urban missionary specialist, discovered people from 63 different nations living in the same square mile in which he resided in Chicago. [30] The world has come to America. More than 100 languages are spoken in most of the public school districts of our largest cities. There are more Jews in the USA than in Israel, more blacks than in any nation in Africa, with the exception of Nigeria. There are more Irish here than in Ireland. We are the third largest Spanish-speaking nation on earth. [31] The second largest Hispanic city in the world is Los Angeles. Miami is the gateway to and from South America. Chicago is the second largest Polish city in the world. Churches are breaking free of homogeneous configurations and becoming multicultural. Times Square church has 120 nations in its pews. Dwight Allen, in Miramar, Florida, has more than 60 nations worshipping there.

Paul did not go to churches—he went to cities. The first stop on the Great Commission journey is the city of Jerusalem. The book of Acts is the story of the early church turning the world upside by evangelizing pagan cities. In Donald Dayton's book, *Discovering An Evangelical Heritage,* he outlines a number of reasons the evangelical church fled the cities.

1. The experience of salvation and the subsequent blessing of God on the poor who had discovered the "good news" resulted in material abundance and created a prosperous middle class unlike anything that had existed in the world's social order before. Sadly, the blessings corrupted the church as they had Israel before. **The church forgot the pit from which they had been dug.** Rather than being transformed, they changed the gospel itself into a missive that justified their comfortable existence and offered them contentment

rather than conviction, **a mission-less gospel lacking the motivational courage that would liberate and rescue others** from the circumstances from which they had been redeemed.

2. The social reformation movements of the 1800's, rising out of the Second Great Awakening, were dealt a blow by the Civil War and World War I. The **church gave up on the idea of a transformed society.**

3. The great social problem of the 1800's was slavery. The church failed to grapple with the problem, and the result was the bloodiest war in American history. After the Civil War, reformation movements narrowed to the personal, rather than the larger social concerns. The crusade for personal righteousness replaced the campaign for societal justice. Temperance movements condemned smoking and drinking, sexual aberrance and gambling. Personal purity was exalted. **An introverted version of faith was set forth,** one that was deeply individualistic.

4. Farms began to dry up. Mechanization and industrialization altered the way men worked. Factories sprang up like mushrooms. Families migrated to towns and cities. Urbanization spawned cities with massive numbers of people. **A new set of challenges emerged for which the church lacked answers.**

5. **The religious character of the Protestant nation was changed** by the huge movement of European and Catholic immigrants at the turn of the last century (1900's). They had no vision of a Protestant nation. It was their forefathers from whom their Protestant forebears had fled. And while it was Protestant Christian tolerance that welcomed them, the character of the nation itself soon changed.

6. Dissident and critical voices attacked the church from within and without. German higher criticism assailed the foundation of the faith, dismissing the Bible as authentic and authoritative. Cultural leaders moved toward the embrace of Enlightenment ideas. Darwin became the rage. Socialism was whispered in some places. The church was no longer "in." Faith and the entire Christian value system was under attack. The rulings on Bible teaching (1948) and prayer in the public schools (1962, 1963) were only the flower on a vine that had been wrapping itself like a python around the culture. **Evangelicals retreated. They adopted a fortress mentality**. They reacted. They defended the gospel. They were singing to the choir but the culture was no longer listening.

7. With the clouds of faith-hostility darkening, the church became obsessed with an escapist eschatology. They would no longer invest in a perishing world. After all, they were leaving. The city was forgotten. The church became an island for retreat from a decaying world. **The certainty of a great falling away replaced the hope for yet one more Great Awakening. The idea of a triumphant church languished. The remnant of the few faithful became a theme.**

8. The pre-civil war church leaders founded colleges that embraced the whole spectrum of learning, including liberal arts. Those eventually became America's premier universities. The post-civil war model was to found Bible colleges that paid little attention to the arts. The field of learning and training narrowed. **The church trained preachers and missionaries, not lawyers and legislators, not civic leaders and governors, not doctors and educators.** Without Bible-based training for secular leadership, radical views were unimpeded. The arts were abandoned altogether, except for their narrow application to worship. The divide between the church and the world expanded. The idea of vocation, other than ministry, as a sacred calling virtually disappeared. The sacred-secular divide was, in fact, aided by the church.

9. **The view of man as a responsible change agent was dealt another blow by an extreme emphasis on the sovereignty of God.** A poor man is poor by the will of God, as is a slave. A rich man is rich because of the sovereign favor and blessing of God. Let them both be! Accept God's management of the world. Let Him be sovereign. Man can do nothing to change the world. If God wants it changed, He alone must and will do it.

10. **A revisionist history began to emerge** without the emphasis in the messages of Finney and Moody, or others that had called for social reform as a part of their revival message. Heart messages were acceptable. Social action messages were scripted out. [32]

Add to these shifts, the national mood. The Scopes trial was one which the fundamentalists both won and lost. Suddenly Bible believers were, in the public view, archaic and uneducated buffoons, holding onto the thin air of faith in the face of hard evolutionary evidence. Almost simultaneously, in reaction to the urban explosion of immigrants and the face of the changing cities, evangelicals began a migration to the edges of the metropolises. They gave birth to the suburbs. The unreached people, the hurting and the hopeless, were left in the cities. The evangelicals created a new world for themselves with a safe boundary.

In 1800, 97 percent of global population was concentrated in rural areas with only three percent in cities. By 1900, the number had risen to five percent. But in the next 100 years, the number rose to 47 percent. In 1950, around the world, 83 cities had a population exceeding one million.

In 2007, the number of cities above a million residents approached 500 (468). The global urban population is now at 3.2 billion, and in the next 20 years will rise to five billion. To reach the world, we must reach the cities. Evangelicals are not in the city! They avoid the city.

91.4 percent of all evangelicals live outside the cities of 1,000,000 or more.

Some 91.4 percent of all evangelicals live outside the cities of 1,000,000 or more. [33] The term civilization is drawn from civic, inferring city, because in ancient times, the more civil and refined people lived in the city. The country-folk were more common, less cultured and refined. Today, the inner cities are known for anything but elegance and education. They are the wild and untamed America. We are dying at the center.

Had evangelicals escaped the corrupting city to create a launching pad for mission into the city, there might be a reason to rejoice. Instead, they became indifferent, as if the inner city, were a different world, on the other side of the planet. Pleasure oriented and materialistic, they embraced the good life with the impoverished poor on the other side of town. But they couldn't escape. Their teens listened to the same music, experimented with the same drugs, drank alcohol, and also had their first sexual experience far too young. By the age of 18, 57 percent of US teens have had their first sexual experience. [34] The TV, their cultural mentor, was on five hours a day, piping the same distorted values into the suburbs that it sent to the projects. The father, absent in the inner city, was emotionally absent in the suburbs, engaging in eye contact with any of his children no more than three minutes a day on the average.

This was the good life. In truth, it was only a veneer. The evil in the inner city is plain for all to see. The disorder there is visible in broken windows and graffiti. It is audible in the sound of gunfire. The back alleys reek of uncollected garbage. The streets are lined with teens looking for action far too late in the night, and with the homeless looking for a shelter for sleep for a few hours. But in the suburbs with the neat lawns and well-kept houses, evil is hidden. It is stealth. [35]

What is the nature of your city—industrial/manufacturing, educational, medical (human services), convention city, transportation center (airport, rail-center, port, interstate hub), banking or economy, a government city (county or state—a ruling city), a judicial center, a pleasure-leisure city (theater, athletic), a river town, a railroad town, a seaside town, a valley-town, a bedroom community?

Washington may be the political capitol of the USA, but New York is the economic capital. Hollywood is the cultural capital—good or bad. Nashville is the music capital. Miami is the gateway to South America, as are West Coast cities to the Far East. Every city has a profile. Cities have purposes, but we rarely even notice. We should. Cities rule the earth, not nations. Trends, ideas, pop slogans, fads, movements are all born in cities. The flash point for change is the city. They control the distribution of power and wealth, material resources, and cultural trends. And today, those trends can go viral very quickly.

In the 1930's, the New Deal forced government solutions onto people in the Great Depression. In the 1960's, the Great Society programs took social intervention to a new level. Money was the answer to povert, but the programs failed. Government compassion, social engineering, a guaranteed entitlement, the State with all of its weight and wealth cannot touch the roots of moral and social disorder in our cities— those are issues of the soul.

"For decades, most academics, journalists, and policy experts ignored or dismissed the role of religion in solving social problems. Health care and social work professionals were taught to be morally neutral and "objective," and to see a spiritual dimension in their work as inappropriate for professional care. Secular foundations and government insisted that for Christian social service agencies to receive funding, they would have to water down or abandon the explicitly religious aspects of their work."[36]

That situation is now beginning to change. The late Senator Daniel Moynihan, speaking to Harvard about the American cultural meltdown, declared plainly, "We do not have a clue!" Glenn Loury, Boston University professor, calls our dilemma "a disease of the soul for which a more powerful balm than money will be required ... Through our government, our churches and our civil society, we must— all of us—be in relationship with them ... The point here transcends politics and policy. It is a spiritual point of the highest order."[37]

The late Senator Daniel Moynihan, speaking to Harvard about the American cultural meltdown, declared plainly, "We do not have a clue!"

By the end of the century, it was becoming clear to even liberal elite, the morally neutral cultural experiment had failed. The evidence is in failing schools, reading and math scores plummeting, inner city violence, family dissolution, abortion and child abandonment rates, unrelenting poverty of body and soul. In the face of secular and government failures, evidence began to surface about successful programs with fewer funds and smaller staffs, but soaring success rates—Teen Challenge, Prison Fellowship, inner city rescue efforts. The evidence suggests that holistic approaches succeed when secular approaches fail. People need faith. Still, liberals resist the notion of partnerships with faith-based organizations, despite a Pew Charitable Trust survey that indicates that 75 percent of Americans favor such partnerships, even if federal dollars are used. [38]

The Self-serving Church

"A feeble nominal Christianity is the greatest obstacle to the conversion of the world."[39] Church historians have observed that in the 18th century "truth" died. In the 19th century "God" died. And in the 20th century "man" died. [40] Russell Kirk observed that "the inner order of the soul and the outer order of society" are intimately linked. "If our souls are disordered, we fall into abnormality, unable to control our impulses. If our commonwealth is disordered, we fall into anarchy."[41] Faith and culture are as inseparable as the two different sides of a coin. T. S. Eliot observed, "What we call culture, and what we call religion of a people are not different aspects of the same thing; the culture being, essentially, the incarnation of the religion of a people." [42]

The salvation of the culture is in the salvation of the church. The destiny of the city is in its congregations. Few parishioners see this. They have a narrow view of the church as irrelevant to the economic or employment dynamics of the city, its civic policies or its crime problems, with the exception of feeble whimpered prayers. This is the result of the reductionist view of the gospel as primarily or exclusively soul care.

Worldwide, Christian churches spend more than 85% of their resources on themselves. Less than 15% goes to outreach, evangelism, or mission causes. In the USA, 95% goes to home-based ministry, 4.5% to cross-cultural efforts in already-reached people groups, and only 0.5% to reach the unreached.

In one survey, 80 percent of people believed that Jesus spent time with the poor? Are they right? If so, should that be the custom of His followers? In the same survey, only one percent said they themselves spent time with the poor. Mother Teresa was once asked, "How did you receive your call to serve the poor?" Her answer must have shocked the listener. "My call is not to serve the poor. My call is to follow Jesus. I have followed Him to the poor."[43] If we are following Jesus, will He lead us to the hurting? If we are not serving them now, can we say we are following Jesus?

We want to be part of a church that does what we, the members, do not have to do. We want a reputation for compassion, without the requirement that we be compassionate; for sacrifice and devotion, while we continue the good life, unimpeded. The notion is clearly irrational to everyone but the church itself.[44] Jude spoke of rootless trees— they wanted the option of a mobile life without the obligatory stationary root system. No such tree exists. Christians today want the benefits of living in a moral and caring world, without the inconvenience of sacrificial and godly living themselves. They want a church they can count on, without having to be present to be counted each week. One that is community involved, but without their necessary night at the rescue mission.

Such a state is contradictory and illusionary.

John Stott observes, "It is a strange, rather tragic, and disturbing paradox. On the one hand, in many parts of the world, the church is growing by leaps and bounds. But on the other hand, throughout the church, superficiality is everywhere. That's the paradox. Growth without depth ... superficial discipleship."[45] Siang-Yang Tan, in his book, is plain spoken describing "self-serve Christianity" as equivalent to primary narcissism, old-fashioned self-centeredness, pride, and character weakness. [46] Tan asks, "What would happen if the church today recovered Jesus' pattern of humble service? ... The answer is clear: The world would stop to watch— and be changed." Tan believes that "Christianity as servant-hood" is the key to transformation, but it also demands leaders and pastors who truly become servants themselves. [47]

We have come to focus almost exclusively on the moment of conversion—the approach to and the experience of "the new birth"—with little focus thereafter. Wesley's objective was beyond conversion, aimed at the formation of genuine followers of Christ. He concentrated on the season following conversion. He formed bands of Christ-followers who together pursued the practice of godliness. It is said that he "organized to beat the devil."[48] His goal was not converts, but saints. The distinctive of Wesley was an emphasis on community and action. Wesley dismissed "solitary religion" and secret Christians in favor of his societies. And he dismissed faith without works. Faith was alive for Wesley; it was evidentiary. [49] For Wesley, a soteriology (salvation) detached from ecclesiology (the church) was neither balanced nor Biblical. [50]

In a seminary class on "Church and Society" I was introduced to the plight of migrant workers in California's San Joaquin Valley. Their living quarters were unthinkable. Their labor in the season of harvest was relentless. On the eve of their pay, in some cases, the border patrol would round them up and haul them back to Mexico. The practice is ancient. James, the brother of Jesus warned, "*Look! The wages you failed to pay the workmen who mowed your fields are crying out against you. The cries of the harvesters have reached the ears of the Lord Almighty,"* James 5:4.

In another experience, students were asked to "take the plunge."

Go to the mission. Stand in the soup line. Panhandle. Wade into the sea of homeless folk. Kids from suburban settings who spend a week in the inner city see poverty up close; they hear the stories; they eat dinner with the neighbors in the 'hood; and often have an epiphany that may change them forever. We have erected invisible walls that prevent our connection with the poor, with people in pain. A Haitian proverb declares, "We see from where we stand." [51]

The Way Out

Carl Dudley in his book, Energizing the Congregations: Images that Shape Your Congregation's Ministry, sets forth "Five Congregational Self-Images." [52]

1. The **PILLAR** church is ***filled with community leaders, anchors, pillars***—good citizens who have a rich heritage of civic activity. They are deeply community sensitive and tend to have access to power.
2. The **PILGRIM** church is an ***indigenous*** church—Haitians, Jamaicans, Koreans, etc. When these people migrate, they are there to offer them a church home. Their reach is typically restricted to their ethnic profile. The church is a cultural repository. They do things "the back-home" way.
3. The **SURVIVOR** church is ***a congregation in crisis.*** They react, rather than act. Their goal is to hold on. They are tenacious, but not usually creative. They passively persevere, rather than proactively do the daring and transformational.
4. The **PROPHET** church ***stands against the world***. In the larger sense, it, too, is a "survivor" church, not with a focus on internal issues, but on social-cultural-moral issues. It may stand down the mayor or the school board. It is offended when "truth" has been violated. It may work for social reform by creating a fire storm of protest by "proclaiming" rather than incarnating.
5. The **SERVANT** church is concerned about the same issues as the "prophet" church, but it ***approaches the problems incarnationally*** by wading into the difficulty and attempting to make a difference from the inside. It operates on the "priestly" continuum. It sees the same truth that the "prophet" church sees, but connects with the community on the continuum of love, waiting for the moment to speak "truth in love." The "pillar" church is consumed with the high end of the city—budgets, power, parks, schools, political is-

sues, and processes. The "pilgrim" church lives in an ethnic enclave. The "survivor" church is self-concerned about its own little existence. The "prophet" church is issue driven. The "servant" church finds individuals and cultural slices of pain, and seeks solutions. It is pastoral in its approach.[53]

A holistic congregation integrates evangelism and discipleship with social action ministry. It demonstrates the gospel as it proclaims it. It cares about the poor, the disenfranchised and disempowered, those in prison and their families, those oppressed by the social and political system, by the economy or ethnic status, or by the devil himself. Such a church is a liberation community. Ministry is relational and long-term. They grow by growing people. They see mission as something near and far.[54]

Here are some important questions.

1. Are your evangelism eggs all in one basket?
2. Are your best prospects confined to the unchurched in your member's relational networks?
3. Is your evangelism essentially "words" or does it also have an action component? Do you demonstrate the love of God?
4. Do you engage in prayer or care activities that bring your members into contact with the poor and the hurting?
5. Do you have a model that encourages members to build relationships with the lost, or is witnessing typically an event?
6. Do you have an identified harvest field—an ethnic group? the six blocks around your church? the teens that attend the school next door? the three bars in a square mile of your church? the police or firemen? some geographic or cultural slice of the city to which God has called you to make a difference?
7. Does evangelism happen only though your church programs? Or are your members spontaneously soul winners?
8. Does your church have an evangelistic outreach plan? Does it offer regular evangelism training?
9. Is evangelism the task of a small group of zealous soul winners or the responsibility of the whole church? Does the whole church know that? Do they assume that duty?
10. Are your evangelism methods tract-based, confrontational, ma-

nipulative dialogue (Evangelism Explosion type approaches), fear-based, door-to-door, cold-turkey calls? In other words, are they dated and irrelevant to this culture?

Ray Bakke says that 90 percent of the barriers to effective ministry are not in the city—they are in our congregations.[55] We tend to feel that in a large city our response needs to be large and city-encompassing. Urban missiologists are discovering the exact opposite to be the more effective strategy. Instead of broad-casting the larger and more diverse city, the more you need to narrow-cast. The more impersonal the city becomes, the more relational your evangelism approach must be. The formula has been: big cities demand big meetings and big strategies. In truth, big cities demand micro, rather than macro, applications.[56]

Sociologist David Brooks has noted that the Pentecostal movement was the most significant social movement of the 20th century.[57] This is a fact ignored by America's mainstream media as well as the middle and upper class, not to mention the cultural elite. Yet, the Pentecostal movement has, in the space of a century, swept the planet offering a heartfelt, personal relationship with a God who cares and whose power delivers. When other movements have fled the inner cities, stubborn Pentecostal missions have remained, pulling people from the fire! They are an exit ramp from hopelessness.

These churches are often led by a bi-vocational pastor without a formal theological education, and sometimes by a lay-preacher. Eighty-five percent of the characters in the Bible are not clergy but laity.[58] Without the credentials of ministry, these grass roots leaders are street smart, worldly wise, with a bulldog tenacity. What they lack in polish, they find through the power of prayer. The missions they lead are half treatment and half faith-based recovery centers. Low on formal liturgy, they are passionate over God's personal concern for the sinner. Compassion is coupled with a confrontational, no-nonsense approach. They are tough and tender, and they are often the difference between life and death for the folks who attend their mission.

Eighty-five percent of the characters in the Bible are not clergy but laity.

We are in an age of copycat, cookie-cutter churches. We allow too little to be creatively birthed by the Spirit. Most programs are imported and adopted. If we know anything about God's work, we find it infinitely diverse. No two mountains are the same. The earth is rich with variety in landscapes, elevations, and multiple climates, not to mention birds and beast, flora and rocks. The mission of your church is locked up in the unique passion and callings of its constituents, and the aggregate gift pool. Identify the unique corporate character of your congregation.

Know who Christ is but know who you have been created to be in Him and for Him. Second, study the community around you. Know the needs. They are avenues to demonstrate the love and care of God. You are equipped to minister uniquely to some community need. Gifts and resources meet needs at the intersection of mission opportunities. Cultivate, prayerfully, ministry vision and mission. "*Look, see the harvest!*" Jesus continually urges, "*Then, pray that the Lord of the harvest would send forth ...*" Literally, that He would "*thrust out*" laborers. This is a forceful word. The mission is never driven by need—the needs and wounds around us cannot dictate our mission. We are compelled by the Spirit. Merely reacting to need is further averted by moving not from vision and mission to tactical deployment, but rather by taking time to develop a long-term, multi-layered, and often multi-year strategic plan. That will mean studying the hurdle to holistic ministry inside and outside, developing alternative plans, lining up the tactical programs to reinforce one another, and translating single action programs into an interdependent strategic process.

Remember, tactical expressions of ministry can be random but holistic ministry demands an incarnational approach. That requires you are true to Christ and a unique expression of His body, to yourself, and to your own gift-mix and congregational calling. Imitations are out. Authenticity is in. Don't start with needs. Start with signs of hope. The needs are overwhelming. Where is God working? Where is there apparent hunger to escape some prison of despair? In Mumbai, India, Youth With A Mission (YWAM) and Teen Challenge are working with the children of prostitutes. At the Teen Challenge center, the children turn their faces to heaven and lift their hands to give God praise. Their mothers may still work the streets, but the children are a sign of hope.[59]

Stories

In his book, *Spotting the Sacred,* Bruce Main tells the story of Rudy. Lynne, his high school teacher, was always obliging when he asked, almost daily, "Miss Lynne, do you have any of those crackers left?" She would dig out a pack, assuming he wanted to add them to his soup for lunch. She became curious. She discovered that Rudy's mother left the house every morning at sun up for a grueling labor job. Rudy, as the oldest, had to get his brothers and sisters up and out the door for school. There was little food in the house and at times the family was without electricity, even though one of the children required the use of an electric respirator due to a severe asthmatic condition. Rudy, the happy kid—the one with good grades, always smiling, extremely courteous—was hungry and living in poverty!

Impoverished kids are sometimes disguised in designer jeans, wearing high-dollar sneakers. Their parents have provided the disguise to help them avoid the stigma of being called poor. [60] The cultural pressures to be cool, to possess the symbols of being "with it," and thereby granted "insider" status by peers is unrelenting, inescapable, and quietly brutal. The images are everywhere.

What do you do in the face of the darkness? How do you start? Helen Cole is a nun! Her home is Camden, New Jersey, rated by some as the most dangerous city in America. Per capita, the city boasts of more murders, rapes, aggravated assaults and violent crimes than places like Detroit, East St. Louis, New York City, or Los Angeles. In one of the most notorious neighborhoods is Sister Helen. She is among the suffering poor, the broken, trying to make a difference. She meets people on the streets, takes their hands, and offers prayer with a blessing. "Give me your pain. Put it in my hands. Let it go!" she tells them. She calls it companioning. Wherever there is crime and pain, you will find Sister Helen sprinkling holy water, lighting a candle, saying a prayer, and sanctifying the defiled ground, asking God to make it holy. [61] For Catholics and Pentecostals, Sister Helen's practice of applying holy water to blood-stained sidewalks seems eccentric. But, for Sister Helen, her public prayer practices are more than symbolic.

What would happen in your city, if after, or even in the face of tragedy, some group of brave and humble intercessors went to the site, and prayed passionately that light would come into the darkness, that the land would be redeemed, and then obeyed the gentle prompting of the Spirit? Our current practice is to hear of violence in a part of the city removed from us, and barely shrug our shoulders with a disinterested "that's too bad!" disposition. We don't weep with those who weep. We don't comfort those who mourn. We genuinely hope someone else will! We hope they are not alone! We don't wish them evil. We simply won't change the rhythm and practice of our lives. So the dark deeds continue, and they inch slowly toward us and our safe enclave. On our doorsteps, we must act. But if we wait to save only ourselves, we may find that we have waited too late.

Discussion Guide

Big Ideas

- In the New Testament alone, there are 160 occurrences of the word *city*. In the Old Testament, the total is 1,090. Some 142 different cities are mentioned. Jerusalem accounts for half of all citations. And 51 times the city of Sodom is mentioned.
- Ten reasons the church fled the cities. Review the ideas. Discuss them.
- Cities have personalities and purposes. What is the nature of your city? What drives the economy? What makes the city tick?
- Seventy-five percent of Americans favor faith-based partnerships on social issues, even if federal money is used.
- Consider the need to "Study the City!" Know your harvest field.

Notable Quotes

- Some 91.4 percent of all evangelicals live outside the cities of 1,000,000 or more.
- "For decades, most academics, journalists, and policy experts ignored or dismissed the role of religion in solving social problems.

Health care and social work professionals were taught to be morally neutral and "objective," and to see a spiritual dimension in their work as inappropriate for professional care. Secular foundations and government insisted that for Christian social service agencies to receive funding, they would have to water down or abandon the explicitly religious aspects of their work." That situation is now beginning to change.

- The late Senator Daniel Moynihan, speaking to Harvard about the American cultural meltdown, declared plainly, "We do not have a clue!"
- Glenn Loury, Boston University professor, calls our dilemma "a disease of the soul for which a more powerful balm than money will be required ... Through our government, our churches, and our civil society, we must—all of us—be in relationship with them ... The point here transcends politics and policy. It is a spiritual point of the highest order."
- "A feeble nominal Christianity is the greatest obstacle to the conversion of the world."
- Take a look at the 10 questions related to being a holistic church.

Questions for Discussion

1. God heard cries coming from the city. Can you hear them? Do you think we are deaf to the cries? Should we hear them? What do they sound like? And hearing them, what should we do?
2. The nations have come to America. We can now evangelize the world, here and now. What nations live near you? How could you reach them?
3. Discuss Kirk's idea—the inner order of the soul and the outer order of society are intimately linked. Agree or disagree? If you agree, what does this do to the popular notion that what someone—politician or preacher —does in their private life should not be a deciding public factor? If you disagree, then what is the point of private ethics? Can a person really be so duplicitous? Does this not cancel the concept of sin's wages, of sin as social leaven?
4. What kind of congregation are you—Pillar, Pilgrim, Survivor, Prophet, or Servant?
5. Ray Bakke says 90 percent of the barriers to evangelism are in the church. Can you identify the barriers you struggle with?

ADDENDUM

101 Ways You Can Feed the Hungry and Help the Poor

by Diana Lewis

Missions Ministries Teams
Arkansas Baptist State Convention

Pray and Remember

1. Pray, first of all, for God to show you any attitudes about the poor that need adjusting.

2. Pray for the poor of the world.

3. Pray for the poor of the United States.

4. Pray for the poor near you. Yes, here, too. Find out how many low income people are in your area.

5. Billy Graham said, "Heaven is full of answers to prayer for which no one ever bothered to ask." Pray for God to bring people out of poverty.

6. Remembering the quote from #5, pray for God to open the heart of your church to the poor.

7. Remember God's grace extended to you when you work with those in need.

8. Remember when you see someone in need how great the Father's love is for them.

9. Remember to see the potential for a new creation in every person you see.

10. Prayer walk a needy area of your town/county. Don't know where to go? Call your local Department of Human Services office and they can tell you where the poorest areas are.

Look and Impact Your Area

11. Look at your community with fresh eyes. Where are the needs? What do you see, hear, smell, touch?

12. Do a community needs assessment to really look at some of the greatest needs in your area.

13. Give out Bibles in your area through all kinds of businesses and organizations.

14. Sponsor a yard sale, with the proceeds going to a poverty ministry.

Examine Your Church's Present Resources

15. Think about the vehicles your church has: Could they be used to help transport needy people to appointments, interviews, outings and to church?

16. Think about the senior adult or youth trips that your church takes. Could a free scholarship be offered to an unchurched needy senior or youth each time?

17. Think of your kids' summer camp outings. Could a needy kid or two get to go every summer with your kids? Think of the impact on their life.

18. Think of all your regular weekly activities for children and youth. Could you bring in unchurched kids for choir, mission activities, other special activities?

19. Does your church have Mother's Day Out? Is there a way a scholarship could be provided occasionally for a low income mother to have a day off?

20. Does your church serve a Wednesday night meal? Are there needy people that could be brought in to that and then they also will experience Bible study and fellowship with believers? Could your leftovers after a meal be sent to a shelter or other ministry?

21. Does your church have parents' night out or parenting seminars? Invite the community to come to these.

Get Out Into the Community

22. Do a door to door survey. Find out about people in a needy part of town- a mobile home park, or other low income area.

23. Survey and ask "What are some of the needs of people in this neighborhood?" Value their comments. They know the area better than we do.

24. Go door to door and simply ask, "How can we pray for you or your family?" This will open doors of opportunity for your church.

25. Offer to pick people up for church and take them home.

26. Sponsor a block party in a needy part of town. Get to know the people and let them get to know your church.

Hunger Ministries

27. Read up about hunger in the United States and then look around for it where you live.

28. Get your church involved in observing World Hunger Sunday every year.

29. Host a carnival, meal, or gather change for world hunger.

30. Check with your school and see if it has the Food 4 Kids program offered by Rice Depot. If not, call Rice Depot at 501.565.8855 and find out what is involved in getting this free service into your schools that helps send food home with needy kids in backpacks.

31. Collect food items that are needed most for an existing food pantry.

32. Volunteer to go help sort and bag food for them.

33. Ask your pastor or church staff if you could fix little bags of non perishable, easy to open food for them to keep on hand in the church office (peanut butter crackers, pop top fruit cans, juice boxes, peanuts, oatmeal cookies, other items that don't have to be cooked).
34. Buy fast food gift certificates to give out to people you see who need a meal.
35. Start a pantry in your church.
36. Fix sack lunches for needy kids in the summer or senior adults for the weekend.
37. Deliver meals on wheels to seniors. Churches can go in together and divide up the days.
38. Serve a hot meal once a week for the needy in your town.

Housing and Other Home Ministries

39. Join Habitat for Humanity and help build houses for needy families.
40. Volunteer to paint the home of a needy person (call DHS or a home health agency for a name).
41. Do yard work: rake leaves, trim limbs, clean up yard of a needy person.
42. Mow the grass for a needy person who is elderly or disabled.
43. Build a ramp for a needy person.
44. Teach basic home repairs (fixing a leaky faucet, a toilet, a roof leak, etc.)
45. Volunteer to clean house for someone.

Children's Ministries

46. Provide funds so a needy kid can go on a school outing.
47. Provide self-esteem programs for children.
48. Teach goal setting.
49. Provide a place for kids and youth to play basketball or soccer in a low income area.
50. Build a park or prayer garden in a low income area.
51. Get permission from the school to eat lunch with kids who don't have a parent ever come.
52. Be a volunteer babysitter for a teen mom finishing school.
53. Donate infant and children's car seats to those who can't afford to buy them.
54. Donate band instruments to your school for low income kids.
55. Host a party at your local Head Start center.
56. Donate coats, gloves, lice shampoo and other needs to your local school.
57. Offer a free scholarship so a needy kid can take art, music or gymnastics classes.
58. Provide affordable, quality child care.
59. Sponsor a wholesome, fun movie night for kids in an apartment complex outside.
60. Be a big brother, big sister, a mentor for a kid.
61. Provide after school activities for kids.

Employment Ministries

62. Call Employment Security office or a Community Action Agency in your county and ask if they need business clothing, shoes, jewelry for women getting job training.

63. Start a job search/help wanted matching service.

64. Provide transportation for low income people to get to job appointments/interviews.

65. Be a mentor to someone out of work.

66. Start a Christian Women's Job Corps and/or Christian Men's Job Corps in your association.

67. Provide classes on how to get a job and keep a job.

68. Teach life skills and goal setting to adults who need a job.

Senior Adults

69. Involve your children and youth in sending cards to nursing home residents.

70. Get floral shops to give you flowers they are getting rid of & deliver to home bound seniors or nursing home residents.

71. Have a senior adult VBS in a nursing home or senior adult housing area.

72. Call your local home health agency and find out who needs a visit that never has company?

73. Fix an extra meal for seniors who live alone and deliver it for the weekend.

74. Find a way to help seniors buy part of their medicines. Any little bit helps.

75. Help seniors change light bulbs, take down their curtains to wash, etc.

76. Make a phone call to an unchurched senior every week.

77. Donate fans for the summer heat for needy seniors.

78. Build a ramp/rail for a senior.

79. Help them write letters, write out bills.

Homeless Ministries

80. Call your local homeless shelters, domestic abuse shelters and find out what kinds of programs they could use.

81. Call and find out what they need donated: washcloths, shower caps, shampoo, underwear, whatever their greatest need might be.

Literacy Missions

82. Start an English as a 2nd Language ministry.

83. Get trained in Adult Reading and Writing ministry.

84. Start an after school Tutoring Children & Youth ministry.

85. Gather school supplies, prizes, flashcards, learning games for a tutoring ministry.

Health Care Ministries

86. Provide free health screenings at your local church.

87. Start a free medical/dental clinic with the churches of your area.

88. Donate used medical equipment (walkers, wheelchairs, shower chairs, etc.).

89. Donate old reading glasses to an organization that works with low income people.

Migrant Ministries

90. Take bottles of water out to the fields where migrants are working.
91. Have a "Cottonpatch" VBS for the migrant children out by the fields where parents are working.
92. Donate gloves, warm shirts in the winter.

Other Ministries

93. Offer free haircuts.
94. Offer parenting training.
95. Fix the cars, do oil changes for needy people.
96. Donate furniture.
97. Sew unusual sizes of clothing for clothing ministries.
98. Donate your good used shoes and clothing.
99. Donate maternity clothes and baby items to a local Pregnancy Care Center.
100. Go on a mission trip nearby.
101. GO!

Resources

Seasonal Serves

- **January**—Give away hot coffee at an area where such a service would be appreciated.
- **February**—Give valentines to single moms and widows.
- **March**—Put up a "Free Prayer!" booth at a Flea Market or public venue.
- **April**—Help Seniors clean up their lawns. Tackle an inner city block.
- **May**—Plan a series of neighbor-based block parties. Do one at the church. Invite the neighbors. Put up inflatables. Offer free services.
- **June**—Do park ministry: puppets, fly kites, create competitions and give-away prizes. Cook hot dogs. Don't go to suburban parks. Go to inner city parks.
- **July**—Hold a patriotic party. Invite the mayor and congressmen. Adopt a city-impact project.
- **August**—Give away bottles of cold water.
- **September**—Have a back-to-school outreach.
- **October**—Go rake leaves. Help the seniors and widows with fall clean-up. Some may need winterization assistance at their homes.
- **November**—Do a thanksgiving outreach.
- **December**—Run a "tree lot" for the poor. Put the word out to other churches: Christmas trees at cost for qualifying families. Be sure to have a prayer team on the site.

Other ideas

- **Create a Call List**—and check on widows at least once a month. Have ministry crews ready to assist with their needs: house repairs, chores, general assistance, cleaning, and more. Take time to visit. Invite them to some event. Get them out of the house for dinner. Expose them to young children and youth. Send flowers.

- **Adopt an Inner City Block**—in a depressed area. Pick an area that is showing some signs of neglect. Pick up trash. Mow lawns. Sponsoring a "clean team" is a way of seizing the opportunity to talk about righteousness.

- **Start a Chow Crew**—Both men and some women still love to cook. Think about all the opportunities to share prepared food—families in bereavement, shut-ins, surgical recovery patients, special events, community activities. Set up a grill near the projects and flip burgers. Feed the prostitutes. Cook hotdogs for the kids. It may be the best meal they have had in days.
- **Set up a Car Clinic**—for the poor, the widows, single-moms, the elderly, and the disadvantaged. Change the oil and the filter. Check belts. Check other fluids. Do minor repairs. Fix windshield wipers. Replace batteries. Have refreshments for your "customers." Treat them with dignity.
- **Have a "Style Day"**"—free manicures, pedicures, haircuts, and hair-dos for the single mom for whom such a treat is off the budget chart. Throw in a fashion show. Make it a first-class event. Self-esteem is often a major need when you are down financially.
- Transform single men and youth into a **volunteer "Break-down" crew.** Offer their services at community events. The fellowship is great. The service is a ministry and testimony to the community. You teach the value of service. You open doors into the community. It's a win-win.
- **Reach out to students**—at nearby college or university campuses. Honor the annual **Collegiate Day of Prayer**. Set up a "prayer tent." Start a Bible study. Find international students and invite them for a cultural and faith exchange evening. Start a student assistance ministry—some don't have cars. Many, surprisingly, are short of funds and sometimes need basic supplies. Others are lonely. Many went to church at home, but here will detach from faith and church.
- **Create a prayer team**—for your local school.
- **Volunteer to serve**—in the library in a reading program.
- **Create a prayer team**—for your mayor.
- **Care for the homeless**—You may be surprised to discover, even in small communities, pockets of occasionally homeless people, including children. These are not always the classic and chronically homeless. Sometimes they are a mother forced out of a home, trying to scrap together a few dollars for the next apartment, but for now, living out of a car.

- **Start a Code-Red team**—Have a small, trained group of people who respond to fires, accidents, and in some cases, police calls. Arrange for motel vouchers for families forced out of their homes due to a fire or emergency. Offer food coupons, blankets, and basic necessity packets. Find out if the local police have a chaplaincy component. If not, volunteer. If they do, work with them.
- **Do Backpack Give-aways** at the beginning of the school year.
- **Start a "Moving Service"** for the poor.
- **Put the word out to police and fire**, to the medical community and others if a family in crisis does not have a pastor or church, you are willing to service.
- **Volunteer to do free funerals** for folks without a church home.
- **Join the community team**—don't reinvent the wheel. Don't compete. Find out what is already happening in your community and join the existing effort. Then, plug the holes.
- **Drive the Drunks**— offer to be available when the bars close from midnight to 2:00 AM, and drive the drunks safely home. What a great ministry to men who are often depressed, coping, numbing their pain.
- **Build bridges to the girls at the strip clubs**—give them flowers, candy, and offer unconditional love. It shocks them. Many would like to flee that life, but have no idea what would happen if they walked into a church, or if in that church, it was discovered they were fresh from club life. Establish relationships that say, "If you ever want out, we care." Typically, they are already convicted. They need a way out, encouragement, and new friends.

Resource Organizations

Operation Compassion—www.operationcompassion.org

Out of 1.4 million USA charities, Operation Compassion is among the largest. From a pool of America's 200 largest charities, Operation Compassion, for the second consecutive time, is number one in efficiency, with 100% of expenses going to global programs. In another ranking, Operation Compassion was listed as number 17 in non-profits in the world, behind such giants as Food for the Poor, Feed the Children, AmeriCares Foundation, and World Vision. Many of those non-profits have been allies of Operation Compassion's network.

Wherever compassion is needed, the ministry is on the ground with its teams or in the background providing logistical support and supplies.

Project Pray

www.projectpray.org

Project Pray is an outreach of Alive Ministries. For almost two decades, the organization has been involved in Schools of Prayer, prayer summits, city envisioning and leadership training. "Prayer," founder P. Douglas Small says, "is at its heart worship, and at its edge mission." To see pastors and congregations recapture the vision of being "houses of prayer for the nations" is at the heart of the ministry and its seminars and conferences. The ministry serves local churches, citywide gatherings, denominational renewal efforts and offers a range of books, DVDs, and CDs.

Other Compassion Ministries

Appalachian Dream Center

www.verdunville.com & www.Miepan.org

The Appalachian Dream Center grew out of the outreach efforts of the Verdunville, West Virginia Church of God. Operation Compassion received a facility donated by the Massey Coal Company as headquarters to assist in benevolence ministry to West Virginia. The Appalachian Center provides a safety net, regular outreach, clothing and food assistance, holiday support, and a number of programs which reach across the nation and into South America.

Blood:Water Mission

www.bloodwatermission.com

A leader in the fight against HIV/AIDS. They offer well programs to provide clean water. They care for the sick through medical facilities. In Africa, they focus on the elimination of injustice, oppression, and poverty.

Children's Cup

www.childrenscup.org

They provide humanitarian help in war zones and after natural disasters in the face of epidemics. The help they provide includes medical, emotional, and spiritual assistance.

Children of the World Ministries

www.childrenoftheworldministries.org

The ministry is currently serving hundreds of homeless children in more than a dozen orphanages around the world. Their goal is over 500 child impact care, feeding and learning centers around the world. They partner with Operation Compassion, Church of God World Missions, and other humanitarian organizations.

Christian Pilot Association

www.christianpilots.org

Established in 1972, CPA is dedicated to assisting God's people in fulfilling the Great Commission by providing emergency air logistics, survival services, and supplies for people in need. The airplane has become the primary vehicle for moving people and supplies to the place of need. Unlimited skyways provide the most economical, most rapid, and safest transportation in the world. We are 10 times safer at 10,000 feet in an airplane than in a car on the highway. CPA's mandate is to enlist dedicated pilots and airmen volunteers throughout the world to fly church and mission projects relating to the Great Commission.

City of Refuge

www.cityofrefugeinc.com

The City of Refuge is a ministry outreach to the poor of Atlanta. The center operates a shelter. The amazing partnership between the city of Atlanta and the ministry helps over 10,000 people each year. It has a clinic and a first-rate kitchen. It treats its clients with respect. It has a special unit for women with children called Eden village which is designed to be a transitional social reentry program. It has been successful for 65 percent of the women. Most recently, the organization has opened Eden Village I and II, redemptive housing centers for homeless women and women with children, and the 180 Degree Kitchen, a culinary arts training program for at risk young adults. The Eden Village program houses 10 percent of Atlanta's female and child homeless population.

Cyrus International

www.cyrusinternational.org

The Cyrus ministry focuses on human trafficking, neglected and exploited orphans, and abuse victims. They resource other organizations focused on the relief of the oppressed. They are committed to raising up a network of partners, a veritable social justice army.

End Poverty
www.endpoverty.org
EndPoverty.org helps enable the very poor of the world to lift themselves, their families, and their communities out of poverty by providing small loans, business training, and community development programs through a network of locally led organizations in 12 countries to equip poor families to improve their lives.

Equip and Empower
www.equipandempower.com
This evangelism effort is committed to global, person-by-person evangelism. Their A21 focus stands for their campaign to abolish injustice in the 21st century, with a focus on rescuing young girls from sex slavery.

Exodus International
www.exodus-international.org
An organization providing support for those wishing to exit the homosexual lifestyle.

Family Research Council
www.frc.org
A Washington, DC organization focused on family issues and national trends affecting family life. Led by Tony Perkins, the organization champions healthy families, provides an array of family support materials, lobbies in behalf of family concerns, and engages in research that supports and documents the power of healthy families.

Feeding America (formerly Second Harvest)
www.feedingamerica.org
Feeding America and its member food banks are leading the fight against hunger with new and innovative strategies and programs, and enhanced outreach to engage the public and private sectors in their mission. Their goal is to create a more efficient and effective food bank network that will deliver more nutritious food to more people in need, including children and seniors.

Habitat for Humanity
www.habitat.org
This organization builds small, sound and economical structures to provide long-term housing for the poor and displaced. In some cases they provide a financing option. They provide an owner orientation

for upkeep since this is the first time some of the families will have experienced home ownership. Habitat depends on volunteer labor and donations to make the houses as affordable as possible.

Hope Charitable Ministries

www.hopecharitable.org

What began as a ministry to the poor in Portsmouth and Norfolk, Virginia, has now expanded throughout the USA and around the world with recent service efforts in Florida, Alabama, Mississippi, Appalachia, Washington DC, Maryland and Native American Reservations; providing relief to the urban/rural poor and migrant camps. The ministry operates THE URBAN OUTREACH CENTER, in the inner city of Portsmouth in the Greater Norfolk Area, and provides a free dental clinic, an after-school program for at-risk children, and a feeding and assistance program. They offer an everyday, all day, all summer camp that includes breakfast, crafts, performing arts, chapel, lunch, athletics and mentoring. At the conclusion of the program, every child is outfitted for school. The ministry, in dollars and commodities, has a budget approaching two million dollars a year.

Humphrey Humanitarian Ministries

www.humphreyhumanitarianministries.org

Home & Abroad Ministries, (HAM), was organized to reach the lost and poverty stricken people of the world in partnership with the Humphrey Humanitarian Ministries (HHM). It was founded by Roy and Ann Humphrey in 1995, first with a focus on the Filipino people, and then extended throughout East Asia and the USA. HAM is based in Cleveland, Tennessee, with a Far East operational office in Angeles City, Philippines. The vision is simply to "extend helping hands and the love of GOD to those in need." They provide medical and dental services, dig water wells, offer community feeding programs, operate a children's home, an educational ministry, job-training and humanitarian aid. They ship clothing and needy items throughout Asia. They plant churches. Their greatest current needs are vehicles for transportation, mobile living units, and delivery and service units for their work. HHM is an approved Church of God World Missions Project, number 102-3038. It is a nonprofit Christian organization that makes no charges and collects no fees for materials distributed or services rendered. HAM is tax exempt under 501 (c) (3) tax code and gifts made to HAM are tax exempt.

Kingsway Charities

www.kingswaycharities.org

Kingsway is a faith-based, Christian charitable organization that runs International Medical Missions—a ministry that warehouses medications and medical supplies donated from pharmaceutical companies, and works with medical mission teams to distribute them to third world and developing countries.

Men and Women of Action

www.cogmwoa.org

Men and Women of Action is an extension of Church of God World Missions providing information related to volunteer ministry opportunities around the world. More than 100 projects are conducted each year for churches in the USA and abroad, in disaster areas, and mission fields. Local congregations field teams for blitz builds or repairs. The ministry is local, national and international.

Mercy Ministries

www.mercyministries.org

Works with young girls with life-controling problems such as drug and alcohol addictions, depression, eating disorders, unplanned pregnancies, abuse whether physical or sexual, and suicidal or self-threatening disorders.

North Carolina Home for Children

The Church of God Children's Home in Kannapolis, North Carolina, was started as an outreach of the Elm Street Church of God when Pastor A. V. Childers found a baby on his doorsteps. With the assistance of C. A. Cannon, owner of Cannon Mills, land was appropriated and the children's home commenced. The home is supported by donations. It houses children through private and foster placement.

Operation Blessing

www.operationblessing.org

An outreach of the 700 Club, the ministry provides disaster relief, digs wells around the world, works at hunger relief and medical care. They also teach life-skills and cooperate in the provision of orphan care and at-risk children.

Outreach Magazine

www.outreachmagazine.com

A great resource with a ton of fresh ideas and a finger on the pulse of creative outreach.

Peniel Ministries

www.peniel.org

Dr. Marion Spellman envisioned a treatment facility which would provide professional, effective treatment for individuals caught in the web of drug addiction and alcoholism, along with spiritual care. Peniel's Drug and Alcohol Treatment Program is recognized as one of the most successful in the nation. Professionals have found help in the 13-month program, young and old, men and women. Hundreds are now free and with family, living productive lives. PENIEL has a unique four-phase treatment approach in which a "determined to succeed" attitude on the part of the individual is essential. The program operates in Johnstown, Pennsylvania. (814) 536-2111. E-mail: PenielDA@aol.com. See: www.penielrehab.com. Limited scholarships are available.

People for Care and Learning

www.peopleforcare.org

People for Care and Learning is a non-profit humanitarian organization working to eradicate poverty in locations around the world—primarily in Cambodia and Southeast Asia—by providing housing, food and educational opportunities to the poor, and giving them a working chance toward a brighter future. The organization partners with Children of the World.

Prosthetics Outreach Foundation

www.pofsea.org

Prosthetics Outreach Foundation is a catalyst for change in developing countries. Their goal is to ensure children and adults suffering from limb loss and deformity have lifetime access to high-quality orthopedic and rehabilitation services. By establishing local capacity to help people walk for a lifetime, POF permanently transforms peoples' lives.

Samaritan's Place Homes

www.samaritansplace.com

The mission of Samaritan's Inc. is to help "build a hope and a future" in the lives of their clients by providing high quality residential care, community based, and training programs in a loving family-style Christian environment. Samaritan's Inc.'s vision for their clients is to be empowered to become healthy, educated, socially, and spiritually developed persons who can experience his/her God-given potential in life. Thus, they will become responsible members of society functioning in positive and meaningful ways for their own families, community, and country.

Samaritan's Purse

www.samaritanspurse.org

This outreach of Franklin Graham focuses on the world's sick and poor and the suffering and the hurting. Samaritan's Purse is often a first responder in the face of natural disasters, war, and nations experiencing famine and disease. They provide food and water, medical assistance, and temporary shelter. Their educational programs aim to break the cycle of poverty.

Save the Children

www.savethechildren.org

Save the Children is the leading independent organization creating lasting change in the lives of children in need in the United States and around the world. They work with other organizations, including Operation Compassion, governments, non-profits, and a variety of local partners while maintaining their own independence without political agenda or religious orientation.

When disaster strikes around the world, Save the Children is there to save lives with food, medical care, and education. It remains to help communities rebuild through long-term recovery programs. As quickly and as effectively as Save the Children responds to tsunamis and civil conflict, it works to resolve the ongoing struggles children face every day—poverty, hunger, illiteracy and disease—and replaces them with hope for the future.

Smokey Mountain Children's Home

www.smch.cc

Just before Christmas, in 1920, four young children were placed in a small frame house in Cleveland, Tennessee, in the care of Lillian Kinsey. Thus began the Church of God ministry to homeless children. Its mission was to provide shelter mostly for homeless and orphaned children. Poverty, illness, and death of one or both parents were the initial primary reasons children needed care. Today many are victims of neglect and abuse. Now called "The Smokey Mountain Children's Home" the ministry continues as a private, faith-based, not-for-profit, multi-service agency offering professional care and treatment for boys and girls referred to the agency due to emotional, behavioral, and life situations. You can sponsor an individual child and make an eternal difference in a child's life for as little as $20 per month.

Foster family care and residential treatment centers have now replaced the large, institutional care programs of the early days. Intensive training for the primary care givers is offered. The multiple offerings of the Home include Residential Care and Foster Care programs, family counseling, individual therapy, educational opportunities, and structured groups.

South Carolina Home for Children

www.sccog.com/homeforchildren

The South Carolina Church of God Home For Children provides a wholesome, well-balanced life for every child in its care, and a family structured program teaching Biblical values, morals, and love. The home has operated for 55 years. Its present location in Mauldin, South Carolina, consists of a 25-acre campus, three homes for the children (a capacity of 40), library, gym, food, and clothing stockrooms, Superintendent's home, and a Relief Parents home. It is fully licensed by the South Carolina Department of Social Services. No child is denied care and services based on race, religion, ethnic origin, or inability to pay for the services. The home offers residential services, residential group care, professional evaluation and counseling, and medical and dental services. It participates in foster care and adoptions on a limited basis.

Teen Challenge

www.teenchallenge.org

Started by David Wilkerson, the ministry centers continue as one of the most effective in drug rehabilitation, discipleship and recovery.

The Prayer and Crisis Referral Network

www.prayerandcrisisreferral.org

Linda Morrison is the founder of The Prayer and Crisis Referral Network, a 24/7 prayer hotline and referral service serving the nation. Partnering with ministries and churches across the USA, they train prayer-line volunteers and provide the infrastructure that allows a congregation to be the center of hope, love, and compassion in a community. Each church brands the ministry with their name and participates in an affordable and effective evangelism outreach.

Waymakers

www.waymakers.org

Waymakers is the ministry outreach of Steve Hawthorne, an author and speaker in the prayer movement, serving on the National and International Prayer Committee. His book on *Prayer Walking* has been used around the world. His annual "Seek God for the City" booklets are used by hundreds of thousands. His website offers additional resources.

Widow's Ministry

www.widowsministry.org

The Church of God "Home for the Widows" is located in Sevierville, Tennessee. It offers limited residential care and an array of educational ministries to equip the local church in ministering to widows. Believing each widow is left for a purpose, Widows International raises Kingdom awareness by teaching and training aimed at transforming the widow from a victim to a victorious agent of change. They offer seminars, conferences on widowhood, speakers, counseling, written materials, and a residential program. Globally, Widows International, in a cooperative effort with international and local ministries, provides evangelistic rallies to care for and empower the widows to take their nation for Christ.

In addition, they launch special care projects. For example, there are over 50 million widows living in India. They are shunned and treated as outcasts. Loneliness drives some to suicide. Their life options are limited. Most are illiterate and can only learn by what they hear or are taught and are double victims. The "Sewing for Souls" project connects these needy widows with a local church for spiritual covering and fellowship. It gives them practical tools to rise above their poverty and despair. Their first projects are sewing clothes for orphans in church-based schools. Then, sewing for profit. Widows can partner with a church and school to care for orphans in a mission field and share the good news of Jesus Christ.

World Vision

www.worldvision.org

World Vision is a charitable organization that aims to help the lives of all people living in poverty. They work on long-term projects as well as emergency relief and the sponsoring of children.

Endnotes

1. Adapted from a story submitted by Marc Morris, Regional Superintendent of Church of God Missions in North/Southeast Asia and Oceania. Marc was appointed in 1987 to direct the WEAC short-term missions and benevolence programs in Asia Pacific. In 2000, Marc and his wife Marilen founded Samaritan's Place (SP) orphanage in the Philippines.
2. http://www.smch.cc/about-us/history.html. *History of the Smoky Mountain Children's Home, formerly the Church of God Children's Home*, Sevierville, TN
3. http://www.npr.org/templates/story/story.php?storyId=125676950; NPR: National Public Radio. April 7, 2010; http://en.wikipedia.org/wiki/Coal_mining#cite_note-16.
4. Walter Brueggermann, *The Prophetic Imagination*, Augsburg Press, Minneapolis, MN 2001, page 112.
5. Don E. Eberly, *Restoring the Good Society: A New Vision for Politics and Culture* (Grand Rapids, MI; Baker Publishing Group: Hourglass Books; 1994), 16-17.
6. *Ibid,* 27.
7. *Ibid,*
8. *Ibid,* 27, 28, 31.
9. *Ibid,* 29.
10. *Ibid,*
11. James Wilson, Quoted by Eberly, 29.
12. Floyd McClung, *Seeing the City with the Eyes of God* (Grand Rapids: MI; Zondervan, 1991), 155.
13. Carl Becker, Quoted by Thomas Reeves, *The Empty Church: Does Organized Religion Matter Anymore (*Simon & Schuster Adult Publishing Group; 1998), 83.
14. Richard Foster, *Celebration of Discipline: The Path to Spiritual Growth* (San Francisco: Harper Collins, 1978), 1.
15. Joseph Mattera, *Ruling in the Gates* (Lake Mary, FL: Creation House, 2003), 42.
16. Eberly, 88.
17. Dwight Perry, Editor, *Building Unity in the Church of the New Millennium* (Chicago: Moody Press, 2002), 40.
18. *Ibid,* 45.
19. Don Otis, *Trickle Down Morality: Returning to Truth in a World of Compromise* (Chosen Books: Baker Publishing House, 1994), 15.

20. *Ibid,* 19.
21. Eberly, 3.
22. Will Durant, Ariel Durant, *The Lessons of History* (Simon & Schuster, 2010), 41.
23. *Ibid,* 41.
24. Eberly, 81.
25. Bruce Main, *Spotting the Sacred: Noticing God in the Most Unlikely Places* (Grand Rapids, MI: Baker, 2006), 149.
26. Eberly, 90.
27. *Ibid,* 89.
28. McClung, 103-104.
29. Ray Bakke, Jon Sharpe, *Street Signs: A New Direction in Urban Ministry* (New Hope Publishers, 2006), 37-38.
30. *Ibid,* 63.
31. Perry, 156.
32. Donald Dayton's book, *Discovering an Evangelical Heritage*, Quoted by Mattera, *Ruling in the Gates*, 41-43. (Adapted for inclusion)
33. Harvie Conn, Quoted by McClung, *Seeing the City with Eyes of God*, 80.
34. McClung, 157.
35. McClung, 92-93.
36. Ronald Sider, Philip Olson and Heidi Unruh, *Churches That Make a Difference* (Grand Rapids, MI: Baker, 2002), 11.
37. Eberly, 89.
38. Sider, 13.
39. Henry Venn, Quoted by Don Otis, *Trickle-Down Morality* (Chosen Books, a Division of Baker: Grand Rapids, MI; 1998), 29.
40. Tim Downs, *Finding Common Ground: How to Communicate with Those Outside the Christian Community ... While We Still Can* (Chicago: Moody Press, 1999), 22
41. Eberly, 51.
42. *Ibid,* 50.
43. Mother Teresa, Quoted by Ronald J. Sider, Philip N. Olson, Heidi Rolland Unruh, *Churches That Make A Difference* (Grand Rapids, MI: Baker, 2006), 130.

44. Main, 224.
45. Siang-Yang Tan, *Full Service: Moving from Self-Serve Christianity to Total Servanth*
46. *Ibid*, 10.
47. *Ibid*, 138.
48. Charles W. Ferguson, *Organizing to Beat the Devil: Methodist and the Making of America* (Garden City, NY: Doubleday, 1971); Quoted by Howard Snyder, *The Radical Wesley and Patterns for Church Renewal* (Downers Grove, IL: Intervarsity; 1980), 2.
49. Snyder, *The Radical Wesley*, 2.
50. *Ibid*, 5.
51. *Ibid.*
52. Carl S. Dudley and Sally A. Johnson, *Energizing the Congregation: Images That Shape Your Congregation's Ministry* (Louisville: Westminster/John Knox, 1993), Quoted by Sider, Churches That Make a Difference, 252.
53. *Ibid.*
54. *Ibid*, 16.
55. Bakke, 122.
56. *Ibid*, 135.
57. *Ibid*, 156.
58. *Ibid*, 39.
59. *Ibid*, 261.
60. Main, 226-227.
61. *Ibid*, 12-13.

For additional copies of this book, please contact

P. Douglas Small, President

ALIVE MINISTRIES
Project Pray
P O Box 1245
Kannapolis, NC 28082-1245

www.projectpray.org
704-938-9111 Office

Retail $15.99. Discount rate is 3/$30. Buy two, get one free.

Call for multiple copies and case discounts.